# MORNINGS AT THE STANTON STREET SHUL

# Mornings at the Stanton Street Shul

## A Summer on the Lower East Side

JONATHAN BOYARIN

*Fordham University Press* NEW YORK 2011

Fordham University Press has no responsibility for the persistence or accuracy of URLs for external or third-party Internet websites referred to in this publication and does not guarantee that any content on such websites is, or will remain, accurate or appropriate.

Fordham University Press also publishes its books in a variety of electronic formats. Some content that appears in print may not be available in electronic books.

Library of Congress Cataloging-in-Publication Data

Boyarin, Jonathan.
Mornings at the Stanton Street Shul : a summer on the
Lower East Side / Jonathan Boyarin.—1st ed.
p.   cm.
Includes bibliographical references and index.
ISBN 978-0-8232-3900-9 (cloth : alk. paper)—
ISBN 978-0-8232-3902-3 (epub : alk. paper)—
ISBN 978-0-8232-3903-0 (updf : alk. paper)—
ISBN 978-0-8232-3904-7 (fordham scholarship online : alk. paper)
1. Stanton Streel Shul (New York, N.Y.)   2. Synagogues—
New York (State)—New York.   3. Jews—New York (State)—
New York.   4. Lower East Side (New York, N.Y.)—
Religious life and customs.   I. Title.
BM225.N52S733 2011
296.09747′1—dc22
2011016366

Printed in the United States of America
13  12  11      5  4  3  2  1
First edition

# Contents

# Illustrations

*People, following page 98*

All photographs are by Elissa Sampson, with the exception of those on pages 64, 140, 142, and 186, which are by Shauna Wreschner, and Figure 8 of "People," which is by Clayton Patterson.

# To the Reader

Aside from the introduction to this book, what follows really is, for the most part, what I wrote down in my journal in the summer of 2008. At the wise urging of my editors Bud Bynack and Helen Tartar, I've cut a few repetitions, improved my syntax here and there, and explained (in text and a few notes) a bit more about some of the "insider" terms that are indispensable for an insider's guide such as this one. You will find an extensive glossary in addition to such explanations of specialized terms as I have provided in the text. Many of the terms there and in the text do not have standardized English orthography, or if they do, that spelling does not reflect the way they are commonly pronounced in and around the Stanton Street Shul; any idiosyncrasies in spelling reflect those conditions.

To be sure, the book remains much more a record of my experiences than a primer on synagogue life. But even as I made my regular journal entries, I wrote as an anthropologist, with an eye toward cultural translation as well as documentation. I fervently hope you will find that the translation is successful, in the main if not at every moment—at least to the point that you are able to imagine yourself a sometime participant in the Stanton Street Shul congregation.

I have, consistent with ethnographic canons, changed the names of almost everyone mentioned in this book. The only exceptions are my own close family members; synagogue elders whom I wish to honor with their own names; and rabbinic leaders of Stanton Street and other local synagogues, whom I regard as public figures.

My continuing respect and love for the late Rabbi Joseph Singer should come through clearly in these pages. Although one of the remarkable features of an Orthodox Jewish congregation is that it does not strictly require a rabbi in order to be able to function, he and the other rabbis who are key figures in this book are of course vital to the long-term viability of such communities, and I am grateful to all of them.

May everyone who recognizes herself or himself in this book, under cover of a pseudonym, similarly consider herself or himself hereby acknowledged and thanked.

Elissa Sampson, may she live and be well, is certainly one of the very few key figures without whose passionate and stubborn persistence there would no longer be a functioning synagogue at 180 Stanton Street. For that and so many other reasons, I dedicate this book to her.

MORNINGS AT THE STANTON STREET SHUL

*The Stanton Street Shul*

# *Introduction*

At 180 Stanton Street, on New York City's Lower East Side, stands a synagogue currently known as the Stanton Street Shul. It is occupied and owned by a group known as Congregation Anshei Brzezan. That name means "men of Brzezany," but not one of the current members comes from that town in Eastern Europe. The building itself, dating from 1913, is one of the last remaining exemplars of an entire fleet of such tenement synagogues that once rode at anchor here, their numbers dwindling for decades as the neighborhood's Jewish population has declined. In fact, the Jewish population of the Lower East Side reached its peak in the 1920s, not long after the synagogue at 180 Stanton Street was built.

The extraordinary survival of the synagogue's congregation is a story involving courage, creativity, some shady dealings, and most of all plain stubbornness. In telling the story of the shul's survival from the inside, focusing on the day-to-day repetitions and changes over the course of a recent summer, I hope also to show how changes on the intimate scale of a religious congregation illuminate the human face of urbanization, migration, and globalization.

It's easy enough to see how a book about an old synagogue on the Lower East Side would find its place within a series of ethnographies documenting persistent Jewish remnant communities. Barbara Myerhoff showed the way with *Number Our Days*, about the cantankerous community of old East European Jews in Venice Beach, California, in the 1970s. Jack Kugelmass took the story back east, telling us about the last Jewish congregation in the South Bronx in *The Miracle of Intervale Avenue*. Then I went across the ocean—not quite back to Poland—to spend a year in Paris and try to understand the astonishingly complicated life history of its Polish Jewish immigrant community, a journey described in my *Polish Jews in Paris*.

All of these books were about *old* Jews, but of course there are, thank God, young Jews, too. I didn't realize I was only writing about old Jews until one of them—a rising star in cultural anthropology named Matti Bunzl—called me on it in print (he also called me the leading authority on the anthropology of Jews in Europe, which relieved a bit of the sting), and until two more young scholars, Caryn Aviv and David Shneer, published a book with the bracing title *New Jews: The End of the Jewish Diaspora.*

They were right. But I guess I'm still not ready to begin looking only toward the future. Meanwhile, I realized I had a great story right in my neighborhood, one I'd been part of for years. Don't you worry: this book is going to keep on telling you, just before it's too late, about the heritage of the immigrant generation, and I think I'm still going to get away with preserving vital memories that would otherwise be lost. Just think about the names, literally engraved in stone, of the founding members and donors whose hard-earned contributions (fifty or a hundred dollars was enough to get you immortalized) made the Stanton Street building itself possible. Look at the old-fashioned lions sewed in the *paroches*,[1] the velvet hanging that covers and dignifies the ark in which the Torah scrolls are kept. Come on in. There aren't that many places where you can see that sort of thing anymore; most of them have been destroyed, some of them since my wife Elissa and I moved here— after all, we've been in the neighborhood for thirty years.

But let's not get too sentimental while we're looking at the memorial plaques and the old paroches, the narrow pews, the water-damaged and crumbling zodiac signs that decorate the walls (each one representing one of the twelve months of the Jewish year), or the women's balcony, another flight upstairs (the last I heard plans were afoot to turn it into a Jewish art gallery). Along with just a few of the old-timers, there's a crowd of "new Jews" at the Stanton Street Shul, and I want you to meet them. Maybe that's why they call this part of the book an introduction.

As we spend time together between the pages of this book, I'll also take you outside the shul sometimes, to show you how the old neighborhood looks today. But don't be fooled: the Lower East Side ain't what it used to be, and it probably never was. The Jewish Lower East Side continues to shrink—stores "go out," as they used to say around

---

1. Terms found in the Glossary are italicized the first time they appear.

here. Most have already gone. Sometimes the awnings are kept, so "Max Fish," once a wholesale dealer of some sort, is now a bar and late-night music spot. Has been for almost twenty years, it seems, so probably I'm behind the times here. It hasn't been clear for quite that long, however, that the neighborhood was fast becoming a global hipster destination. Until the world's economy crashed in 2008, oversized apartment buildings, taller than anything ever attempted on the swampy low ground of that part of Manhattan Island, began popping up like weeds, and glassy condos began to tower over the synagogue.

These changes aren't just part of shifts in the global political economy and the symbolic economy that fuels and reflects it. They're the effect of quite local politics and economics, too—such as New York City planners' decision to designate all of Lower Manhattan a "recreation area" in the wake of the trauma of September 11, 2001, and the massive departure of jobs from the so-called financial "industry." Whether the changes in the neighborhood ultimately have more to do with these local forces or with the flows of global capital, the shape the changes will take is hardly something that I or anybody can predict in advance. Take a walk down Grand Street east of Essex—the "main street" of the Jewish Lower East Side since the 1960s. Its subsidized, union-sponsored co-op buildings, many named for Jewish socialist leaders, which replaced the older tenements, have been privatized over the past decade. Long-term residents have profited by selling and moving away, leaving behind a younger, more affluent, and also more transient population in the neighborhood of Stanton Street and other local synagogues. But to get a sense of how many of the younger people moving in are Jewish, and of those, how many might be interested in populating and reinventing old-fashioned *Orthodox* congregations, we need to go inside the shuls, start looking around and talking to people.

Along with the remaining elderly who've been at Stanton Street ever since I came there, along with a few folks more or less my age (Elissa not least among them) who've been around the neighborhood as long as I have, along with, it seems, quite a few more young adults who've come into the neighborhood more recently and might depart at less than a moment's notice, one of the people I'll be talking to most in this book is myself. At the risk of sounding a bit too fancy, I'm what you might call something of a postmodern Jew. What I mean by that is, I'm Jewish because of my birth but also because of choices that I've made in my life and continue to make. Jewishness isn't something that I could escape even if I wanted to, but its content is determined by my physical surroundings, by those with whom I congregate, and by the directions I set for myself. And I see the rest of the congregation at Stanton Street as Jews in the same way, even if they don't use the same academic terms I'm accustomed to.

*Anthropologists* today commonly talk about group identity using a model that focuses on persons as they actively and consciously reinvent themselves and the group of which they are part. The question then becomes what particular people in particular situations do with the tools (symbolic and other), the assets, and the liabilities at their disposal. At Stanton Street, for better and for worse, the main asset is the building itself. It's not particularly old, as Lower East Side synagogues go. It's not large, being one of what I call the "tenement shuls," squeezed long and narrow into lots laid out for crowded immigrant housing.

There's no denying that the building is a liability. It's too small for many of the social functions a synagogue is expected to host these days. The new roof put on in the last few years drained the congregation's resources and caused acrimony among the leadership. As for the zodiac murals, some members would just as soon see them go, along with the crumbling plaster they're stuck to, while others adamantly insist they are irreplaceable folk art that must be preserved. In the summer the main shul upstairs is often too hot for holding services, and in the winter it's often too cold, so the narrow *beis medresh* or "study room" in the cellar has to double up as sanctuary and social hall.

Yet the building's very poverty is an asset as well. Its lack of ostentatiousness helps the congregation project a message about what makes us special: we're not going to judge you by how you dress or how you look. This much was equally true back in November 1983, when I first stepped into what was then known as Rabbi Singer's Shul, as it is today, when the shul itself is nearing its century mark. One mainstay of the shul until 2008 was a pediatric neurologist and mother of two who struck me as belonging more in the fashionable world of Upper West Side Orthodoxy than in the downtown mix of stodgy *heymishkeyt* and scruffy hipsterism. She explained that this nonjudgmental atmosphere was what made Stanton Street special. Alluding to advertisements for a health club that welcomes those of all shapes and sizes, she said, "We're the 'Crunch' of synagogues."

The same sentiment is also expressed in a more local and quirkier idiom. Some of the younger, newer congregants years ago noticed that,
when the synagogue's president for life, Benny Sauerhaft (he should live
and be well), wanted to urge someone he'd just met to come back and
visit the shul again, he'd say "Don't Be Strange," his Yinglish variant on
"Don't be a stranger." For the brief time around 2005 when the shul
published a regular newsletter, "Don't Be Strange" was the name on its
masthead. Making the phrase their own, these newcomers borrowed an
immigrant idiom and quickly cast themselves as those at home, welcoming in turn others who, the phrase promises, won't long be strangers.

I am no stranger at 180 Stanton Street (although the combination I
still favored in the summer of 2008—a long ponytail and a big black
yarmulke—might strike some people as strange). Back in the day when
Rabbi Singer was still running the place, I marveled at his remarkable
success at maintaining a small but regular crowd for services—initially,
both in the morning and the afternoon, and in his last years, mornings
only. Rabbi Singer was the product of distinguished Hasidic ancestry.
His style, both as a rabbinic leader and in the form of worship he su-
pervised, reflected that movement's intense personalism, traditionalism,
and emphasis on proper intent. He mentioned to me once that he was
descended from Reb Gershon Kitever. Reb Gershon Kitever was, in
turn, brother-in-law of the Baal Shem Tov, still regarded as the founder
of modern *Hasidism*.

Rabbi Singer was a native of the East European region of Galicia,
though from the town of Pilsno rather than Brzezany, the hometown
of the immigrants who founded the shul. Like other congregations'
rabbis,[2] he served at the members' pleasure; unlike most American Jewish congregational rabbis, and certainly those of the more liberal
branches of Judaism, he was paid little or nothing to do so. In fact, the
congregation could have performed the core of its ritual functions—
daily, Sabbath, and holiday services—without any rabbi at all, so long
as enough male participants had the knowledge and ability to perform

2. The word *rabbi* means an ordained religious authority, often but not necessarily a
congregational leader. In this sense, it will only be capitalized when linked to a named
individual. By contrast, references to "the Rabbis" indicate the masters of the Mishna
and Talmud, and "Rabbinic" texts are the body of legal and related literature that ultimately derives its authority from that of the Rabbis.

central ritual functions. Yet during the years I knew him, it was clear
that Rabbi Singer was the animating force that kept the congregation
alive, as teacher of Torah, conjurer of the minyan, calmer of the angry,
and even a kind of informal social worker.

In the years after my first visit to what I then called Rabbi Singer's
shul in 1983, I found there, early each morning, a cantankerous *minyan*,
a quorum of ten assembled largely so that they might help each other
meet the obligation of commemorating the dead.[3] Title to the building
was still held in the name of a society of immigrants from Brzezany,
who, as is customary with Jewish congregations, were quite autonomous
from a legal standpoint, though hewing to standards shared with the
larger Orthodox Jewish community regarding matters such as dietary
laws, separation of men and women, and restrictions pertinent to the
Sabbath and holidays.[4] Yet not one member of that society was still active in the synagogue, and it seemed clear to me then that without
Rabbi Singer the building would have closed its doors long since. I was
fascinated by the relation between the saintly Rabbi Singer and his less
than saintly congregation. I was inspired in part by my friend Jack
Kugelmass's work in the South Bronx, and a bit envious of the larger-
than-life elderly survivors he found in that neighborhood, which was
even worse than the Lower East Side, who met in a synagogue that was
in even worse shape than the one on Stanton Street.

Though I set aside the project for the chance to do fieldwork among
other old Jews in Paris, I remained a more or less full-time resident of the
neighborhood until just a few years ago. Now that I earn my living as a
professor away from New York and only return for summer and winter
breaks, it's actually easier to step back a bit from the everyday irritations
and pleasures of participating in the Stanton Street congregation.

---

3. The memorial prayer is said daily (and three times a day if possible) for eleven
months after the death of a loved one, and annually on the anniversary of that person's death. Often a communal representative—such as the rabbi or the synagogue
president—will also recite the memorial prayer for the sake of those who have no
family member carrying out that responsibility. During the period covered by this
book, a minyan was most pressingly needed when one of the regular members was
in mourning or wished to observe the anniversary of a family member's death.
4. While many Orthodox congregations also belong to an umbrella group known as
the Orthodox Union, such membership is not compulsory, and the Stanton Street Shul
is in fact not a member congregation.

Which, in the meantime, has become a very different place. Despite Rabbi Singer's best efforts, his aged congregation continued to decline throughout the 1980s and 1990s, while a handful of younger people became attached to the rabbi and "his" synagogue. Around the year 2000, synagogue regulars discovered that, unbeknownst to them, the rabbi and his family had undertaken the sale of the synagogue. A court struggle ensued, in whose decisive phase I served as one of the congregation's attorneys and in the course of which much of the congregation's oral history was recorded. The hearings were held in the New York State Supreme Court—actually the lowest rung of the state court system. The transcript of the first hearing during the litigation to block the sale contains some classics of American Jewish diction. In the excerpt below, Judge Lippman, himself a product and life-long resident of the Jewish Lower East Side, explains the hearsay rule. The attorney for Rabbi Singer's family, attempting to establish the length of Rabbi Singer's service to the shul, had elicited testimony from one of Rabbi Singer's descendants concerning events in the middle of the twentieth century. That was too much for the judge, as the transcript reads:

THE COURT: . . . if this man is now stating he's fifty-seven now, I think that Mr. Beerman's questions, several of them, are somewhat—you're asking this man to testify about things that happened when he was two.

Now, with all due respect, I mean, it's just not possible.

The Court, on its own, is going to throw out a lot of his testimony.

MR. BEERMAN: Fine, Judge.

THE COURT: Because he may be brilliant, but at two and four, how brilliant he was, I don't know. He's talking about things that happened in 1947.

I'm taking this to heart as a warning. I may have some things to say about what happened in the shul before I came along in 1983, but not too much, because I don't want this book to be thrown out of court. Of course, an ethnographic memoir like this isn't subject to quite the same rules of evidence as a court hearing, so I'll let myself keep as part of the record a lot of things that someone heard that somebody else said. I'll also keep in some answers that might seem of doubtful relevance at first, since part of an anthropologist's job is to make sense of answers and arguments that seem to come from out of left field.

One of these, also contained in the hearing transcript, concerned Rabbi Singer's age. He was certainly well into his eighties at that point, but it's entirely conceivable that even he could not have stated his exact age. His answer, at any rate, was simply: "I'm not a Zionist!" As good an anthropologist as I like to think I am, I'm still not quite sure why he said that, but as a good Jewish reader, I have a few plausible interpretations ready. One is: "Whatever my age is, I'm old enough to have grown up at a time when Jews weren't necessarily Zionists." But the most plausible, I think, is: "I'm not one of those modern Jews, those Zionists, who don't think it's bad luck to say how old you are."

As it turned out, whatever evidence the rabbi's family brought to the court hearing wasn't enough to convince a judge to permit the sale of the building. In the end, a settlement provided for the building to remain in the possession of the congregants and for Rabbi Singer to receive modest payments in lieu of a pension. I was amazed, because when I'd first heard about the sale, I'd assumed that the building was lost and that was the end of the story. Instead, as a result of the demographic changes in the neighborhood and the outcome of the court struggle itself, a congregation now consisting largely of younger and newly arrived Jewish singles and families retained control of the building. For the past several years, that new cohort has struggled: we've struggled to get along with each other, to find the means to restore structural integrity to the building, and to find ways actively to inherit something of the distinctive character of the old congregation.

Legally, the ownership of the building never changed hands. It was built by, and still belonged to, Congregation Anshei (the people of) Brzezan. In fact, the court process worked a remarkable feat of alchemy: A group consisting of a few old-timers and a number of younger folk (all new to the synagogue, nearly all new to the neighborhood) have become the membership of a society known as "The People of Brzezany." The legal drama turned centrally around the definition of the congregation's membership. Accordingly, the court papers and hearing transcripts not only describe a particular moment of crisis at which the institution's history easily could have come to an end but also mark a dramatic shift from the older to the newer membership cohort. Some of the older members survive and remain as a perishable storehouse of memories. Spending time with them in good times and bad over the past decade has been one of the crucial ways I've tried to make a Jew out of myself. I'm grateful that they waited for me to come to the Lower East Side, even though I'm not always as patient with them in turn as I probably should be.

Part of this is just my job. To the small extent I can do so as an individual, I try to be a living bridge to the world of East European Jewishness, preserving gestures, idioms, and anecdotes for those who come after and will never have the chance to learn them from the immigrants themselves. Part of it is what helps me make sense of my own life. It's not only me, but many of the younger members as well who model themselves on these totemlike elders and thus, in part, create the congregation's continuing identity.

But these younger people are in some ways profoundly different from the immigrant generation. They speak a different native language. They learn how to pray from books and from each other more than they do from their parents. They consciously choose which aspects of Jewish law and tradition they will follow, which they will discard, and which they will modify, rather than letting it all happen under the guise of a seemingly continuous "tradition." I don't want to turn this account of the shul, its congregants, and its rabbis into another meditation on "Jewish identity." Yet I will be talking about how the Jewishness of the new members compares with that of the older congregants. I call them "fictive Bzezaner," with a nod to the anthropological notion of fictive kinship, but I suppose I could call them "adopted Bzezaner" just as well. The notion is sentimental, but not only so, since in a legal sense the new members "inherited" the synagogue by becoming members of the Society of the People of Brzezany. And, to be sure, the kinds of Jews these new people are and become has something to do with the place they come to be Jewish in.

Many times in the history of the Lower East Side, a group of later immigrants, with different standards and customs but sharing a strong common identity amongst themselves, simply took over a building from an earlier group that had left the neighborhood, and a documentary history of Stanton Street would show how dwindling societies of emigrés from other towns—Lancut, Bluzhov, Rymanow, all in Poland—surrendered their own buildings and retreated to the Brzezaner Shul. Their reluctance to do so was based on a pattern still found in some Jewish communities, whereby the shared identity of a group of Jews is based on and known by their place of origin. Such geographically based identities are certainly not different religious "denominations" but may indicate distinctive standards, arrangements of particular prayers, musical styles, and other differences in both public worship and daily practice. Toponymics are especially important among today's Hasidic communities, such as that of the Satmar Hasidim, named for the town, now in Romania, where their former leader lived but based now in the Williamsburg neighborhood of Brooklyn, across the East River from the Lower East Side.

But in this first decade of the new millennium, the new congregation certainly cannot be said to come, as a group, from elsewhere. Indeed, it doesn't exist until it comes together at Stanton Street. And even at Stanton Street, its character is constantly shifting. How does the fact of their coming to be Jewish in *this* place with *this* history affect the Jews, the people, they are always still becoming?

Any answers to this question cannot assume that the character of the old congregation is safely known and only that of the new is to be discovered. Thus, for example, I might be tempted to view the new congregation as an "intentional community," a group of individuals who had come together as a matter of deliberate choice, rather than simply through the force of shared circumstance. Indeed, no social web compels them to attend a synagogue at all, and certainly not this one.

We tend to think that, unlike emancipated individuals in "freedom-of-choice" America, our immigrant ancestors went where the winds of history drove them. But let's think a little bit harder about it; let's imagine, without even digging into the archives, what we would have done in their situation. When we try this mental exercise, it's hard not to suppose that even poor immigrants a century ago made decisive choices about who they were going to become in the new country. Would they donate money to help build a synagogue? Doing so might tie them to the neighborhood, but it might eventually force them to choose between staying in the awful tenement conditions and leaving the comfort of daily contact with their friends from the old country. Or would they keep their savings and get away as fast as they could?

If we do see traces of the immigrant generation at all, we tend to see the record of the ones who stayed close together. Even they must have known that their world was fantastically different from the one they had left. Even their synagogue was different from the one back home. It seems to me more than likely that the immigrant generations at 180 Stanton

Street were conscious that they were not merely continuing, but attempting to replicate and in some sense imitating the forms of worship they or their ancestors had known in Europe. So the current decade's new congregation, both native born and "immigrant" to the Lower East Side, aren't the first Jews at Stanton Street who've had to make it up as they went along.

Other distinctions between the old and the new congregation are undeniable. The older congregation consisted largely of those who had somehow refused or been unable to leave the Lower East Side when most Jews with the means to do so had gotten out. Some of the younger congregants likewise grew up in the neighborhood and could afford to leave but choose to stay. Their reasons might be practical (it's close to work, or they "inherited" an apartment from their parents), or they might feel the same fierce and nostalgic love for these gritty blocks that Elissa and I share. Many of the newer arrivals have, however, chosen to "return" to this new old country, something that has become an expensive proposition as the neighborhood acquires a new cachet. Among the new members, there are heterosexual and gay singles, along with young married heterosexual couples just beginning families.

Promising as their arrival is, there is no certainty that these new arrivals will stay very long. It's true that folks have been leaving the Lower East Side as fast as they could for well over a century. But it seems they come and go even faster now.

Nor does everyone who comes to the Stanton Street Shul to keep making it a Jewish place live in the neighborhood. Some are brought in by a tour guide, passing through for a couple of hours rather than a couple of years. If you walk through the neighborhood on any given Sunday afternoon, you might hear a voice singing an old-fashioned children's song:

My mother and your mother live across the way,
214 East Broadway.
Every night they have a fight and this is what they say:
"Lady, lady, turn around.
"Lady, lady, touch the ground.
"Lady, lady, buckle my shoe.
"Lady, lady, how do you do?"

The person singing the song, to paraphrase an old vaudeville routine, is no lady—she's my wife. This bit of folklore was recorded as Elissa conducted a tour of synagogues on the northern portion of the Lower East Side, the "East Village," part of the Allen Ginsberg–inspired "Howl" festival of the arts in 2004. Elissa's a Brooklyn girl, and that's where she learned this song from her own mother, who had grown up on the Lower East Side. Now she demonstrates and recirculates it back on Manhattan Island, where 214 East Broadway really is across the way, or at least at the far edge of the same neighborhood. Elissa's version was recorded for posterity by an Australian producer of radio documentaries and eventually broadcast over the Australian Broadcasting Company (she never thought she'd be singing on the radio). And I got to hear it over the Internet on the other side of the rainbow from New York City, in Kansas, where I was teaching when that radio documentary came out.

These days, when I'm not in New York, I'm in North Carolina, so I've gotten some long views of the Lower East Side from the west and from the south. When I return to New York, I can say I'm doing ethnographic fieldwork. But I know a lot about this place and these people for someone who's just entering the field.

In fact, even though Elissa and I had only been living in the neighborhood for a few years before I started going to Rabbi Singer's Shul, it wasn't our first shul on the Lower East Side. That place in our hearts belongs to the old Eighth Street Shul, off Tompkins Square Park between Avenue B and Avenue C. Around 1980, when we were going to Eighth Street, its immediate surroundings were more dangerous than Stanton Street. The blocks were a combination of vacant lots, abandoned buildings used for drug dealing, poor housing, and, toward the end, a few buildings just starting to be reclaimed by the squatters who turned out to be the harbingers of gentrification.

The Eighth Street Shul somehow just couldn't hang in until enough of a new generation might come to reclaim it, and after a bitter fight it ended up being sold to a developer. It still stands, but now as private housing. The building lives, but the shul died, of two causes. One was legal limbo. Like Stanton Street, the Eighth Street Shul belonged to a "society" that had dwindled down to a couple of families. The other was neglect; like Stanton Street, its roof was going, and even though, unlike Stanton Street, it had a boiler, the boiler almost never worked.

Part of the reason there's a different story to tell about Stanton Street is that Elissa wasn't willing to let this one go by without a fight. She started asking Rabbi Singer where the people were who *really* owned the shul; she started looking into the possibility of getting grants to do basic repairs on the building. She started thinking about ways to find the new people who, she was confident, would want to keep the shul alive if only they knew about it. So Elissa and one of the "pioneer" newcomers to Rabbi Singer's Shul, a scholar of Jewish mysticism named Sura Ziskind, started a *shabbes* afternoon group to discuss the weekly Torah portion. They held it at the Orensanz Foundation, a former synagogue turned arts center on Norfolk Street, just a few blocks from the Stanton Street Shul. One of the first attendees at that discussion group was a corporate lawyer who had insisted (against his new wife's better judgment) on remaining in the neighborhood where he'd been born. He was attracted to Stanton Street and eventually became one of the stalwarts of the new congregation, though he and his family have since moved uptown. In the meantime, the Orensanz Foundation—housed in a building that's vastly more imposing than the Stanton Street Shul—served as a wet nurse for the nucleus of a new Stanton Street congregation.

Of course, every community dreams that its continuity won't be fragmented in this way. If there's a remnant community of stubborn old people, it means either that they don't have children or that their children are far away. If there's a resurgent community of confident and questing younger people, it means they're looking for some connection to a tradition that they're not getting with their parents and grandparents. It's great to have young people around, but even Elissa and I mourn the lost traditions. Our feelings were mixed when we realized that within far less than a decade we had gone from being almost the youngest members of the congregation to a couple of its old-timers, to be alternately consulted, respected, and ignored.

For Rabbi Singer, being old certainly had its virtues, for he associated age with wisdom. Years ago our son Jonah, then aged about eight, asked him how Methuselah could have survived the great Flood. His first response was to exclaim in Yiddish: *a kashye fun an altn yid,* "That's the kind of question an old Jew would ask!" (Rabbi Singer's substantive answer to Jonah's question was, "Methuselah was very tall.")

It's not clear how many people, if any, are now going to grow old as members of the Stanton Street Shul. New people come into the

neighborhood, but young people are likely to leave as well, as their ca-
reers take them elsewhere, as they get enough money to buy larger
homes in less expensive neighborhoods, as they have children whose
educational needs cannot be met on the Lower East Side. Meanwhile,
some of the older members of the congregation don't seem to come
as often because they may not feel at home. The younger people try
all the same to make everyone feel welcome, as the shul's Web site insists: "All will be welcome! All will feel welcome!" And of course the
older people pass away, as Benny Sauerhaft puts it: "Time passes by,
and we pass by too." Sometimes it seems the younger people don't become old as quickly as the elderly pass by.

All the same, I like to think of the younger people becoming
Bzezaner in their turn, but maybe that's just me. The artist Jason
Frankel, one of the younger people interviewed for the Australian radio
program, wasn't too impressed by this notion. He suggested that I, the
anthropologist, might be romanticizing the pseudo-genealogical connection between the older immigrants and the newcomers. It's funny
that he should be the one to say that, because he's perhaps the most patient and loving of the younger members toward the remaining old-
timers. Jason marked his reverence for Benny Sauerhaft, on the occasion
of Benny's ninetieth birthday, with a commemoration in a novel
medium: a chopped liver bust.

There does seem to be some kind of magic about the place that
seems to encourage the reproduction, even in the youngest members,
of a certain style distinctive to the Lower East Side. One of the
youngest at Stanton Street, not quite out of diapers, once stuck a couple of toothpicks into a piece of flattened-out Play Dough and approached his mother with the proud announcement: "Mommy,
look—herring!"

With adult members as well, it's tempting sometimes to see the
ghosts of congregants from back in Rabbi Singer's day. Many of the
echoes stem from the fact, which I've noted in my earlier work about
Stanton Street,[5] that you don't have to be a particularly pious Jew to be
included in the minyan. One morning in the fall of 2006, we were working our way through the Rosh Chodesh prayers, an extended service in
honor of the new moon. In the middle of *musaf*, the additional prayers

---

5. See "Death and the Minyan," in my Thinking in Jewish.

that mark that holiday, Benny Sauerhaft called out in his typical blunt
fashion a reminder: "Take off your *tefillin*," boxes containing passages
of Torah worn on the forehead and upper arm. Lenny Rivers, one of the
young parents in the congregation, was sitting in the back. Though he
was tremendously devoted to the shul, he was no doubt eager to leave
shul and get to work by this time. Echoing Benny's tone, he called out,
"Stand on one leg!" Our young Rabbi Yossi Pollak shushed Lenny. At
the podium, where I was leading the service, I giggled, and an image
popped into my head of an odd man named Yoyne, who used to sit at
the same back table, not participating in the service at all, but still
counting as the tenth man to make sure we had a minyan. Yoyne's version of the prayer book was *Time* magazine.

   While Lenny sat and waited for the service to conclude, he carried
out one of a Jew's important religious duties: he was counted in the minyan, at least by the shul's standards. With or without a rabbi present, of
course, virtually all of the other tasks involved in an Orthodox service
(such as leading the prayers and chanting aloud from the Torah scroll)
can be, and often are, carried out by members who need not be clergy
or officers of the congregation.

   The next day, somebody else was sitting where Lenny had been the
day before, where Yoyne used to sit in years gone by. This one was a bit
better dressed than old Yoyne had been, and actually he wasn't needed
as the tenth man, but still—there he was in the same place.

   I know these people aren't really ghosts, but spirits are more substantial things than we often are willing to credit. And my own eagerness
to see those spirits speaks to my desire to perceive, somehow, a continuing if not quite intact cycle of generations, a generation coming as another generation leaves. There are plenty of moments where this kind
of continuity can be seen by someone who's on the lookout for it. One
was the morning when two members of the minyan were marking three
rites of passage. I was observing the first anniversary of my father's
death, while a young father at Stanton Street was both observing the
*shloshim*—the thirtieth day after the passing of his father—and giving
his newborn son a Jewish name in shul.

   Longer-term relationships between some of the congregation's oldest
and youngest members also suggest this comforting image of a cycle of
generations. Lying around somewhere still in the downstairs beis
medresh are two photographs of our now-deceased member Abie Roth,

one of Abie as an infant in his mother's arms and another of Abie, still innocent of face, but well over ninety years old.

Before his recent death, Abie, a tiny, quiet, and gentle man, who opened the shul every morning for years, became almost a sacred figure at Stanton Street. The little bit of dancing as part of the Friday night service to welcome the Sabbath was enhanced by a hand wave we came to call "the Abie shuffle." When Abie was gone, the dancing gradually stopped. Abie himself told us, during his last years, that people were asking him for a blessing, "So I give it to them." Years earlier, when our disabled son Yeshaya was learning to walk after long delays, he and Abie would spend part of each shabbes morning service walking together around and around the *bima*, the central platform where the Torah is read. Later, when Lenny Rivers had a son of his own, old Abie and young Seth became the closest pair of friends in shul, and after Abie passed by, Lenny invoked Abie's memory in his High Holiday appeal. The picture of Abie and Seth together certainly invokes a comforting notion of the Stanton Street Shul as a place where lost grandparents can find new grandchildren and young children, even if not lost, can find a few extra grandparents.

The shul's gay membership, however, is a creative interruption of any attempt to measure continuity against a sentimental normatization of the cycle of generations. As it happens, none of the gay male members of the shul so far has had children. Perhaps in compensation—but why does one thing have to be compensation for the other?—they are among the most insistent on the value of cultural continuity. They are the sharpest critics of pretension to superficial Orthodox pietism and the most reliable creators of the kind of ironic, creolized humor that ultimately redeems a marginal institution like the Stanton Street Shul.

One, a longtime board member, persistently complains about the new rabbis, mostly on general principle. (Why should any congregation be satisfied with any rabbi?) He also has more particular grounds for complaint, especially their abandonment of traditions such as the East European–style *Ashkenazi* pronunciation of Hebrew during the prayer service. Though not a native speaker of Yiddish himself, he also promotes the use of Yiddish in shul. Once he drafted a mock flyer for a *kiddush* (the festive refreshments following a service) with the slogan "Think Yiddish, Eat Kiddish." He told us once that, when he's talking to neighbors of his parents in the Orthodox Brooklyn neighborhood

of Midwood, he tells them, "I *daven* at the Bzezaner beis medresh."
That's strictly true—Stanton Street is the Bzezaner synagogue, after all,
and we do pray downstairs in the beis medresh. But in Brooklyn, and
certainly to someone who doesn't know the Stanton Street Shul, the
phrase "Bzezaner beis medresh" evokes a style of traditionalist Orthodoxy that's quite far from Stanton Street's reality today.

This member's complaints about Stanton Street are classically "cranky"
(a term of art in Jewish culture). Yet they also point out the sharp and progressive loss of any *nusach*, any distinctive and traditional customs and
patterns, which might once have characterized services at Stanton Street.

One year another gay male member wrote a script for a brief
*Purimshpil,* a performance on the festive holiday of Purim commemorating the bravery of Queen Esther and the rescue of the Jews of Persia
from an ancient threat of annihilation. Purim performances have long
been used as an opportunity for a kind of communal autoethnography
and especially self-critique. This one took the form of a presentation
about a fantasized plan to renovate the shul. Its author pointed out both
pressures to transform the building and the congregation and pressures
to sustain the illusion or reality of continuity with the congregation's
past and the Jewish past. The script accordingly proposes a range of
modifications to the existing building, such as reuse of the old women's
gallery as a showcase for Jewish art.

> Since all that art will be up there, the men's section might look kind of
> bare, so it has been decided to add a sculpture garden. Since we have so
> much room, it'll be easy to stand a statue here and there. They'll also
> be useful to put the extra *talleisim* on too.
>
> Of course we haven't gotten many statues yet, but we have commis-
> sioned the work "Waiting for the Tenth Man." Nine male figures sitting
> and standing around staring at the door. Almost like the real thing, but
> with a reproduction of Salvador Dali's "dripping clock" on the wall to
> set the mood!

At that time, one of the most pressing issues threatening the building's,
and the congregation's, future was a leaking roof: The Purim proposal?

> We are getting rid of the roof.
> "So what will keep the rain out?" You must be asking.
> I'll tell you.

A complex of eleven apartments!

Why eleven? Simple! We need ten men for a minyan. But if someone has to go the bathroom, we'll have one extra! Naturally, the leases require that every tenant has at least one male over thirteen years of age, and you'll get a discount in rent if there are more of them.

We've wired the intercoms on each apartment to Benny Sauerhaft's seat, so that if you guys oversleep, he can get you down immediately! (Benny's voice: "Call apahtment seventin!")

The script goes on to imagine all the amenities an American Orthodox community expects today. It proposed, in the immediate vicinity of the shul, on the blocks where so much redevelopment work had been going on anyway: a *mikva* or ritual bath; a kosher supermarket; a health club and café; and the crowning glory, a new yeshiva.

So where does this leave the Stanton Street Shul today? Is it just hanging in the air, or hanging by a thread? It might seem so, in the context of a Lower East Side in which all that is solid seems to melt into air.[6] The boundaries of the neighborhood themselves are always shifting—not least because of "new-old" institutions such as the Stanton Street Shul itself, which draws congregants from beyond what we're used to thinking of as the Lower East Side, from those precincts further west with names like Soho and Tribeca.

The Stanton Street Shul is at the edge of the Lower East Side both geographically and halakhically, in terms of Jewish law and practice. At the same time, the Orthodox "core" along Grand Street is growing ever more porous, largely due to the privatization of the co-ops. The free market in the co-op buildings has brought an influx of money and its concomitant, freedom of choice, into the neighborhood. Our congregation is positioned within a range of congregations and movements that are struggling to balance *halakha*, the binding tradition of Jewish law, with widely shared egalitarian principles. It is the first congregation to do so in a community that has prided itself on a form of authenticity that scrupulously avoids the cutting edge.

On the holiday of Simchas Torah in 2006, 180 Stanton Street saw a

---

6. I take this phrase from Karl Marx, via Marshall Berman's *All That Is Solid Melts Into Air: The Experience of Modernity*. I have been especially influenced by Berman's chapter on the destruction of neighborhoods in the Bronx as part of Robert Moses's regional development efforts.

reading from the Torah by and for women only, to my knowledge the first time such an event had ever been held on the Lower East Side. Events like this one help define the congregation's special mission and help push along the new syntheses of traditional authority with contemporary values that must always be one aspect of a living Jewish community. Yet they also arouse suspicion from outside.

Stanton Street, in addition to being located on the geographical margins of the Lower East Side, might be considered on its religious margins as well. With the decline of the neighborhood's Jewish population, the resulting excess of synagogue space relative to potential participants, and the arrival of young Jewish adults with excellent secular educations, the most natural position for Stanton Street to continue functioning as an independent congregation is at the most "progressive" end of the traditionalist form of Judaism known as Orthodoxy. That means that Stanton Street is committed to the authority of Jewish law as handed down through the centuries of rabbinic scholarship, but also to outreach in many directions: increasing women's participation, welcoming Jews who have limited religious competency or who are not observant, and balancing Jewish identity with universal human sympathies. To some in the neighborhood, this has at times made it seem as though Stanton Street were not truly an "Orthodox" congregation, but perhaps *Conservative*—a designation that, in this context, actually suggests a step toward the left in religious terms.

A few years ago, my brother, Daniel Boyarin, a Talmud scholar whose graduate work was done at the Conservative Jewish Theological Seminary, was invited to speak at Stanton Street. His talk received a friendly write-up on a shul member's blog. A commenter took the event as further evidence that Stanton Street is outside the Orthodox camp. He bitterly complained that someone with a degree from the Conservative Seminary should not be allowed to teach in an Orthodox shul. The exchange was puerile, but it reflected a real tension. In August 2006, Stanton Street hired Yossi Pollak as its first rabbi since Rabbi Singer. Another young rabbi on the Lower East Side told Yossi that Stanton Street would have to decide whether it was inside or outside the Lower East Side Orthodox community's camp. But how new all of this is may be more a matter of time frame than anything else.

Maybe even these controversies are themselves signs of a healthy tradition. Certainly it wasn't sweetness and light back in the old days.

Questions were raised in Rabbi Singer's day, too, about whether some of his practices were entirely consistent with Jewish law. Some people would mutter that the little *sukka*, the holiday booth he built on the fire escape in the back of the building every year, was not up to halakhic standards. And even some of the men who loyally attended daily morning services to be with Rabbi Singer objected to his practice, when short one man for the minyan, of opening up the Torah ark and counting the scroll inside as the tenth.

When Rabbi Pollak first came, he struggled to summon a daily minyan, just as Rabbi Singer did in his day and Rabbi Josh Yuter does now. And in his first couple of months, he too insisted there was no justification in halakha whatsoever for opening up the ark to make the minyan. Here, it seemed, was one point where tradition would not be allowed to stand in the way of Orthodoxy. But eventually his resistance to opening up the ark for a "tenth" evaporated entirely. No one would have expected it, and maybe no one else thinks it yet, but I began to suspect that perhaps the ghost of Rabbi Singer lived on in Rabbi Pollak. Was it just a coincidence that both of them were redheads . . . and that our next new rabbi, Josh Yuter, is a redhead too?

The summer of 2008 was, in any case, a moment of particular uncertainty for the Stanton Street Congregation. Rabbi Pollak had announced that he was moving on to another post—no surprise, as his wife was expecting their first child and the rabbi's salary at Stanton Street is hardly that of a full-time employee. Hence much of this account is colored by his impending departure and by our concern about changes that were certain to come.

A brief note on synagogue practice seems in order before we begin. The Stanton Street congregation at the beginning of the twenty-first century generally follows the religious standards of Modern Orthodox Judaism, or the more liberal fringes thereof. Men and women are seated separately during religious services. Women are not included as members of the minyan. At the same time, Stanton Street is known as a synagogue that creates new opportunities for participation by women, such as the annual reading of the Scroll of Esther by and for women on the holiday of Purim. Various key Sabbath restrictions—such as not turning electric appliances on or off, not using microphones, not cook-ing—are observed inside the synagogue, though members' private be-havior is not scrutinized too closely. All food brought into and served at the synagogue is kosher according to Orthodox standards.

Jewish tradition mandates three daily prayer services: morning (here called *shacharis*), afternoon (*mincha*), and evening (*maariv*). An individual Jew may fulfill his obligation in private, though it is con-sidered meritorious to pray with a minyan. If the congregation is large enough, all of these may be held, with a minyan, on a daily basis (though the afternoon and evening services are often combined into one session). Key aspects of the service may only be performed if there is a minyan present; the most salient here are the brief readings from the Five Books of Moses ("Torah reading") on Monday and Thursday mornings and Saturday afternoons, as well as the full weekly portion or *parasha* on Sabbath and holiday mornings; the *kedusha* (roughly, "sanctus") recited by the prayer leader; and the mourner's prayer, or *kaddish*, which is recited by an individual mourner, but only in the presence of a minyan. As of the summer of 2008, there was no after-noon-evening service at Stanton Street during the week. Hence, serv-ices were held seven mornings a week; on Friday night, to welcome the Sabbath; and on Saturday starting in the late afternoon, to usher the Sabbath out.

For practical as well as sacred reasons, the daily liturgy is less elabo-rate than that for the Sabbath and festivals. On an ordinary weekday, a morning service at Stanton Street lasts around forty minutes or so, and perhaps ten minutes longer on a Monday or Thursday, when a Torah reading is included. This service begins with a series of blessings, recita-tions of Rabbinic texts and psalms, all of which can be recited without a minyan present if necessary. If a certain point is arrived at, however, without a minyan present, a decision must be made whether to wait for a tenth to arrive or to continue as a group of individuals with a curtailed service. In either case, key further elements of the morning service in-clude the *Shema*, the declaration "Hear, O Israel, the Lord our God, the Lord is One," with related Bible paragraphs and blessings before and af-ter; the *Shemona Esrei* ("Eighteen Blessings") or *Amida*, a set of suppli-cations and praises addressed to God; and the *Aleynu* ("It is incumbent upon us"), an assertion of faith in the ultimate dominion of God throughout the world and His recognition among all peoples. Not, to

be sure, that most congregants at Stanton Street are thinking about all
this theology as they recite the prayers every morning.

During weekday morning services only, male participants (and recently, but still very rarely, a female participant as well) will wear tefillin,
as mentioned above. These consist of boxes made of cured and hard-
ened leather containing prescribed Torah excerpts, handwritten on
parchment by a scribe and worn on the bicep and the forehead, to
which are attached long leather straps. The tefillin are worn in fulfillment of the biblical commands to bind "these words which I command
thee this day" "for a sign upon thy hand, and . . . for frontlets between
thine eyes" (Deut. 6:8).

Sabbath and festival prayers take longer (and almost always start later
in the morning as well). As a matter of community standards, no one is
supposed to be rushing off to work, which is forbidden by Jewish law on
these days. The additional elements include more preliminary hymns, a
longer Torah reading, an additional reading (*haftora*) from the Prophets
or *Writings*, and an additional musaf prayer that symbolically represents
the extra sacrifices made on these special days when the Temple still stood
in Jerusalem. For better or for worse, rabbis generally give sermons on
these days as well, though this is not a requirement of Jewish law.

I have referred above to the weekly Torah portion. An Orthodox congregation will, in the course of a lunar Jewish year, complete the public
recitation of the entire Five Books of Moses, from "In the beginning" to
"in the eyes of all Israel." A parasha, or proportionate segment of the
reading, is allocated to every Sabbath of the year, and that parasha gives
its name in turn to the Sabbath on which it is read. My chapter divisions
here refer both to the Torah readings of the various Sabbaths during the
summer of 2008 and to the weeks that culminated in those Sabbath days.
They begin with Leviticus 25:1, and end with Numbers 36:13.[7] They
deal with matters such as genealogy, census, journeying, interethnic con-
flict, ritual obligations, retribution, and social justice. Their readings will,
with God's help, never be exhausted. I hope that my allusions to them
here will help give some sense of how eternal repetition and utter singu-
larity come together in the Jewish experience of social time.

7. My quotations are from the Jewish Publication Society's 1955 bilingual edition
*The Holy Scriptures.*

# Week One

*And if thy brother be waxen poor, and his means fail with thee;
then thou shalt uphold him: as a stranger and a settler shall he live
with thee. . . . I am the Lord your God, who brought you forth out
of the land of Egypt, to give you the land of Canaan, to be your
God. . . . Ye shall keep My sabbaths, and reverence my sanctuary: I
am the Lord.*

—LEVITICUS 25:35, 38; 26:2

*Detail of Embroidered Lion on Paroches (Covering of Holy Ark)*

## Day One of Parshas Behar (Sunday, May 11, 2008)

Things happen, schedules get disrupted, places get renamed, places get destroyed, sometimes not entirely forgotten. If you think you know what you're going to see and describe before you get there, you're often going to find you're too late.

Sitting in front of my Thinkpad to start this book, I shift my gaze from a screen showing a photograph I took last week on my cell phone while driving in the countryside between Lawrence and Baldwin City, Kansas. It shows a historical marker before a flat, plowed field reading: "Brooklyn. Early Trading Post on Santa Fe Trail. Destroyed by Quantrill August 21, 1863." Remind me, come August 21, and I will mourn the destruction of Brooklyn.

Again the summer starts abruptly, a few days too early. The first time, two summers ago, I had unwisely chosen to stick to my plan to celebrate the end of my first year teaching at the University of Kansas by participating in the annual Wheat State Whirlwind Tour, a bus trip through the heart and guts of the state, even though my wife Elissa was scheduled for neck surgery the same week. On Wednesday, the third day of the tour, as we settled into our motel in Dodge City for the night, I got a cell-phone call from a cousin closely watching Elissa's recuperation, telling me she had contracted hospital pneumonia and I should come home as quickly as possible. So I made the 5:30 A.M. flight to Kansas City, took a taxi back to Lawrence, and began the marathon drive to New York in time to accompany Elissa home from the hospital. A visiting cousin innocently said, "You must be glad to be back in New York," and I just glowered at her in response. I was heartbroken not to be able to finish the tour, but as some kind of recompense, for the rest of my life I'll be able to tell people about the time I had to get out of Dodge City before sunrise. And if some of my friends get sick of hearing the story, it will just mean I have lived long enough to become an old bore.

This time, two years later, I had again chosen to stay on out of town for a couple of weeks after my semester ended. I was looking forward to a visit back to Kansas, followed by a few days hiking with a friend in the mountains of my new professional home of North Carolina. Today is Sunday, the first day of the new Jewish week. I had planned to fly to New York from Raleigh for the summer Monday, tomorrow, but on Thursday night Elissa called, reporting herself dreadfully sick, suffering from the neck spasms that have plagued her ever since her surgery and from severe nausea caused by a changeover in medications. So my friend and I ended our excursion early and drove north all day Friday.

Perhaps it was because I was eager to begin this writing, but this time I was indeed glad to be back in New York, unlike the time I left Dodge City in the middle of our whirlwind tour. Here I am in New York for the summer, as far as I know, but as I say, things happen, schedules get disrupted. It's not likely, in any case, that Elissa will recover enough for us to be able to travel much this summer, so I should be here.

So this journal begins on a Sunday, the first day of the weekly Torah portion of Behar, "on the mountain"—a day when, to indulge a cheap pun, I might otherwise have been climbing a mountain but am instead at my desk in our dining room on the Lower East Side. The notion was that each weekday morning I would get up and go to the morning minyan at the Stanton Street Shul, where I've been a regular on and off now since November 9, 1983 (I know because I immediately started keeping field notes, on a diskette that's probably unreadable now if I could find it, on a word-processing program few would remember ever existed). I'd come home and write a thousand words and see if I had a book by the end of the summer. "Sounds simple, no?" I hear Zero Mostel as Tevye rhetorically asking.

But things happen, people die: this time Mr. Erving Krause, one of the older regulars who started coming to Stanton Street several years ago out of friendship for Benny Sauerhaft, himself well into his nineties (he should live to a hundred and twenty). Benny's the president of the Stanton Street Synagogue, which I'll mostly be calling our shul here. So for today and the next few days, no morning services will be held at Stanton Street; instead, the regulars are invited to attend the shiva minyan at Mr. and Mrs. Krause's apartment in the Grand Street co-ops, providing a quorum of ten Jewish men (that's the minyan) so that his son may recite the mourner's prayer while observing the initial seven-day period of ritual mourning (that's the shiva).

I walked into the Krause apartment at 8:30. A minyan was already present, only one or two of them folks I recognized from Stanton Street, including Benny Sauerhaft and Jack Fish, a former vice president of the shul who has since returned to his old congregation on Sixteenth Street (uptown!). Our rabbi for just a few more months now, Yossi Pollak, straggled in after me, along with a couple more Stanton Street regulars. A cooler of bottled water had been placed in the hall leading to the living room where the minyan was being held. The cooler bore the logo of the organization that provides for mourners' needs, the logo in Hebrew and English script using the distinctive font that indicates the organization is somehow connected to the *ArtScroll* publishing organization.

Mr. Krause's son, whom I could not see during the service because I stood just outside the living room itself, led the service in a fluent Ashkenazi Hebrew. For one long moment during the service, Benny and I looked at each other. I'm not sure what his eyes were saying, but I think mine were saying the same thing, and it was something like, "Here we are, both alive, and it's nothing to take for granted, because after all, here's Erving Krause already gone."

## Day Two of Parshas Behar, May 12, 2008

On a rainy, cool spring morning like this, dream, gossip, prayer, and memory seem to share no interest in their borders with one another. Our bedroom overlooks the corner of Avenue A and East Third Street, which makes it light on sunny days, noisy on weekend nights, and cold whenever a wind is blowing. Drowsy and half-awake, I see it is light and wonder if I am late, unused to setting an alarm after months in the North Carolina countryside.

Not late, surely, for the shiva minyan on Grand Street that I attended yesterday, though today being Monday and a work day, it will begin an hour earlier than Sunday. But I dread the thought of walking to Grand Street in the rain (my mother would say: "You're not made of sugar, you won't melt") and the notion of taking the bus there seems too silly. Besides, that living room will be full of men wet like me, if they've come from as far as I would, rather than (as more likely) from other apartments in the same huge Grand Street co-op building or from similar ones nearby.

But a bit late, not entirely too late, for the other option, one that Rabbi Pollak had put in my mind when he told me that Stanton Street would not be holding services during the shiva for Mr. Krause: "They seem to be getting enough men at the shiva minyan, so if you want to go somewhere else for a few days, this is the time to do it. Anyway, after the shiva, we're really going to be needing you back at Stanton Street"— after all, Mr. Krause himself had been one of the regulars, and he certainly won't be there. Another regular, Dudi Dembitser, is going on a trip to Israel and will be away for some time. (I asked him, "Are you planning to come back?" and only when he answered that he was did I wish him, in Ashkenazi Hebrew and then in Yiddish, "Go in peace and return in peace," explaining that I had learned this practice from Rabbi Singer *alav hasholem*, may he rest in peace. Since, in principle, one who manages to find his way to the Land of Israel is then supposed to stay there, Rabbi Singer never wanted to assume that a fellow Jew was making a one-way trip instead.)

*Reader, do you not know Rabbi Singer? I shall have to introduce you to his memory, later this summer, if we find the time. No, not Rabbi Singer from the Bialystoker Shul. No, not Rabbi Singer from Boro Park; they were his cousins. This was Rabbi Yosl Singer . . .*

The other option, one that I chose this morning, was the regular minyan at the Community Synagogue on East Sixth Street between Second and Third Avenues. I'd been a regular there, too, for years while I worked long hours as a lawyer in midtown; starting a few minutes earlier, ending more promptly, and leaving shul already several blocks closer to work added up to billable hours. Besides, even then the crowd at Stanton Street often had to wait fifteen, twenty minutes, half an hour sometimes until there was an actual minyan. At Community, now as then, more than half of the congregation are men who live outside Manhattan, drive in early, join us, and work nearby, some at Beth Israel Hospital just up First Avenue. The Community Synagogue minyan is scheduled to start at 6:30, and does, but I was still impressed to walk in at 6:40 and find them already beginning the Amidah, the core of daily prayer as far as the ancient rabbis were concerned, so called because it is recited while standing. But there are many pages in the morning service before the Amidah—so you take a look at an Orthodox prayer book and tell me how they could possibly do that in ten minutes!

Sam Lemberger, owner of the Second Avenue Deli (his older son is the manager now, at the new location at Thirty-Third and Third—no kidding, that's where it is, this isn't a joke about *toity-toid street*; I asked Sam why he relocated there after he lost the lease at Tenth Street and Second Avenue, and he answered, "I bought the building!") immediately comes over to me as I'm putting on my tefillin: "So I heard you're looking for a rabbi [at Stanton Street]. Maybe you'll take Charlie?[1] Is Chovevei helping you with the search?[2] Sure, moving to Westport is the right move for Rabbi Pollak. He'll earn a living there, he'll get a house there. The only question is whether he'll move on to a bigger city eventually. I wish Community and Stanton Street could coordinate in some way—we're appealing to the same crowd."

I get impatient with Sam's kibitzing and eventually indicate that I want to focus on praying: "Okay, let me daven." But it's not as if I really had some *kavone*, some intent to communicate with God this morning. I just want to be with Jews doing something relatively innocuous (though surely sexist) and old-fashioned, and I want something to write about every morning this summer. Most of the faces are familiar to me, though I can't put names to many of them: anyway, Shimon the Israeli contractor, Barry the restaurant-furniture manufacturer, Stan the guy with the English accent who loves to bang on the synagogue's old piano. And they notice me, too, and remember my Hebrew name, and call me to recite the blessing over a portion of the weekday Torah reading.

For the second of three times this week—Sabbath afternoon, and then again Monday and Thursday mornings—the minyan hears the beginning of Parshas Behar. After I recite the blessing, I stand in front of the Torah scroll next to the *baal kore*, the Torah reader. Silently I mouth the words of the passage as he chants them aloud, and the text once again tempts me to florid allegorizations of homecoming, of the Lower East Side as another promised land: "When you come into the land which I give you, then shall the land keep a sabbath unto the Lord"

1. Currently rabbi of the Community Synagogue but, as Jack had complained to me and as I can confirm as of this morning, not a regular at the morning minyan there. Elissa and I are both very fond of this rabbi.
2. Yeshivat Chovevei Torah is the recently-established "open Orthodox" rabbinic seminary, where our Rabbi Pollak received his ordination.

(Lev. 25:1)—but the Sabbath, when we're forbidden to write, is just the day of the week when I won't be making entries in this journal. In "the fiftieth year . . . you shall return every man unto his possession, and you shall return every man unto his family" (Lev. 25:10). Well, the apartment is in our joint names, though I think of it as Elissa's, and I like to joke when I come back for a spell during the semester, "Nice place you got here, lady!"

There is a mourner at the Community Shul minyan, as well; I presume that, wherever he lives and whatever his family situation, he is with us to say kaddish in the absence of a minyan at his home. At the end of the service, he comes forward and sits on the low step to the platform in front of the ark where the Torah scrolls are kept. One by one we approach him and murmur, as we did before Mr. Krause's family yesterday, the Hebrew formula "May you be comforted among the other mourners of Zion and Jerusalem."

## Day Three of Parshas Behar, May 13, 2008

A better night's sleep, and a brighter and calmer morning, leave me awake in time to get to the Community Synagogue by the beginning of the morning service today. This morning there's no particular reason to go to Community rather than the shiva minyan, except that it starts earlier and I want to get my day going. Anyway, I can't get inside the Stanton Street Shul, deeper into the heart of the Jewish Lower East Side, can't get to the ultimate "there" of this journal, while it's closed during Mr. Krause's minyan. Though of course I'm doing (in the phrase of the feminist anthropologist Kamala Viswesaran) homework, rather than fieldwork, somehow I feel like an old-fashioned anthropologist stymied in his journey toward the native village by a colonial bureaucracy, a flood, a war . . . a shiva at the mourners' home.

So I take notes meanwhile at some other village, at the margin of the field site, a little closer to the metropole, a little farther uptown. Deduction: at least two of the young men who seem to be regulars at the Community Synagogue minyan are, as I had guessed, students, since on their way out this morning one of them asked his fellow: "So, did you pull an all-nighter?" (It's exam time, though some, like me, have already finished the spring semester; that's why I'm in New York, after all.) It would be inaccurate to say that the Community Synagogue minyan, in the decade or so since I've become familiar with it, was ever a congregation primarily made up of old men, unlike several other minyanim on the East Side. But it does seem nevertheless that the average age has dropped in those years. New people, such as these students, have come. Too many of the elderly have departed, along with others, may we be preserved, who hardly seemed to be at the end of their term.

Bill Feinerman, who is still alive and well into his nineties, but barely able to move on his own, was a regular in the years I first started coming to the Community. A well-built man with a solid mustache, carefully dressed, articulate, of firm opinions about many things, including proper synagogue behavior and customs. Whatever he still remembers of the old days in the neighborhood I will never learn from him now (how much documentation I have *failed to do* over the past three decades will haunt me, as long as my own consciousness holds out).

Across from Bill sat Mr. Irving Feld, the synagogue's *gabbai*.[3] One morning years ago Feinerman and Feld were having a conversation during the morning services. I have no idea what the topic was. Feld didn't understand something Feinerman said, and Feinerman repeated it. Feld said he still didn't understand, so Feinerman growled, "I'll write you a letter!"

No, I'm remembering wrong. It wasn't Feld sitting across from Feinerman that day, it was Max Isaacs, a local businessman (primarily real estate), one of the surviving founders of the congregation from 1948, who boasted of his friendship with Eleanor Roosevelt. What do I remember about Max Isaacs, without digging deeper? First, his gait, supported by a cane, but always determined and even impatient; and second, a joke he repeated several times, looking at the supermarket circulars: "Shrimp is still high!" As though he were still just waiting for the price to come down on this obviously nonkosher food. Certainly he was not meaning to signal that he ever intended to buy it at any price, but perhaps all the same he was reminding the congregation that none of the members might be quite as observant as he appeared when among the congregation.

3. *Gabbai* is a word no one has quite learned to translate into English, partly because the functions of the role it designates have changed through the centuries. In certain Jewish institutions the *gabbai* (plural *gabbaim*) were the trustees, but here it means something like "the one who's running the show."

Another missing member is evoked, in the word *levracha* ("for a blessing") that Barry the furniture dealer interjects at a certain moment in the Amidah. Barry began saying *levracha* because for years he sat next to Hy Genee, a longtime neighbor better known as the stalwart of Kehilla Kedosha Janina, the Romaniote Greek synagogue (as Elissa says, the only true *synagoga* on the Lower East Side) down on Broome Street off Allen. Even at this Ashkenazi minyan, Hy kept and displayed a few nonobtrusive aspects of a non-Ashkenazi prayer style.

I take a moment to mention to Barry that I appreciate his recalling Hy in this way, and he responds by mentioning another other congregant who used to sit next to Barry: "You know Phil Mandel died about a year ago?" I had indeed heard about Phil's death at the time, though I'd been away in Kansas. Elissa and I had known Phil so long that we were practically the only people in the neighborhood who still called him Fishl, Efroyim Fishl ben Shloyme Aryeh, if my memory serves me. (*Reader, never assume that my memory serves me. If I don't remember, I try not to make it up, but my recall is far from photographic, even when I do trust it.*) We knew Fishl, a lifelong bachelor, from several shuls in the neighborhood. The first was the old Eighth Street Shul several blocks closer to the East River, between Avenue B and Avenue C—to us it is something much like a person who has died. (Maimonides tells us that when one passes the place where a synagogue was formerly located, he is to recite the same prayer, "Blessed be the true Judge," as upon hearing for the first time of the death of a fellow Jew.) For years Fishl/Phil came to Rabbi Singer's Shul—now Stanton Street—on Sabbath mornings, until Rabbi Ackerman on Sixth Street (he should live and be well, though in fact he's got numerous health problems he was detailing to me after the morning minyan today) absolutely needed him to come back and help run the services. I've spent my time at Rabbi Ackerman's shul, too. And Phil came every morning to Community, until his heart attack. I guess he may have been seventy. That seventy starts to seem young to me suggests that I'm getting to be no spring chicken myself.

## Day Four of Parshas Behar, May 14, 2008

I'm out the door at Third Street and Avenue A, and turn right one block past the schoolyard. I'm always scoping out the parking patterns to determine the best time to move my car in accordance with alternate side of the street parking regulations, since I need to move it twice a week as long as I don't drive anywhere. Then I take a right on First until I catch up with Rabbi Ackerman, slowing down to walk at his pace out of respect, affection, and long acquaintanceship. I'm not in any particular rush to get to the Community Synagogue anyway.

After the quick service, I talked with Barry about exactly when in the reader's repetition of the Amidah he interjects the word *levracha*, but I'm still puzzled. Here's why: The Community Synagogue follows the Ashkenazi *nusach*, one of the two most common orders for the daily prayer services among East European Jews. The other is called "Sefardi." Although it's actually followed by Ashkenazi Jews, those stemming from the Hasidic communities of Europe, the Sefardi ritual shares some features with the order of prayer followed by *Sefardim*, Jewish communities descended from Iberian Jews. Now, in the Amidah text according to the Sefardi ritual, the words *morid hatal* ("He makes the dew descend") are included during the part of each year that falls in the summer, between Passover and the end of the fall holidays. Barry told me that he adds *levracha* in memory of Hy Genee: "I'm 100 percent Ashkenazi, but it's become second nature to me. When I get to Heaven I might have to answer for it. I get funny looks when I go to other shuls and say that. I even say it when I'm praying at the Wall." But he also told me that when he interjects *levracha*, it's in response to *morid hatal*—words that never appear in the Ashkenazi order used at Community Synagogue. So when did Hy say it when he attended Community Synagogue, and when does Barry say it? The mystery has not been solved as of this writing. Either there's something I'm missing or something I've still gotten wrong.

If this confused me, and it seems like it may have confused Barry as well, you can be forgiven for still not quite understanding what "Sefardi" means, what kind of Jew Hy was (he was a wonderful Jew!) or exactly what combination of words evoke the response *levracha* from Barry today. But the analysis is not trivial. What lesson do you learn from it? *Shma mina tarti*, "Learn two things from this," say the Rabbis of the Talmud. First, that an ethnographer might not always get the "correct" explanation for a given practice, even when she gets that answer directly from the practitioner. I know I'm not the first scholar to share that caveat. Second, more particularly here, that Jewishness is not only profoundly a culture of memory, but also, and perhaps more precisely, a culture profoundly infused with substitutions. Let me be a bit pedantic for a moment. *To substitute* may be either an intransitive verb, "to act or serve in place of another," or a transitive verb, "to put or use in the place of another."

So many substitutions are involved in Barry's little interjection here. I see at least four, and possibly five. The first and greatest is that which constitutes nearly all synagogue prayer, which substitutes for the sacrifices and purification rituals of the lost Temple in Jerusalem. Second is the substitution of whatever land the congregation happens to be located in for the Land of Israel; the seasons for dew and rain follow, of course, the ancient climate cycles of the Middle East, and not the northeastern United States, so we praise God for making the dew descend and for making the rain to fall and the wind to blow during the dry and wet seasons of a very distant land. Third, perhaps, it may be that Hy, when he still lived and interjected *levracha*, was substituting a generic non-Ashkenazi practice for the more particular ritual of the Romaniotes, the ancient Greek Jewish community, which he did his very best to maintain and to transmit but which has been largely lost despite his best efforts. Fourth, when Hy individually interjected *levracha* at this Ashkenazi synagogue, he was acting or serving in the place of an entire congregation that followed his own native ritual but no longer held daily services. Fifth and most surely, when Barry interjects *levracha* he is substituting for Hy (and also for Phil Mandel, who sat next to them and adopted the custom from Hy around the same time Barry did). I wouldn't be attending to any of this right now, of course, but for the fact that the shiva minyan at Mr. Krause's is substituting for the daily morning minyan at Stanton Street, permitting or obligating me to substitute Community for Stanton Street for these few first days.

There is (at least) a third insight to be learned from this little cultural item, suggested to me perhaps by Barry's mention of his prayers at the Wall in Jerusalem. Adopting from his synagogue neighbor Hy Genee an aspect of a very different ritual tradition, Barry was making (and continues to make) an assertion about the unity of all Jews, a gesture toward the reunification of all diasporic rituals into one. This substitution of *levracha* then is not only a gesture toward what has been lost (the Land, the ritual, a friend) but a supplement, a brick contributed toward the rebuilding of the other walls of the Temple.

## *Day Five of Parshas Behar, May 15, 2008*

Back to Stanton Street at last. An e-mail had been sent out announcing that we would return to the morning minyan in shul today, but not to the downstairs beis medresh. Rather, we were upstairs in the main shul, because during the morning Torah reading a new baby girl was to receive her Hebrew name. The festive occasion mandated the use of the more formal, though somewhat dilapidated space that a more modern congregation might call the sanctuary. The baby's parents are named Paris and Rivka. They live on Grand Street, and Rabbi Pollak had performed their wedding, though I'd never seen them in the shul before and wasn't sure they'd ever been inside themselves.

When I arrived, there were nine men present, but with me, there still wasn't a minyan. How could that be? Well, one of the men wore neither tallis nor tefillin, so I had to guess he wasn't Jewish. Remember, an Orthodox minyan isn't just ten men—though you might hear references to "the tenth man"—unless you're Jewish, you literally don't count. A chance to record one of my favorite stories about Rabbi Singer. One Friday evening more than twenty years ago, I passed through the lobby of our apartment building, and a neighbor about my age asked me what synagogue I was headed to. I brought him along to Stanton Street. As we walked, he explained to me that his grandfather had been Jewish, his wife was an Israeli Jew, and he was now beginning to study for conversion to Judaism. We entered the shul and were the ninth and tenth men. I approached Rabbi Singer and explained quietly, "This young man wants to convert to Judaism"—so Rabbi Singer understood that my companion could not complete the minyan. Meanwhile, the rest of the congregation, assuming that there were ten male Jews present and we already had a minyan, wondered why Rabbi Singer wouldn't start the service: "Let's get going! I want to eat supper! You've got a minyan! What are you waiting for?" Of course Rabbi Singer didn't want to shame my companion by explaining to everyone that he wasn't Jewish. He stalled as long as he could, but no one else came in—and finally he said, "Okay, we'll start davening." In other words, Rabbi Singer chose to ignore the need for the tenth man—sorry, the tenth male Jew—rather than shame another.

This day when I entered, the prayers were being led by someone I didn't recognize, but should have. I had met him on Sunday morning at the shiva minyan for Mr. Krause, and he is Erving Krause's son. Later I overheard him say that he hadn't been in the shul for twenty-five years (he lives on Grand Street, in the same building as Benny Sauerhaft). I also heard the tail end of a conversation he had with Rabbi Pollak: "and there's always a late minyan at 9:00 if I need that." I'm guessing that what preceded that sentence was an exchange about the younger Krause attending our minyan regularly while he's saying kaddish, followed by Rabbi Pollak's very proper caveat that some days we might not get a minyan and it won't be possible for Krause to say kaddish with us. We'll see over the coming weeks whether that's what happens. There's something a bit too ethnograpically neat about the son coming to take the place of, to substitute for, the father in such a direct way. But the minyan wouldn't mind; it would be a blessing.

If I were quicker, or a bit more inquisitive and had a sharper memory, I'd know more about the families of the parents of the new baby who received the name Orli Rachel this morning. I did hear that the parents have a four-bedroom apartment on Grand Street (so they're not poor; very few young couples on the Lower East Side these days are, it seems). I did hear that the mother's father (no, it must be her grandfather), the patriarch of the family, a Holocaust survivor, had recently arrived from Israel to live . . . hmmm, in Soho? . . . with the parents of the young mother. Far from being disgruntled at his displacement, he is delighted to be among a growing family.

This is by no means the first new baby that's been welcomed into the congregation at Stanton Street in the past few years. It's some contrast to the days when our son Jonah was routinely the only child present. Still, we don't exactly have a junior congregation yet, either. But I'm not so much trying to sketch the changing demographics here as explain the nuance of my own reaction to the special event: it is fine to see new people in shul, but I was actually looking around to see who was part of the regular minyan, not just a flash in the pan for the special day. When I arrived, the regulars present were Benny, Rabbi Pollak, Dan Cantor, and an older man who's a friend of Benny's too, I guess, but whose name I've never learned. Gradually a few more regulars drifted in, including Buddy Bardin, who lives up on Eighth Street and whom I have known for a long time from the old Eighth Street Shul days; Charles Copeland, whom I know from our "beginners" class at Rabbi Feinstein's yeshiva on East Broadway, also back in the early 1980s; Pete Silver, our weekday

Torah reader, who comes regularly despite being in shockingly poor
health. I counted eleven regulars all told by the end. Yes, I counted
them, though tradition has it that it's bad luck to count Jews. And
should I count young Krause, as well?

Another regular showed up whom I hadn't seen in the morning for
some time: Melech Goldfeld, a character I'm tempted to describe as
straight out of a Sholem Aleichem story, except that he's too smart
and too competent. Melech is in the discount long-distance telephone
business and has a partner who's a Satmar Hasid from Williamsburg.
I hadn't seen Melech for some time, and a couple of years back he'd
consulted me, informally, about some potential litigation against his
partner. Now, he reported, he'd finally gotten the case to the *beis din*,
the rabbinical court administered by Yeshiva University. Overhearing,
Rabbi Pollak asked in astonishment: "How did you get a Satmar
Hasid to go to a YU beis din?" Indeed, I would hardly have expected
anyone from the highly traditionalist Satmar community to accept
the authority of Yeshiva University's Modern Orthodox rabbis.
Melech's answer was that, in the minimal contract he and his partner
had signed, there was a stipulation that this was where all disputes
were to be resolved.

Although a beis din procedure does not follow the formalities of a
civil court, apparently it is in practice possible to have a lawyer present.
Melech reported that his adversary was represented by Nat Lewin, famous for arguing various cases on behalf of Orthodox Jewish organizations and institutions.

But I argued a lot better than he did, because I know the case so much
better and because I knew who the judges were. One of them is Rabbi
Prusansky, from Teaneck. He's a big Zionist. So it was great that the
beis din was on Yom Ha'Atzmaut, the Israeli independence day; that
drove the Satmar guy crazy. I wore a *kippa sruga* [a knitted skullcap],
just like the Orthodox Zionists. Do you know Prusansky? He wrote a
book about the Book of Joshua explaining that we should do to the
Arabs what Joshua did. I'm not going to argue about politics with him
now, I'll save that for after the beis din. So at one point I said to
Lewin, "You know, over shabbes I was reading Rabbi Prusansky's
book on Joshua. And at one point Rabbi Prusansky's talking about
an interpretation by the commentator Radak, and he says that's a

*drash r'chok* [literally, a 'distant' interpretation]. I think the claim you made just now is a drash r'chok."

At the beginning of a beis din, the judges are supposed to announce whether they know either of the litigants. One of the judges, the econ-omist—he's not a rabbi—said he didn't know me, and I said, "Sure you know me, you were my economics professor at YU." So later, when I was presenting all of my forecasts and financial analysis to explain how I valued the business, he was absolutely *kvelling* [swelling with pride]. The third judge, Rabbi S——, also said he didn't know me, but the next day he called up the lawyers for the other side and said, "I remember Melech Goldfeld now. He's the one that ran for student body president on a platform of letting girls in the dorms."

Melech told me some more things, too, but I don't think they belong in this story. If he shows up at all regularly to the morning minyan, as he promised Rabbi Pollak he would (promises, promises . . .), I'll cer-tainly have plenty to write about this summer.

Here I go, acting like there were absolutely no women present this morning at all. There were, perhaps five or six, the mother of the new-born girl and her relatives and friends. But the truth is, if this journal really focuses on the morning minyan, as I anticipate, there won't be so much about women in it, even by the end of the summer.

## *Day Six of Parshas Behar, May 16, 2008*

No minyan at Stanton Street this morning, that is, the shul was open and eight men came, but we didn't get a minyan. As a cheap gesture of analogy between narrative and community, I have fragmented notes on each of the men who were there this morning and one or two who weren't.

Item: Young Krause had evidently told Rabbi Pollak that he would plan on joining us Sunday mornings only; that day, indeed, there's a 9:00 minyan that he could always go to if we don't get one at Stanton Street. In any case, he was not there today.

Item: Mr. Krause's son has in fact made a very positive impression on all of us. Rabbi Pollak mentioned that at Erving Krause's funeral last week (a day or two before I returned to New York for the summer), var-ious speakers from the neighborhood had referred to our shul as the

"Brzezaner Shul." But the son Krause had referred to us as the Stanton Street Shul, and Rabbi Pollak, looking forward, counted that in his favor. Nate Hacker responded in a mild tone of voice, "But we *are* the Brzezaner."

Item: Most of the prayer books in use at Stanton Street are the *Nusach Sefarad* (Sefardi ritual) version of the bilingual ArtScroll edition, but there are a few older, Hebrew-only books still around, and I prefer to use them when I can take the trouble to find one. The one I picked up yesterday morning had an inscription documenting its donation on January 16, 2001, "to Rabbi Singer's shul on Stanton Street." Obviously, then, Rabbi Singer had not yet abandoned the shul in early 2001. (This is easy enough to confirm, from documents or from interviews with others, but my memory of dates is poor, so I find this document useful.) But why did the donor need to specify "on Stanton Street"? Although there were other Rabbi Singers, so far as I know, this was the only shul called "Rabbi Singer's shul." Perhaps she already thought of it sometimes as just the "Stanton Street Shul" (although apparently not as the Brzezaner Shul).

The transition to naming a shul by its location is not unique to our case, because the former Young Israel of Fifth Avenue, now separated by litigation from the National Council of Young Israel, is now officially named the Sixteenth Street Synagogue. Sixteenth Street is pretty far uptown from the Lower East Side, although I suppose within walking distance; I don't suppose that particular synagogue is likely to make another appearance in this book.

A number of the minyan "regulars" were there this morning.

The aforementioned Nate Hacker, father of two young children, the shul's treasurer, stalwart and even tempered. As folks were leaving this morning, Benny, the president, asked Nate to come on Sunday morning, since Krause is expected and we really need to have a minyan for someone who's in mourning. (Krause is not the only one.) Nate said he would try, but Sunday is the day of the week he usually takes off from coming to shul. "It's my shabbes," he added.

Pete Silver, whom I've already mentioned. I'll add this detail today: Pete often appears in a sweatshirt saying "Stern College." Once I said to him, "What's the reason for the Stern College sweatshirt?" He answered: "I always wanted to go to Stern College," which is Yeshiva University's college for women, "but they would never admit me, so at least I get to wear the sweatshirt." Oh, and this too: every time I return to shul after a stint out of town, Pete says to me the same thing: "Welcome back to Fun City."

Rabbi Pollak, whom I described glowingly in the voice-over narrative for an Australian Broadcasting Company radio documentary about the Stanton Street Shul made about two years ago, just after Rabbi Pollak had joined us. He'll be leaving us soon for Westport, so this summer is a good time to say whatever I'm going to say about his role at Stanton Street.

Me, about whom nothing more needs to be said today except that, of course, I'm a minyan regular when and only when I'm in New York—summers and winters for the most part, since I teach in North Carolina. It struck me, during my long solitary walk the day before yesterday down through Lower Manhattan's West Side to the Battery, up through Wall Street, and home through the historic East Side, that any time I'm in the neighborhood, it will not be true that there are no Jews left on the Lower East Side. For what that's worth, which may not be much; when I had the thought, it seemed to have some bearing on theoretical discussions of ethnography and temporality, but enough about that for now.

Sol Decker, up from the Washington, D.C., area for a long weekend, a stalwart of the minyan when he's here and an energetic member of the shul's board. Sol originally came to us because he'd known Rabbi Yossi during the year Yossi served as assistant rabbi to Shimen Goldfeld (Melech Goldfeld's brother; remember Melech, from yesterday?) in Washington. It looks like he'll stay with us after Rabbi Pollak leaves.

Isaac Maxon, an earnest and rather strictly observant young man, a student, I believe, single, who's been a regular for the past year and a half or so.

Benny, the president for life, originally from the town of Lancut, Poland, and also president of the Bluzhower-Rymanower Society, which paid "rent" to the Brzezaner Society for decades to share use of the building. That's how Benny became the president, and it has something to do with the reason Benny and Rabbi Singer never seemed to get along.

Dan Cantor, who rides from Grand Street in Benny's 1968 Dodge every morning and gets out of it after Benny parks it on the side of the

street where parking is illegal, but where Benny's car will never be tick-
eted, right next to the shul. While eight of us waited for another to
come in—with nine we could have continued with the regular service,
adopting Rabbi Singer's legal fiction of counting the Torah scroll as the
tenth—Dan stepped outside to the sidewalk to wait for another Jew to
come along.

Apparently he had tried that once, and when someone came past and
Dan asked him, "Are you Jewish?" the man replied, "Is this the Stanton
Street Shul?" He was the father-in-law of a member and had actually
been looking for the shul. So it worked that time, but Dan says now he
doesn't want to try it too often, because he doesn't want to importune
God for such miracles.

*Upstairs, Electric Candelabrum*

# Week Two

*For the land shall be forsaken without them, and shall be paid her Sabbaths, while she lieth desolate without them; and they shall be paid the punishment of their iniquity; because, even because they rejected My ordinances, and their soul abhorred My statutes. And yet for all that, when they are in the land of their enemies, I will not reject them, neither will I abhor them, to destroy them utterly, and to break My covenant with them; for I am the Lord thy God.*

—LEVITICUS 26: 43–44

*Depiction of Rachel's Tomb, Upstairs Sanctuary*

## Day One of Parshas Bechukosai, May 18, 2008

The renovated beis medresh, which seemed beautiful but stark, almost cold, when it was first opened last fall, is starting to acquire atmosphere. The floors have become a little bit scuffed. The half-flight of steps leading down to the beis medresh, which before the renovation were not only worn with decades of footsteps but also markedly tilted to one side, are neither worn nor tilted yet, but the dark stain that was intended to make the new ones look old is already somewhat scuffed as well. Meanwhile, the empty spaces begin to fill with sounds: A young man who grew up in the Belz Hasidic community in Boro Park, who is in the neighborhood as a guest of Isaac Maxon's for shabbes, sings snatches of luxuriant liturgical melodies of the Belzer Hasidic community as we wait on Friday evening for the minyan that never happened, and something of the echoes of his tunes remains in the air even after he has left.

I still have the overwhelming impression, though, that when the downstairs was renovated, all the ghosts departed, as well. Some I can and will recall by name or by some other characteristic: Moshe Sternberg, a former dressmaker (the only reason I know is because, once during my first years in the morning minyan, Mr. Sternberg was given the honor of covering the Torah scroll after the reading, and another member spoke up, "Mr. Sternberg was a dressmaker, I think he knows how to cover the Torah"); the gentle Itshe Duhl; nervous Mr. Teigman, who had a print shop in the neighborhood and bitterly opposed Rabbi Singer's practice of opening up the ark to count the Torah scroll as the tenth for the minyan, threatening at least once to walk out so that there wouldn't even be nine living Jewish men in the room, let alone ten; Heshy Gleicher ("Cheap Heshy"), who for decades owned a discount store around the corner on Clinton Street; Heshy Kolber (Benny was so contemptuous of him that once he muttered, *un dus hot gehat a siti dzhob,* "and *this* had a city job"); Shimen Perlman (a showman with snatches of Yiddish vaudeville and comedy theater; he could imitate a stereotypical *Litvak* Hebrew school teacher or a mock impresario announcing "Ladies and gents, *katshkes un gendz,*" "ducks and geese"); Mr. Berger, who used to yell at Heshy Gleicher and others, including me (Rabbi Singer calmed me down by saying, "He just talks loud"; when Elissa would walk in, he became a perfect gentleman; and when Jonah would come in as a toddler, Berger would call affectionately, "Hey, Pupik!"); Ari Lemkin (he should live and be well), a sad young man who eventually became Rabbi Singer's right-hand man in the shul and resolutely sided with the Singer family once the dispute over the future of the shul broke out; other Heshies and Harries, Moishes and Abes, over the years.

I like to think of their ghosts as being available to make up the minyan, but no one thinks that's how Jewish law works, not even among the minority of us who continue to accept the custom of counting the Torah scroll. May I share an image, without intending disrespect to any of them, simply because it continues to echo, insistent in my mind? It's reported that, when the workmen doing the renovation tore up the old, badly worn floor of the beis medresh, they found nothing below it but dirt. Trapped in the dirt, along with a number of live rats, who scurried away but continued to trouble the building as long as the renovation work was in progress, were dozens of dead rats. I'm glad I didn't see them, and I'm sorry to associate them with memories of past human residents, *lehavdil b'elef havdoles,* that is, to distinguish with a thousand distinctions. Blame the image on that endearing character, the Death of Rats, a sidekick of the equally colorful and sympathetic Death in Terri Pratchett's Discworld novels, or maybe on a joke made by a character in Kugelmass's *The Miracle of Intervale Avenue,* about another old shul in another borough, that you could put a yarmulke on a rat and include him in the minyan.

If we cannot count those who are physically absent, there is no apparent prohibition against one live male Jew doing double duty, attending one minyan and then moving on to fill the complement for another. This happened regularly, weekday mornings in the 1980s and early 1990s, when, in addition to the minyan at Rabbi Singer's shul, the Chasam Sopher shul around the corner on Clinton Street had (as it still does) a morning minyan, and when Rabbi Heftler's shul on Attorney

Street still stood. (It has since collapsed, been demolished and replaced by an apartment building that, in its architectural detail, seems to me, at least, deliberately to recall the outlines of the neoclassical shul that once stood on the spot.) Occasionally, during the months after our first child, Jonah, was born, I would proceed on to Attorney Street after finishing at Rabbi Singer's and come home around 9:00 in the morning, sometimes having had a shot or two with the old men, but Elissa put a stop to that after a month or two. More frequently, we would call Chasam Sopher and ask them to send one man, or maybe two, but we would always be careful to send them right back if another of our regulars straggled in. Occasionally, though not nearly as often, Chasam Sopher would likewise be short one congregant (they paid yeshiva students to come to the morning minyan, an option our even poorer shul didn't have), and Rabbi Singer would be absolutely prompt about taking advantage of this opportunity to even the credit/debit balance of this Lower East Side shul economy. One winter morning, he personally left his shul to make the minyan at Chasam Sopher, in such a rush that he slipped on a patch of ice by the doorway, broke his leg, and was in the hospital for weeks.

This exchange system has broken down in recent years. The Stanton Street congregation is in some respects marginalized or even ostracized by the broader (though still rather narrow) Lower East Side Orthodox community, both because of bad memories left over from the struggle between Rabbi Singer's family and the congregation early in this decade and because of certain issues in Jewish law (the appropriate realm of women's participation; the possibility of creating an *eruv*, or boundary marker to permit carrying on the Sabbath, on the Lower East Side) that appear to some to put Stanton Street outside the Orthodox camp. Things came to such a pass that, about a year ago, the rabbi and the president—or perhaps just the president on his own—of Chasam Sopher declared that they would no longer agree to send men to Stanton Street when we needed someone to make the minyan; we had apparently been put under some kind of communal ban.

Well, yesterday in the early evening, at the time for saying the afternoon service of shabbes, Sol Decker decided that he would go to Chasam Sopher to see if he could borrow a tenth. I guess he just decided that the ban wasn't necessarily going to last forever. He returned promptly with two young Lubavitch Hasidim that I hadn't met before.

One of them, Israeli, but with a reasonably good command of English, told me later that he and his friend had been walking around and went into Chasam Sopher. (He implied that they found the shul more or less by chance, though my assumption has been that when young Lubavitchers walk miles from their base in Crown Heights on shabbes afternoon, they know exactly where they're headed.) A few minutes later, when Sol walked in, he was told by the Chasam Sopher regulars, "Let the Lubavitchers come with you." Perhaps the ban is over. In any case, I suppose it was easier to ignore it this time because these two Lubavitchers, "surplus" Jews, were available for dispatch anyway—no regular member of the Chasam Sopher minyan had to be sent. And perhaps next time they need someone, they won't be too proud to call us, and perhaps next time we need someone, they won't refuse to send one of their regulars.

A returnee to the shul: Andrew Pearl, one of very few daily minyan regulars my age or younger who remembers Rabbi Singer nearly as well as I do. He and his wife, the Bible scholar Sura Ziskind, were very close to Rabbi Singer and among the members angriest at him and his family for attempting by stealth to sell the building. Andrew and Sura gradually drifted away from the congregation in the years after the court battle, though Sura did much for the shul's future by suggesting that we ask the new Yeshivat Chovevei Torah to send us a rabbinic intern until we could hire a new rabbi. When I arrived this morning, Andrew was already arrayed in tallis and tefillin, at the front of the beis medresh. I hope we will see him often.

## Day Two of Parshas Bechukosai, May 19, 2008

Shortly before waking this morning, I dreamed I walked into a modest restaurant in New York and sat down at a separate table next to a large picture window—no, I want to begin with a bit before that, part of the same dream, but in this earlier part, I was sitting outside at the same café. I could overhear two young men sitting at a nearby table, mocking academics for speaking always in generalities. I couldn't help turning to them and retorting that sometimes academics could be *very* specific.

Later, then (but is there really any before and after in dreams?), I sat, as I say, at a table inside. The waiter came over, and I ordered a hot dog. It wasn't a kosher restaurant, but the waiter knew—presumably because

I was wearing my big black velvet yarmulke—that I wanted a kosher hot dog. He said with a smile, "I've got something new for you!" He brought one hot dog, and when I'd finished it he brought a second one, saying "It's a new brand-Halevi!"

When I returned from shul this morning and told Elissa about the dream, she said "You don't need a psychiatrist to explain this one. It's about being able to go someplace and get what you want."

Now that I'm into a rhythm of writing each weekday morning, I start thinking before shul, as I sip my coffee and as I walk from the house, about a theme for the day. This morning as I got ready to put on tallis and tefillin, I quickly settled on the theme of tefillin. So.

I carry my tallis and tefillin in a plastic bag; right now it's a bag from Eichler's Hebrew Book Store in Boro Park, which I suppose makes me seem religious. The important thing is not what they're carried in, but that the tallis should lie on top of the tefillin, rather than the other way around. (I knew that even before Rabbi Pollak taught this rule this morning.) The proper order is to put the tallis on first and say the appropriate blessing, and only then to put on the hand and head tefillin; but if one were to reach in and grasp the tefillin first, then he would be obligated to fulfill the *mitzvah*, the commandment, of tefillin first. This is something I'm usually pretty good about remembering.

My tefillin are reasonably new and relatively large. (I hope this isn't boring you.) The sack I hold them in was my grandfather's tefillin bag. It is of maroon velvet and bears the word *tefillin* (in Hebrew letters, of course) on it—as though anyone could have mistaken its contents for anything else. My grandfather, my mother's father Yeshaya/Cyrus Weltman, must have had smaller tefillin, because mine barely fit inside his sack. But I think he knew a lot more Talmud than I do now or than I ever will.

The tefillin, when not in use, are protected by boxes made of the same lacquer used for the tefillin cases themselves (inside of which are small parchment scrolls with biblical inscriptions). Each of these boxes—one for the head tefillin and one for the arm tefillin—open with the help of two hinges. The hinges for my head tefillin fell out a couple of years ago, and when I brought them to the scribe, "young" Eisenbach on Essex Street (once, of course, he really was young, by comparison to his father, "old" Eisenbach) for repair, he substituted small pieces of thin nails. One held, and one fell out years ago, but as long as the one stays in, I'm in business.

I learned how to "lay" tefillin, to place them on my arm and head in the proper sequence and arrangement, when I was preparing for my bar mitzvah, but I hadn't put them on for almost fifteen years when I started coming regularly to Rabbi Singer's minyan in late 1983. He showed me again how to do it, doubtless in a slightly different fashion from that I had originally learned, since he followed the Hasidic custom in these matters. But I had trouble because, on initially placing the arm tefillin over my bicep, it would tend to slip. He showed me how to wind it once more to hold it in place, saying, "Now you're the boss!"

Tefillin go on the right hand, unless you're left-handed, as I am, in which case they're placed on the right hand. Once, in the years while I lived in New York but wasn't going to Rabbi Singer yet, I was cajoled into the Lubavitchers' "mitsvah tank" and reintroduced to tefillin. I told the young man who was helping me that I was left-handed and so needed to put them on my right arm. He was stymied: "I just got here from Tennessee a few months ago. I don't know how to do it for a leftie."

And around the time I started going to Rabbi Singer, I visited the Telz Yeshiva community in Cleveland, to which my family is connected through my grandfather Yeshaya (the one whose tallis bag I'm still using, though it's gradually wearing out). My brother, already a Talmud professor and for years Orthodox, was there too. But I had forgotten to bring tefillin. He was a bit annoyed: "I'll lend you mine, but then they'll think I've forgotten mine." I don't recall clearly how we resolved the problem; I'm sorry now I didn't just approach someone and say, "I forgot my tefillin—is there a pair I can borrow?" (I hope to visit Telz again this year—I haven't been there for decades—and am a bit worried how they will react to my very long hair, so perhaps I haven't learned so much after all.)

Tefillin were "thematized," as academics sometimes say, in shul this morning, but after I had decided to thematize them in my notes for today. First Nate Hacker came in and explained that he had forgotten his, and Rabbi Pollak showed him where there was a pair he could use for today. Then, after we'd finished, Rabbi Pollak announced that, after a few weeks when we'd let our daily study of halakha lapse, it was time to take up a new theme. Having finished the laws of *tsitsis*, fringes on four-cornered garments, it was now time to take up in detail the laws of tefillin. The first (or almost the first) of these is that your tallis should lie in the bag on top of the tefillin, so that you can grasp them in the same order in which you are supposed to put them on. But, as I wrote above, I knew that rule already.

Another regular, whom I hadn't seen for the past week: Mendel Trebitsch, a learned bachelor who is quiet in shul and very fond of musical theater.

## Day Three of Parshas Bechukosai, May 20, 2008

Two conversations yesterday, both outside on the sidewalk, and in both of them, it seems to me, I was more the listener than the talker, as my two conversation partners set the agenda. But both of them, ostensibly, had to do with the fate of the elderly Rabbi Pesach ("Paul") Ackerman's shul, Anshei Mezritch, several blocks north and west of Stanton Street, on Sixth Street between Avenue A and First Avenue. (Curiously, nobody calls it the Sixth Street Shul—on the contrary, the new board of the Community Synagogue, one block over on Sixth Street between First and Second, have started styling it on their Web site as the "Community Synagogue on Sixth Street.")

Yesterday I spent more time than I have in years on the sidewalk right in front of our building, the Ageloff Towers, on the corner of Third Street and Avenue A. Most of an hour, first, babysitting my car after the street sweeper had passed, after securing a spot while I still could before that side of the street filled up again, until the "no parking" time was officially over at 10:30 A.M. A beautiful, cool, windy morning of extraordinarily clear air for Manhattan. Ready to go inside, I was stopped at the door by Rabbi Charlie, the still relatively new rabbi at the Community Synagogue, who's just moved into our building. He wanted to know what I thought about the future of Rabbi Ackerman's shul; the reason he was asking now was because he'd heard rumors that the city was interested in giving the building landmark status. But before I could give him a substantial answer, our neighbor Jeremy Sandel (who had also been busy moving his car and moving it back) walked up. I introduced them, and we talked for about half an hour about numerous other things besides Rabbi Ackerman and his shul: details on parking tips; the gradual disappearance of the elderly Jewish ladies Elissa refers to as the "beach chair brigade," who used to spend most of the day in fine weather seated in front of the building, giving advice to parents of small children; growing up in New Hampshire, South Carolina, and

New Jersey; recent history and changes, especially in the attitude toward gay members, at the Sixteenth Street Synagogue, several blocks farther west and uptown. (This last theme—earlier hostility toward gay members and an easing of that prejudice that seems to have coincided with the retirement of one rabbi and the hiring of a younger one—seems to have had much to do with the beginning and end of the deep involvement at Stanton Street of Jack Fish, a pillar of Stanton Street during much of the interregnum between Rabbi Singer's departure and the hiring of Rabbi Pollak.) After the conversation broke up, Charlie and I went inside, and I just had time to say to him quickly: "I think it would be great if Rabbi Ackerman's shul was formally annexed to the Community Synagogue organization and used as a cultural, educational, and social center. Elissa knows a lot more about what's going on there than I do. And Sam Lemberger is really interested in this idea, too—you should talk to him about it."

Indeed, Elissa's heard that Rabbi Ackerman's shul is once again "on the market." Certainly he, or rather the society (with only a few remaining active members) that legally owns the synagogue, seems to have retained the services of Andrew Goldman, a lawyer who also represented the Stanton Street congregation in the dispute with Rabbi Singer. (It seems—though I'm surmising here—that Andrew now is representing parties who want to sell a synagogue, whereas earlier he represented parties who wanted to prevent a sale. Either way, he does know a lot about the law of selling real property belonging to a religious corporation in New York State.) We know or think we know that Andrew is working for Rabbi Ackerman and the Mezritsh Society primarily because a few months ago Elissa received a stern letter from Andrew after she accompanied local documentarian Darrell Cooper when Darrell made a videotape of Rabbi Ackerman leading the afternoon prayers one weekday. (Elissa, when she sees this, will certainly insist, and rightly, that I clarify that the taping was done with Rabbi Ackerman's knowledge and agreement; so I might as well add that now.)

The second conversation took place in the late afternoon, by a bench outside the coffee shop at Third Street and First Avenue. Elissa and I were walking—slowly, since her legs don't work so well lately—toward our pharmacist over on Sixth Street and Second Avenue, and we saw a man we know as Izzie sitting on the bench. We've known Izzie and his brother Naftali for decades, it seems. Izzie is the older brother and, we've heard, has a history of bullying Naftali. They are *kohanim*, descendants of the priestly clan of Aaron, and when both are present at Rabbi Ackerman's shul, the rabbi tries to make sure he alternates which one he calls for the first *aliyah*, to recite the blessings over the first segment of the Torah reading, since Jewish practice retains this much of the priestly clan's ancient prerogatives. But Izzie doesn't come as regularly as Naftali. Anyway, the man is well into his nineties (he should live to be 120). Short, but not tiny, plump, but not especially soft, balding and bareheaded, he certainly doesn't pretend to be especially religious, and so far as I can tell, when he does come to shul, it's because that's part of his routine and part of the neighborhood that he still knows. Elissa wanted to ask him what he knew about current doings regarding the disposition of the Mezritsh building, but Izzie insisted he didn't know and didn't want to know anything about it. Somehow, though, most of the conversation was about Izzie's insistence that he had never been and still wasn't somebody you could fool: so he spoke about the time the Amalgamated Clothing Workers Union had tried to deny him his pension, and he got it restored; the time he discovered one of the banks where he held a certificate of deposit had credited him only with simple, rather than compound interest, and how he got that fixed by threatening to report them to the FDIC. Izzie also mentioned an annuity he had with one of the insurance companies; so far as I could understand, he told Elissa that he didn't take the annual payments because he didn't want to pay taxes on them, but that he wouldn't lose out in the end. But Elissa was still worried that the contract might work against him. (She does work in the insurance industry, after all.)

So what you know about Rabbi Ackerman's shul as a result of my report of these two conversations is: It exists for now, but it might not be there any longer by the time you read this. Maybe one day this summer I'll get you in there for a more intimate description: the place is worth seeing, and worth remembering.

## *Day Four of Parshas Bechukosai, May 21, 2008*

Years ago I posed in an article the question whether what happened (almost) every weekday morning at Rabbi Singer's shul was ten men coming together to make a minyan or the coming into being of a minyan consisting of ten men (sometimes nine). The question, of course, was

rhetorical, a suggestion that there are things to be learned both from
the perspective of various individuals and from the perspective of the
community. This morning. there were eventually nine, though I had
decided that today was one of the mornings when I cannot force myself
to wait—I just proceeded saying the prayers on my own, and waited,
once there were nine including me, for the rest to finish so that the
mourners could say kaddish.

While we were waiting, Benny remarked at one point, "Ted Kennedy
has the same problem that took Erving Krause." And Dan Cantor told
us a few minutes later, "I asked five rabbis if they want to be the rabbi
here, but all of them said no." At one point, Benny, sitting toward the
front, couldn't see me, standing at the back, and declared, "He left!" I
waved at Benny, and he said, "God bless you!"

Here is an exercise for this morning's entry, based on another point
in the laws of wearing tefillin that Rabbi Pollak had taught from the
*Mishna Berura* yesterday morning, to wit: According to the *Shulchan
Aruch*, one who wears an undergarment with tsitsis, ritual fringes,
should put it on at home and then also put on his tefillin at home, before going to the synagogue. But the Mishna Berura adds several quali-
fications to this rule, including the stipulation that one need not walk
to shul already wearing tefillin if he will be passing Gentiles on the way.
Now, the Chofetz Chaim, author of the Mishna Berura, was nothing if
not a traditionalist and certainly never suggested that one should be
anything but a "Jew in the street"—retaining in fealty to tradition and
as a bulwark against modernity distinctive markings of hair and clothing that mark the male Jew as such. Yet for some reason it seems that
even he could not imagine a Jew passing through a mixed neighborhood
with tefillin on, perhaps because it seemed to run too great a risk of pro-
voking mockery or even violence. So I'm prompted to reflect: *What
memories or other images do you have of a Jew, any Jew—perhaps even
yourself!—being visibly Jewish in a "mixed" public sphere?*

Oddly, the answers do not come as readily even to me as I would have
guessed, but here are a few.

—Greenwich Village, thirty years ago; for all I remember, it might
be thirty years ago to the day. I am in a coffee shop, eating poached
eggs on rye, wearing a knitted kippa and my hair long, as it is now but
hasn't been for most of the intervening time. A rabbi (maybe not a
rabbi!) in black coat and substantial beard approaches me and gently

reproaches me for wearing a visibly Jewish head covering while eating in that restaurant. He did not take me to task for eating nonkosher food, but rather for wearing an ostensibly Orthodox head covering while eating in a nonkosher restaurant: "It could mislead other Jews into thinking the restaurant is kosher." At my question, he explained that he had been there to counsel a young woman and had only had a cup of coffee.

For most of my years since then, I have been willing to go into nonkosher restaurants and simply avoid (as best one can; I don't want to deceive anybody here) meat and shellfish. In New York, I will not do so while wearing a Jewishly marked head covering; in other, less "Jewish" cities, such as the university towns where I've worked the last few years, I have fewer compunctions. Once, about a decade ago, I had lunch with a distant relative at a modest restaurant in downtown New Haven and left my kippa on. "Don't you feel funny eating here with a kippa on your head?" she asked. "If I go here with my husband, he always takes his off first." I told her I do feel funny about it—but I feel funny uncovering my head as I walk into a restaurant, too.

—For years, if Elissa and I would pass congregants from the Chasam Sopher shul on Clinton Street on shabbes, we had a very difficult time getting them to return our *Gut shabes*! greeting and thus acknowledging us as fellows. I think this has more to do with their living in their own world than any deliberate refusal to acknowledge us, but Elissa's never been sure about that.

—One shabbes afternoon many years ago, I forgot to cover my head as I left home for Rabbi Singer's shul. I borrowed a yarmulke from the shul and took it off as I went out. An elderly regular—I forget his name, but not someone I remember as especially intelligent or sympathetic— said to Rabbi Singer in wonderment as I walked out, *Er geyt mit a bloyzn kop?* "Does he walk around with his head uncovered?"

—As I was walking near Fifth Avenue and Eleventh Street one twilight long ago, a group of three or four teenage white boys passed me on the street. I didn't hear what they were muttering as they approached me, but after they passed, one of them glanced at my face and said, "Oh, he's a faggot, too!" I never had a clue why they decided to amuse each other by pointing out my Jewishness or on what basis they had decided I was queer. They did not harass me further. The moment stays in my memory partly because it was, after all, quite unusual for me, but also because of the glee they took in scoring an extra point in bagging a Jew who was a faggot as well.

—I love to tell this one, and I don't know if I've ever written it down before. Several years ago, a wintry Friday, early afternoon, on Avenue A and St. Marks Place. Two Lubavitcher teenagers are standing at the corner; they seem to me to be hesitating. I slow down as I pass them, trying to figure out whether they need directions. Seeing me slow down, they ask whether I'm Jewish. I say yes of course, and they ask whether I'd put tefillin on that morning. I told them yes again. They were flabbergasted. They know how to find Jews, and they know how to cajole them into doing mitsvos, but evidently they didn't have a script for someone who didn't look the part, but was already doing whatever it was they had set out to make that person do. It was like someone running toward a closed door with all his strength, prepared to bust the door down by brute force, and then having the door opened just as he approaches it with his leading shoulder. I was delighted. And that's not only a "Jew in the street" story. That's another tefillin story, too.

*So what are some of your "Jew in the street" stories?*

## Day Five of Parshas Bechukosai, May 22, 2008

Another kosher-meat dream, inspired no doubt by a recipe for a five-pound "barbecued" brisket (actually to be braised for three hours and then seared in the broiler) in yesterday's *New York Times*. I'm at some affair, and my brother Daniel—a dedicated carnivore in waking life—is telling me, "You have to get a brisket sandwich, you'll really be sorry if you don't." At first I'm in one of my "I'm not going to do it just because my big brother told me to!" moods, and I refuse, but very soon I'm by the table laden with food. As with the hot dogs (unbelievable—I just typed "hot gods!") the other day, the food is generally not kosher, but here's this woman behind the counter holding up a five-pound slab of brisket, and I'm tearing hunks off it and stuffing them directly into my mouth, planning on buying not just a sandwich but the whole thing (actually it's a bit dry, but oh so tasty). The fact is, kosher meat's a lot easier to get in this neighborhood of New York than where we live in North Carolina, but I still can't run across the street to the local supermarket and buy a kosher steak; there aren't enough customers in the immediate area to make it worthwhile for the supermarket to carry kosher meat. For that we'd need a different neighborhood, one with a lot more Orthodox families.

Pictures of myself walking from the Ageloff Towers to the Stanton Street Shul wearing my arm and head tefillin—and perhaps following the rule of the Ramah, Reb Moshe Isserles (interpreter and adaptor of the Shulchan Aruch for East European Jews), wearing my "large" tallis over my clothes, as well (I have never really adopted the discipline of wearing an undershirt with ritual fringes)—are running through my mind as I sit down to my computer, unsure what to write about for the first time since I began this journal just under two weeks ago. A rainy morning, very cool for late May in New York, encourages this mood of halakhic fantasy. Would I draw curious looks? Certainly I would, but somehow I imagine I would not elicit any rude remarks: It's the East Village; they've seen stranger things before.

Even if they didn't know what it is I'm wearing. I heard a story along these lines a few years ago, when I was visiting Minneapolis for a job interview and stayed over for shabbes there. As I was walking around the Orthodox neighborhood with a congregant of the shul I was visiting, he told a story from the days when his wife's grandfather (or great-uncle?) had been a pioneer rabbi in that region.

> He would have to travel a lot, of course, to visit people for various reasons. One night he stayed over at a farmhouse, and when he woke up, he saw that the woman of the house was putting out clothes on the line, wearing tefillin on her arm. So he went outside and asked her about them.
>
> She told him, "Well, a man was here a couple of years ago, and I saw him putting these on in the morning. I asked him what they were for, and he said, 'They're for my rheumatism.' I have rheumatism too, so I bought them from him."
>
> Of course my wife's grandfather thought this was a desecration of the tefillin, so he said, "I'll buy them from you."
>
> But the farm woman refused: "No, I want to keep them—they work!"

Beyond that halakhic fantasy of walking around the East Village in tallis and tefillin, this question of the encounters elicited by being visibly Jewish in downtown Manhattan continues to evoke further responses in my mind. Here's a memory going back twenty years, or probably a bit more: our Jonah, who's now a few months past his twenty-second birthday, was in the stroller that I pushed along Avenue B one shabbes

morning (ignoring, as I did during childrearing years, the ban on carrying on the Sabbath where there is no eruv, not to mention ignoring
the venerated Lower East leader Rabbi Moshe Feinstein's ruling that
there never could be such an artificial boundary in Manhattan). I was
wearing a dark suit and a black hat. A quite elderly man stopped me and
asked if anyone ever gave me trouble for being Jewish when I was on
that block. I told him that I had never had trouble, and he said, "Well,
if you do, let me know, and I'll take care of it. You'll remember my
name—Al Siegel. I used to have a cousin named Bugsy."

Now, that happened: That's not a dream, though I never saw Al
Siegel again (I didn't walk down Avenue B often in those days). It never
occurred to me until just now that even though Al Siegel told me he
was Bugsy's cousin, that wasn't necessarily the case—he could have
been making it up, or he could have just been kidding me. But still: I
go on the Internet to see how Bugsy Siegel's name should be spelled
(and I adjust the way I write Al's last name accordingly) and find that
the Wikipedia article on gangster Bugsy includes a photo of his memorial plaque at the Bialystoker Shul on Grand Street: *Berish ben Reb
Mordkhe Dov Halevi.* So I guess I should have asked Al if he was a
Levite, too.

Then just yesterday afternoon I'm walking down Fifth Avenue and
a man who seems to be in his early sixties looks at me and asks, "Is that
for real?" For some reason I assumed he was referring to my Kansas
Jayhawks sweatshirt; after all, they've just won the NCAA basketball
championship. So I reply, "Yes, I taught at Kansas for two years." But
it's not clear that is what he has in mind at all, since his next utterance
is, *Shabbat shalom.* It was a Wednesday, so he could only have been
signaling to me that he was Jewish, though he also told me (since
I mentioned university connections) that he'd attended NYU law
school on a Root-Tilden Scholarship (very prestigious, for students
who plan to go on to do public-interest work). I told him I'd been a
lawyer, too, but wasn't cut out for it. He said he was cut out for it, that
he'd been a tax lawyer, and that he receives a nice check for $18,000
every month from his last employer, Milbank Tweed. As I shook
his hand, he waved and said, *Layla tov!* which just means "Good
night." A friendly, but unnerving exchange, and one that took place,
it strikes me now, just a few feet from the spot where I was called "faggot" years ago.

## Day Six of Parshas Bechukosai, May 23, 2008

One of my major pastimes this summer is going to doctors with Elissa, who is struggling with arthritis and the aftermath of spine surgery. Yesterday, after a visit to a neurologist on Union Square, she felt up to walking east with me along Fourteenth Street and asked me to step with her into the little Russian souvenir shop between Second and Third Avenues. (I had been pleased to notice, on a walk just last week, that it was still hanging on, amid all the changes on that block.) She had discovered recently that the elderly owner, a man named Alexander, is a Jew from Belorussia. He was in the store by himself when we walked in.

He was glad to converse in Yiddish, though sprinkled by now with English words. When I asked where he was from, he said "Vitebsk," and started explaining to me where it was in Eastern Europe. I interrupted him and said that my grandfather was from Beshenkovitsh, near Vitebsk, a town whose name Alex immediately recognized. As we talked, my attention was divided between the items in his shop, the content of his speech, and the form of his speech.

The shop is dusty and crowded, as though very few things in it had been moved in years. Small bolts of cloth are racked on the walls toward the ceiling. Bundles of miscellany—long-playing records, sunglasses— are stacked on or near the small counter. Assorted pins are displayed next to an array of Soviet-era medals, the latter commemorating such events as the seventieth anniversary of the October Revolution or the Seventeenth Congress of the Soviet Communist Party. While we talked, a man wandered in and asked whether Alex had any musical instruments for sale, but there were none. Elissa ended up buying two pieces of textile, one a scarf with a brief legend woven in, marking the fortieth anniversary of the "great victory" over fascism, the other a hand-embroidered Ukrainian pillow cover.

Alex told us something of how he and his family had survived the Nazi occupation—in the forests.

There's a magnificent forest in that area, around Beshenkovitsh and my town, Horodok. You get into it, and you can't see ten yards away. If it weren't for the forest, we wouldn't have survived. A cousin of mine came to my town to study. He arrived on the very day they slaughtered the Jews in my town. He approached the houses at night, and he saw they were all lit up and people were partying inside, but it wasn't the Jewish owners, it was the Gentile townspeople celebrating the fact that the Jews were gone and they were going to inherit their houses. He went to a peasant house outside of town, and they said, "We'll take you in, but only for a few days." After that they give him some clothes and they sent him out at night—he walked across the [frozen?] lake and into the forest, in the dark of night. A sixteen-year-old Jewish boy!

Some of the people in my family had dark eyes and hair, and they looked Jewish. My older brother was like that. So when we were in the forests, he had to stay hidden the whole time. I was younger, but I was "white" [had lighter coloring?]. So one night they sent me to a peasant house to buy food. I knocked on the door, she let me in, and I said, "Here's a ruble, I want to buy some food." The peasant woman said, "You can keep that Jewish money"—no, she didn't know I was Jewish, she was just calling it "Jewish money" to show she despised it—everything they didn't like was "Jewish," money, Communism ... "Here," she says, "in the name of Jesus, is some food." So she gave me a pot of potatoes and a pot of sour cream. I carried it back to the forest, and we shared it out, a little bit for each one of us.

Alex's White Russian dialect of Yiddish is what my ancestors on my father's side spoke and what I will rarely have the chance to hear from a living voice again. What most excited me about the speech were the features that only Yiddish linguists notice, and they rushed past me in a torrent that allowed me to recall only a few: *titsert*, one of many variants of the word for "now" in various Yiddish dialects; the expected blending and interchange of *s* and *sh* sounds, and of *z* and *zh* sounds, which are distinct in other regions; occasional affixing of the suffix *et* at the end of prepositional particles, as in *zhi izh gegaan aroyset* "she went out"; and, to my astonishment, something that sounded very like *tote-mome loshn*, the dialect in which the usual *ah* vowel (as in *tate* and *mame*, "father" and "mother") becomes a shortened *aw* (hence *tote* and *mome*). Astonishment, because it's supposed to be confined to the area of Bukovina, in Rumania, hundreds of miles away from the White Russian Vitebsk. And all this on Fourteenth Street, the upper boundary of the historic Lower East Side.

I can't say how similar Alex's Yiddish is to the way my grandfather

Yisroel Boyarin spoke. Grandpa died when I (a youngest child myself)
was eleven. Though his image is clear in my mind, I would have to focus
hard to remember his voice at all, and to me he spoke only in English.
Nor can I say how similar Alex's Yiddish is now to the way he spoke,
let's say, on the eve of the day the Nazis occupied Vitebsk. Sixty-five
years is a long time, with plenty of room to acquire not only foreign
words but the phonology of others, as well. Still, Alex made it clear he
hopes we'll come back and converse with him in Yiddish again, and if
I do, I hope I can bring a Yiddish linguist friend along—maybe Charlie
Nydorf, with whom I worked back in the early 1980s, when we interviewed our professor, Shlomo Noble, at the YIVO Institute for Jewish
Research, about his childhood and education. After all, the days are
pretty much past when I could hear such a rich native Yiddish a few
blocks downtown on Stanton Street.

*Central Staircase Leading from Upstairs to Street*

# Week Three

*And they assembled all the congregation together on the first day of the second month, and they declared their pedigrees after their families, by their fathers' houses, according to the number of names, from twenty years old and upward, by their polls. As the Lord commanded Moses, so did he number them in the wilderness of Sinai.*

—NUMBERS 1:18–19

*Lectern and Platform for Torah Ark, Prior to Downstairs Restoration*

## Day Two of Parshas Bamidbar, May 26, 2008

I know the Torah portion this week is Bamidbar because I heard Rabbi Pollak announce it when the minyan came to the Torah reading this morning, Memorial Day, the day after Jonah's graduation from Wesleyan University in New England. Already in Connecticut by Friday afternoon and staying over with faculty friends, I took it easy Saturday morning and didn't go to the Conservative synagogue, the only minyan in town—so I missed the culmination of the chanting of Leviticus, with the congregation standing at the last verse and reciting in unison "strength, strength, and let us be strengthened!" (to keep going on, that is).

The weekend had plenty of Jewish moments, though. Jonah and I led the *kabbalat shabbat* services to welcome the Sabbath at the Jewish house, the *bayit* (or *bayis* as Jonah, an ardent proponent of old-fashioned Ashkenazi Hebrew pronunciation, calls it). We had done the same once before, almost four years ago, when Jonah was a freshman at Wesleyan and I, by what seemed pure coincidence (but "pure coincidence" only ever means "without a logical connection that we are able or care to discern") a visiting professor there for a term. Then as now, we conducted the service in our middling but enthusiastic singing voices, with a few Shlomo Carlebach melodies roughly executed and with a little bit of dancing. For me, it felt less awkward than it did that earlier time to be standing in front of a congregation of mingled men and women. It also seemed that there were a lot more in the congregation this time—students mostly, I would guess—who were fully familiar with the Carlebach tunes, welcomed them, and sang along.

One of the rigors of Sabbath observance that I try to hold onto, not driving or riding in a car, went completely by the board this graduation weekend. Elissa's ability to walk is quite limited, so she could not have participated in Friday night or Saturday activities without being driven, and I wished neither to separate from her nor to stay away from these activities. So after the kabbalat shabbat service, we drove across campus to park near the new student center, where a kosher Friday-night meal was served to a crowd of perhaps eighty people. After folks were fed, the campus rabbi, Daniel Leipziger, announced that the dinner was especially in honor of Professor Jeremy Zwelling, who will retire in two years after decades running the Jewish Studies program and, as we learned, after becoming one of the university's first Jewish professors in the 1960s. Jeremy recalled that the 10 percent maximum rule for Jewish students admitted to each freshman class had been lifted only in 1961, when a new dean, named Jack Hoy, came in and pushed to increase both Jewish and African American admissions. (We usually think of those barriers as having come down one after the other, not at the same time. Since then, the university's Jewish student population has ranged from about 25 percent to 30 percent, but alas, it seemed to me the graduating class of 2008 was still, or once again, overwhelmingly "white.") "And at the same time in the early sixties," Jeremy continued, "they hired three of us [male] Jewish faculty members. Our names were Carl, David, and Jeremy, and a lot of our older colleagues had trouble distinguishing us from each other."

Michael Roth, who I guess is the university's first Jewish president and just completing his first year in that role, spoke on Saturday afternoon at the Phi Beta Kappa initiation. (Why yes, we were there because our Jonah was being inducted, though I feel funny boasting about it here.) He warmed up the audience, eliciting a bit of mock sympathy with a story about his parents' refusal to understand the significance of his making Phi Beta Kappa when he had graduated from Wesleyan, exactly thirty years ago, back in 1978. "They said, 'But you're already in a fraternity—why do you need to be inducted into another one?' And anyway, they told me they couldn't be here on Saturday, because they had to be at my cousin's bar mitzvah in Brooklyn—and they insisted I should be there, too. So I drove down to Brooklyn for the bar mitzvah on Saturday, missed my Phi Beta Kappa initiation, and came back on Sunday to graduate."

Just now as I write, I turned to Elissa and asked, "So it looks like Roth is probably the university's first Jewish president, right?"

She answered, "Yes, it does—and part of the reason I didn't like his Phi Beta Kappa speech was that I agree with his parents: Going to his cousin's bar mitzvah was the right thing to do!"

I said, "I agree, but he could have buried the whole thing if he'd really wanted to—after all, he didn't have to talk about being Jewish at this year's Phi Beta Kappa ceremony at all."

"Yes," she replied, "it's kind of like *Seinfeld*, the way you and Henry [Bial, a scholar of Jews and media and my former colleague at Kansas] talk about it—acknowledging Jewishness, but using it as a play for sympathy at the same time."

Late Saturday afternoon, after the Phi Beta Kappa ceremony, we drove again (such short drives are not usually the stuff of memoir, but seem to bear some new significance when recorded by someone whose personal and professional identity turns so much on his never, ever driving on Saturday; alas, the confessional-autoethnographic mode) to the lawn of an old house near campus where Jonah had arranged a casual barbecue for some eighteen of his friends and their families. There Elissa had the chance to catch up with various family members of Jonah's friend Tali Melman, the daughter of the Reform rabbi of Birmingham, Alabama, and a young woman to whose stalwart organization and good sense we attribute much of Jonah's academic success at Wesleyan. Tali's grandmother admitted to Elissa that she was still sorry Tali hadn't gone to Brandeis, where, after all, Tali's parents had met each other. It's true in any case that Wesleyan today is a place where you can be as Jewish as you want, or not at all. Jonah's started the Yiddish club there, been able to eat as much kosher meat as he wants (although he didn't arrange for any at the barbecue, which made the whole thing a lot less festive, as far as I was concerned!), and I think informed student Jewish life in a more traditional, but not necessarily Orthodox direction.

Clearly, his own childhood exposure to a Yiddishy ambience (if I may coin the adjective) has rubbed off on some of his classmates, as well. He reported to me after Thanksgiving vacation of his freshman year that his friend Sarah (another part of the gang that stayed together all four years, who was also present at the barbecue on Saturday), visiting back home in Philadelphia, had, upon being asked by her mother whether she was ready for supper, shrugged her shoulders and emitted a long, ambivalent "Ehhhhhh . . ." At which her mother said in exasperation, "What happened to you at that school? You sound like my grandfather!" Eighteen-year-old Jonah reported this to me proudly, as evidence he was having a positive influence on his peers. As for Jonah's friend Tali's grandmother's preference for Brandeis and the possible reasons for it, let me say that Jonah's romantic life at Wesleyan has left him as likely to end up with a Jewish mate as not. Anyway, we all know that in this odd little demographic slice of America where we live and where places like Wesleyan find their applicant pool, being born Jewish isn't quite the same thing as "being" Jewish.

It was a warm day, and between anxiety about parking arrangements for the commencement ceremony (which was more of a to-do than expected because of the last-minute substitution of Barack Obama for Ted Kennedy as commencement speaker), sitting in the sun for two hours, packing as much of Jonah's worldly goods into the hatchback of my Prius as we could stuff without blocking my rear view, and the long drive back from Connecticut, I was quite cranky and had one of my rare headaches by the time we returned to the city. I slept badly—who knows what I dreamed about; it wasn't kosher meat again, I think—and stumbled to shul.

Today being a secular holiday, the minyan started at 7:00, just fifteen minutes later than the usual scheduled starting time, but young Krause had begun the set of blessings that commence each daily service by the time I walked in. I stayed at my own pace, even more than usual, rather than trying to catch up with the minyan. I read slowly, too, perhaps because I have trouble now with the print in the old-fashioned prayer books I prefer to ArtScroll, and I am still reluctant to switch over to my reading glasses in shul. But even though I read each word of the preliminary psalms, I wasn't concentrating on them, but rather reviewing the commencement weekend in my mind. And I wasn't the only one: When Rabbi Pollak walked in, a few minutes after me, the first thing he said was, "I was watching, but they switched it off after the first name was called out. And they didn't carry all of Obama's speech, just the first ten minutes."

In the middle of the service, Rabbi Pollak announced, "No *tachanun* [the penitential prayers] today—there's going to be a *bris* in shul." And a bit later, Shalom Kluger, the president for life (and son of the previous president for life) of the Chasam Sopher synagogue around the corner, came in for a second, and I heard Rabbi Pollak say to him, "The bris will be at 11:00, so we'll be over to you by around 11:30." After the service ended, Rabbi Pollak explained: "The bris is for the son of Debbie and Alex Frank—you know Alex, he's Benny's grandson. And we're going to do the bris here in shul, but our downstairs isn't big enough for the crowd they expect, so they'll have the meal around the corner at Chasam Sopher." Taking into account the moment last week when Sol Decker successfully "borrowed" a couple of men from Chasam Sopher to complete our shabbes afternoon minyan, I wonder whether this is a sign of détente between the two congregations, following a long period of suspicion.

The nadir of that relation was the time, perhaps a year and half or two years ago, when it was rumored that Shalom Kluger had approached Reb Dovid Feinstein, the son of Reb Moshe Feinstein and head of the local yeshiva, to report on some of our congregation's halakhic violations (having to do with carrying on shabbes and women's participation) and had obtained a declaration from Reb Dovid placing Stanton Street in *cherem*, under a ban. In truth, no writing was ever seen to evidence such a declaration, nor did we see much to suggest that anyone was following it; for example, our regular Torah reader, who is certainly a follower of Reb Dovid, never stopped coming on Sabbath mornings. Still, there's no doubt that the rumor, whatever its basis in actual incident, did reflect real suspicions about how "kosher" the Stanton Street Shul, its congregation, and its rabbi were and are.

Some personal notes on my prayer habits follow.

—One would think that someone engaged in solitary prayer at his own pace is concentrating more closely on the meaning of the text, but as I suggested above, after thousands of mornings over the same text, it is entirely possible to recite them carefully yet by rote, while your mind is long ago and far away.

—One phrase that I do attend to, still, comprises the four words that translate as "panic seized the residents of Philistia." Stopping at them with particular intent is my little personal safety valve for whatever hostilities I might harbor toward the Palestinians as a group. Outside of this, I am not only not a Zionist but an implacable, although lately not very vocal advocate of equal rights for Palestinians in Israel and Palestine— so interpreting these words in this way lets me express, quietly and really only to myself, a certain satisfying measure of in-group chauvinism and resentment.

—Because I have long, thick hair, the band into which the straps of my head tefillin is shaped is too small to fit as it should over my skull, and inevitably the box that, halakhically, should rest just at my hairline slips down onto my forehead. Someday this summer I will make it down to Eisenbach the *sofer*, the scribe's shop, and convince him to enlarge them for me.

The father of the baby wasn't Alex Frank, not Benny's grandson. Presumably Rabbi Pollak didn't tell me that it was, but rather said "Arnold." I said "Alex" to Elissa, and Elissa said, "Oh, Benny's grandson." And then I put those words into Rabbi Pollak's mouth. It was Arnold Frank, no relation to Benny as far as I can tell (in any case, Benny wasn't at the bris), but, along with his wife Debbie, a member of the shul indeed. When Elissa and I arrived, a few minutes after eleven in the morning, the upstairs shul was rather full, with perhaps seventy people, a few more women than men, and a few men sitting with the women in the back. A minyan, most wearing tallis and tefillin, were concluding the morning service, and several of the other men were following the service more marginally. (Rabbi Pollak said later: "They told me they wanted to recite shachris. I said, 'Well, 10:30's a little late, but if you want to, go ahead.'")

I immediately felt out of place (underdressed, for one thing) and among people I didn't know—except for the rabbi, Rachel Wiener (a longtime active member and native of the Lower East Side who is expecting her own first baby soon), and a woman from the congregation named Rose. I was seized with a sense that I had failed to keep up with the changing membership of the congregation and with regret for not having taken more care to invite newcomers to our home for a meal, not only to help them feel they were indeed joining a community but, I suddenly realized, even more to help keep hold of some sense that I was part of a community. It wasn't clear where in the room I should be. I felt, indeed, like an *anthropologist*.

The *mohel* was Rabbi Paysach Krohn, a well-known author of several books documenting the life and teachings of a great preacher of Jerusalem in the twentieth century. While we waited for the baby to be brought upstairs, he told this story:

Many years ago Rabbi Aharon ——, who recently retired from a congregation in Connecticut, was in the Soviet Union. He visited one of the few functioning synagogues, and someone came up to him and said, "If you want to participate in a very special Jewish ceremony, you should know that there's going to be a circumcision performed shortly. Go down that alley, make the first left, and where you see candles in the window, you should knock and they'll let you in." Rabbi Aharon followed the directions, knocked on the door, and explained in Yiddish that he was a Jewish visitor from America and happy to be able to be present at the bris. While the crowd waited, Rabbi Aharon explained a bit in Yiddish what the ceremony consisted of and what is significance was. "And," he said, "at a certain point just after the operation itself we'll all say, 'Just as the child entered the covenant, so too may he enter into the marriage canopy, the study of Torah, and the practice of good deeds.'" At that, there was some angry muttering in a corner of the room. The rabbi walked over and asked in Yiddish, *Vos hob ikh gezogt?* "What did I say that made you so angry?" And the people answered him: "The way that the child entered into the bris—in hiding, in a basement room with everyone afraid of being discovered—that's how you want him to spend the rest of his life?"

Rabbi Krohn made his message clear: How fortunate we are, and how particularly apt it is to remember on Memorial Day, that we are in a place where we can congregate safely to celebrate an occasion such as a bris!

The ceremony over, the crowd slowly filtered out down the narrow side stairways, and I stayed behind to speak with Yossi and to introduce myself to Rabbi Krohn. I asked Yossi, "How come I've never seen these people before?"

Yossi explained to me that Debbie is from the Upper East Side, where her family belongs to an Orthodox congregation called Orach Chaim. Arnold is not observant and doesn't read Hebrew. They are indeed members at Stanton Street, but "they never come to shul. But this— they really wanted to do it here."

Elissa and I followed the crowd around the corner to Chasam Sopher, a much larger building than ours, for the festive lunch. I remarked that the cooperation in using their downstairs room for our celebration seemed to be a mark of détente between the two congregations, but she corrected my impression that this was something new; several times before, ceremonies at Stanton Street had been followed by meals at Chasam Sopher.

This is what puzzles me about today's event: Yes, the parents of the baby are members of the shul, but no, the crowd wasn't a shul crowd. No, the crowd wasn't from the shul or even from the neighborhood, but yes, plenty of the people who were there were perfectly comfortable with the ritual and with Orthodox prayer services. Why didn't they just hold the bris uptown, at Debbie's parents' shul? The tempting answer, for an ethnographer of the Jewish Lower East Side, is that Stanton Street somehow speaks to Debbie and Arnold emotionally, even if they rarely show up. (As we left the meal, I stopped to have a celebratory drink with Arnold and introduced myself as being from the Stanton Street Shul. "Yes, Debbie really loves the shul!" Arnold replied with a sincere tone.) It could also be other things, or that and other things— such as a young couple simply declaring that this is their household and their neighborhood now. If I were my own student, I would insist that I track Debbie and Arnold down and ask them about it.

### Day Three of Parshas Bamidbar, May 27, 2008

Elissa slips out the door, heading for the hospital for her monthly treatment for arthritis, wearing the purple floppy cap that always makes me think she looks like Woody Allen. I tell her so, and she mutters, "He's from the wrong part of Brooklyn." Well, of course, Woody's older; I'm not sure Elissa's flattered by the comparison; but the resemblance is striking . . . I'm not the biggest Woody Allen fan in the world myself. I've tended to count him as one of those creative people who get too much mileage out of their anxiety about Jewishness without ever being able to convey why it's something anyone might not want to lose and might in fact see instead as a source of creativity.

I did meet Woody once, in a dream. It wasn't my dream, it was my friend Fred's dream. In the dream (as Fred reported to me shortly after he had it, this nearly thirty years ago by now, when Fred and I were both living in an old-law tenement on Fifth Street between Second and Third Avenues), Fred and I were at a party together. Woody walked into the room, approached Fred, and greeted him: "Hi, Fred!"

Fred said, "Hi, Woody."

Then Woody walked up to me and said, "Hi, Fred!" explaining as he did so that whenever he joins a group and meets people he doesn't know, he just calls everybody "Fred."

I have no doubt that this dream of Fred's was inspired in turn by an old nightclub routine of Woody Allen's, recorded on an LP, about a costume party that Woody had been at which was also attended by someone wearing a moose outfit. "Moose goes in . . . does well . . . scores . . ."

I actually did know someone once who had had a good friend who had known Woody Allen well, way back when they were all in high school. The man I knew was Sy Sina, and his friend was a young woman upon whom the adolescent Woody apparently had a crush for a long time. "So he always used to hang around my friend's house, partly because he had a crush on her and partly because he really liked her mother's cooking. Decades later, her mother asked, 'Whatever happened to that nice Allen Konigsberg?' My friend said, 'Ma, he's Woody Allen!' And her mother just replied, 'He always made me laugh!'"

With a long gray beard, Sy looked like somebody's dream combination (quite possibly mine) of professor, beatnik, and Hasidic rebbe. He played the part, but only in part. He was a frustrated theater professor and embittered public-school teacher, carefully getting by on a limited income and ready to expand, with relish, on the ingenuity with which he managed to do so—resisting his landlord's attempts to remove him from his apartment or finding a bargain on kosher turkey legs in the supermarket and cooking them with a delicious recipe. I believe that when he started attending Rabbi Singer's minyan, it was the first time in his life that he had been a regular shulgoer, and it was clear that he was still learning how to recite the prayers in Hebrew. When he would belch in shul, he would quote Shakespeare's Falstaff (I heard it so many times!): "A plague on these pickled herrings!"

I never knew how he had found his way to Rabbi Singer's shul (I'm going back to the late eighties or early nineties here), but his grandfather had come from the same town of Pilsno where Rabbi Singer had spent his childhood. Once Rabbi Singer told us: "Sure, I remember his grandfather! He used to have an orchard, and one time we kids went into it and stole some plums. He caught us, but instead of scolding us for stealing the fruit, he demanded to know, 'Did you make a *brokhe*?'" Did you say a blessing before you ate it?

Sy passed away at his farm near Ellenville, in the Catskills, years before the big to-do about the Singer family's attempt to sell the building.

I make no promise to you that, in the course of this summer, I will have the chance to evoke all of the sometime members at Stanton Street. There have been so many, and my memory is so poor, and your patience (and my willingness to try yours) so limited. Other, new information floods the dining room where I write. A set of papers, printed in yellow: the membership survey that just went out with a mailing announcing the shul's upcoming annual meeting, to be held June 15. It's clear enough that for years we (meaning here the set of people who somehow are stuck worrying about the future of the congregation and the building at Stanton Street) have been faced with the problem of determining what reason the shul has for continuing as a living Jewish institution, now that the demographic reason—the presence of large numbers of participating Jews in the surrounding blocks, and especially Jews from Brzezan and its surroundings—is conclusively gone. I helped get the mailing out last Wednesday evening but haven't brought myself to review the survey text itself (composed largely by Sol Decker and Lenny Rivers, though Elissa reviewed it and lobbied to add the question: "How important to your involvement is the retention of the *heymish* feeling of the shul building?"). We'll have to keep facing this question of the shul's changing reason to exist, since it's part of the effort to keep the shul alive, whatever changes are necessary to make that happen. It's easy enough for me to imagine that at some point it may have changed so much that I no longer would want to participate myself; one such change would be the obliteration, a real possibility, of the traditional Jewish astrological symbols decorating the walls of the shul upstairs, a feature Elissa has become especially determined to preserve.

## Day Four of Parshas Bamidbar, May 28, 2008

Since I started writing a few weeks ago, I've been avoiding research, even to the extent of looking into whatever archives might be available right here in our apartment. Among the latter are the transcripts of the court hearings when the congregation resisted the Singer family's attempts to sell the shul and a volume of typed minutes of meetings of the Lanzuter Benevolent Association (Benny's old society) from December 11, 1966, through June 12, 1977. (As I open that volume, just to

check the dates it covers, I spot the following item from the very end
of that period: "At this time a man from another org. a Lanzuter came
into our meeting room requesting a book from Lanzute in order to
teach the Kerbusher org. the history of Lanzute, to this Bro. Naftal
Rubenfeld gave his address, as he has an extra book for him." This is
something I would love to have seen when Jack Kugelmass and I were
writing the introduction to *From a Ruined Garden: The Memorial
Books of Polish Jewry*. We asserted there that the memorial books, col-
lective albums devoted to the lives and deaths of particular Jewish communities in Poland and other regions subject to Nazi terror, were
written not only by but also for the survivors and émigrés from the
towns whose Jewish communities they commemorate, and here's a
lovely example of their circulation in practice.)

But I probably will do at least some archival work, starting perhaps
as soon as tomorrow. Elissa's been in correspondence with a small group
of art historians and conservators about those Stanton Street *mazoles*,
the zodiac signs, one of whom has raised a question about how to determine when the mazoles were painted. I've always assumed they were
original to the building—or at least, to the date when two older buildings were reconstructed to become a synagogue, in 1913. Elissa agrees
that's likely and has confirmed with Gedalya Getzler, one of the oldest
(and earliest-arrived) members of the shul, that they were there when
his Rymanower Society moved into Stanton Street in the 1950s. But
last night, as we were going to sleep, Elissa asked me to go to YIVO
(part, now, of the Center for Jewish History) to check the Brzezaner
*landsmanshaft* records that were deposited there decades ago. I'd looked
at them around 2001, in connection with the court case, to determine
whether and when Rabbi Singer had received a salary (if he had, it was
never anything to write home about), but couldn't remember anything
about the mazoles. I couldn't imagine there would be anything about
the mazoles in those records (though why should I assume not?). And
I'd already promised Elissa I'd have a look at the memorial book—even
though it's devoted to the town of Brzezan itself, if we're lucky, it might
include, as some memorial books do, an article about Brzezan Jewish
émigrés and their institutions elsewhere in the world. (After all, they're
the ones who wrote and produced the memorial books.)

So I was a bit annoyed to get these extra assignments as I was trying
to get to sleep. I was hoping it would be a relatively solid night's sleep,

since I'd gotten plenty of exercise during the day. Even when I don't sleep well, I wake up relatively rested, and I'm hardly overworked this summer. But when I'm restless at night, I have troubled dreams, in which bad things happen all around me and implicitly to me, though I'm never too directly threatened and never terrified. To that extent, the structure of my dream world reflects the structure of my life world for the past several years, certainly since I became at last a tenured professor: earthquakes, floods, devastating and inane wars, people losing their houses, while I receive a steady income and manage to live within my means. In the event, I did not sleep well last night. I was troubled, as I often am, by noisy groups of young adults spilling out of the neighborhood bars at closing time (on a Tuesday night!). I remember these two dreams, in fragments.

Dream One: Jonah and I get into a taxi to make a delivery. The person who puts us in the taxi insists we should take along two pit bulls as protection. They do not initially seem threatening, but they become more so as the dream progresses. When we reach our destination, we try to instruct the taxi driver where he should return the dogs, but no longer have that address. Much of the rest of the dream is taken up with a quest to get the dogs back where they belong. At its end, I am standing outside an old apartment building. I see a series of windows in the building, bulging as the dogs attempt to burst out of them, and they finally succeed, landing in a kind of huge tub that instantly bursts into flames. I watch the fire with schadenfreude, and as I transcribe this dream, I know the last part reflects some TV news I saw yesterday, with the sound turned off, showing a NASCAR racer whose vehicle massively caught fire during a race, though he himself walked away. This whole dream takes place at night; it's all terribly noir. (Yesterday Elissa was playing briefly with a friendly young pit bull who lives in our neighborhood, until it nipped her hand slightly. I am very interested in such bits of our happenstance world that find their way, rescripted, as it were, into our dreams.)

Dream Two: I'm with Dudi Dembitser, a regular at the Stanton Street minyan. We're walking somewhere between Stanton Street and my apartment, somewhere near where the Chasam Sopher Shul is in my waking life, and he takes me up a flight of stairs into a big room that's obviously in the process of being renovated. A minyan is in process there, and he says to me, "Yeah, that's the Boyaner minyan." It's clear that this is a group of people who are working on renovating and creating a synagogue, preparing for a new crowd. Now, in waking life—in that world where I can, day after day, find other speakers who will confirm what I see and remember—the Boyaner *kloyz*, the former home and headquarters of the Boyaner Rebbe (part of the Rizhiner Hasidic dynasty) is on 247 East Broadway, where a regular minyan is still held, though that rebbe's successor now lives in Jerusalem and most of the Boyaner Hasidim in New York live across the river in Williamsburg. For years, as far as I know, that place on East Broadway was Dudi's regular shul, though he had occasionally come to Rabbi Singer's, as well. When he joined us at Stanton Street some three or four years ago, he told me he still loved the feeling of the services at Boyan, but couldn't stand the politics. I chose to guess he was referring to reactionary expressions about Israel, or more specifically, about Israeli Jews and their non-Jewish neighbors, but didn't pursue the subject, and I may have been entirely wrong. My placing the dream in an unfinished attic may have to do with the account the friend in Connecticut at whose house we stayed this past weekend gave us about how he had turned an unfinished attic into two cozy bedrooms. But still, why I dreamed that the Boyaner kloyz had moved into this odd, unfinished space I really don't know.

As nearly every day for the last two weeks, we got a proper minyan this morning, though hardly at 6:45, the time it's called for and the time Dan Cantor begins the opening series of brokhes, blessings. When we do get a minyan, Rabbi Pollak sends me up to lead the rest of the service, and as I do so, I reflect that it seems that even on the mornings when there are only four or five people present when I arrive, eventually we do get a minyan. After we finish, I tell him: "We should call this 'the eventual minyan.'"

Meanwhile there are a few plastic boxes of rainbow cookies on the table, next to which Benny Sauerhaft sits, quietly and rather absent-mindedly, waiting for the rabbi and a couple of others to finish their study session so he can lock up and drive home. I approach him and say loudly (he's lost some of his hearing as well): "I love these! Did you bring them?"

"They're not cheap! Take a box home to your wife."

I say, "No, she can't eat them."

"Take a box home," says young Isaac Maxon, imitating Benny, learning how to be like Benny.

I turn to him and repeat, "My wife can't eat them."

He repeats, with a little smile but with straight intonation, "Take a box home!"

When young Isaac first started coming to us, not too long ago (I'm weary of writing "a year," "two, three years;" these are all guesses, because I completely lack the historian's sense of dating), he seemed so earnest in his Orthodoxy that I was afraid Stanton Street would seem too lax for him, and he would move on. But now it seems he's completely captivated.

It's true that Elissa couldn't eat the rainbow cookies, since she's been on a gluten-free diet for the past . . . three or four years . . . But even before then, they never appealed to her, and she'd complain, "Those colors never existed in nature!"

## Day Five of Parshas Bamidbar, May 29, 2008

Yesterday morning, as we sat with Rabbi Pollak to study another item in the Shulchan Aruch's treatment of the laws of tefillin, the Hebrew phrase *brokhe levetole* came up. Then, as I walked back uptown along Avenue B with Buddy Bardin, Buddy asked me what that word *levetole* meant. I told him it meant, in various contexts, "idle," or "wasted," or "annulled." But it's not necessarily pejorative. Somewhere the Talmud says that a Jewish city must have ten *batlonim*, which in this case means ten men who are free from labor so they can spend their time studying Torah.

We do not quite have a minyan of batlonim, but do have a number of men—sometimes as many as ten, students, journalists, a professor here and there—willing and able to stay after the service ends to study for twenty minutes or so. This seems quite a change from the years when the minyan mostly included older men who preferred to have a shot of whiskey after davening, or folks who had to rush off to work. Rabbi Pollak himself seems to enjoy this daily study session immensely; perhaps all of us treasure it a little bit more because we know he's going to leave us soon.

My own progress in traditional Talmud study may be gauged by the following. The halakhic issue we studied yesterday dealt with the rules and rationale for reciting separate blessings prior to placement of the hand tefillin and the head tefillin, even though both are considered the fulfillment of one mitzvah. In response to one of my questions, Rabbi Pollak noted that the pertinent discussion in the Babylonian Talmud was found in the tractate *Menachos*, Folio 36. I said that I'd have trouble checking it, since I always study Talmud from the bilingual ArtScroll edition and didn't have the volumes of Menachos with me in New York. But when I got home, I decided to try to see what I could make of the Hebrew by itself. I knew that Menachos is printed right after *Zevachim* (Sacrifices), the tractate I'm studying on my own in ArtScroll right now. Of course, with ArtScroll's translation and extensive commentary, Zevachim by itself takes up three volumes, whereas in the standard editions without translation, Zevachim and Menachos are printed together in a single volume. I picked up that volume, opened to Folio 36, quickly parsed it as best I could, and was struck by how similar the language and topics of Menachos (which I've never studied yet) seemed to be to Zevachim, though I didn't see anything directly relevant to the tefillin question. This morning, I checked the volume of Menachos in shul and immediately found the pertinent text:

> Rav Chisda said: If one spoke between [putting on the arm] tefillin and [putting on the head] tefillin, he repeats the blessing. If he spoke, yes [he repeats it]; if he didn't speak, no. However Rav Chiya the son of Rab Huna sent [word] in the name of Rabbi Yochanan: On the arm tefillin one says, "Blessed ... who sanctified us with his commandments and commanded us to place tefillin" and on the head tefillin he says, "Blessed . . . who sanctified us with his commandments and commanded us concerning the commandment of tefillin." Abaye and Rava both said: "If he did not speak [in between putting on the arm tefillin and the head tefillin] he only says one blessing; if he spoke, he says both blessings." (My translation)

Sounds good, no? But why didn't I find that when I looked yesterday? As it turns out, yesterday I opened up to Folio 36 . . . of Zevachim . . . which, again by "pure coincidence," I'm about to study for the first time today. Right now, in fact.

A walk down Essex Street (the continuation of Avenue A south of Houston Street, which was widened beyond recognition in the 1960s) to Grand Street, then fairly far to the east, to the co-op neighborhood where most of the Lower East Side's visibly observant Jews still live, for kosher grated cheese—one of the few food products, other than meat, whose *kashrut*, fitness for consumption according to Jewish dietary law, I'm particular about and can't find any closer. I consider composing a catalogue of as many remembered Jewish sites, mostly stores, along that route as I can, but I'm overwhelmed. My memory is poor, compared with what I know has been there, even in my experience, and I'm reluctant to slip into the easy nostalgia of "when the neighborhood was really Jewish." Still . . . Ben-Ari Arts, a Jewish ritual and home decoration items wholesaler, is still on Avenue A; you wouldn't exactly call its wares folk or indigenous art. Below Houston, Stavsky's Book Store is gone, Shmulke Bernstein's (Bernstein-on-Essex; KoChinFoo, the fabled originator of what was called "kosher Chinese food"), the building with the tiled façade bearing the proud words "Max Plotnick" above the ground-floor level has been torn down, too. On Grand just east of Essex, there's the kosher pizza shop, the Moshe's Bakery outlet, and Kossar's bialy bakery. Down Grand, in the same block or so where the kosher grocery store is, there's the kosher butcher, another bakery, and the mikva, ritual bath (the sign actually says "ritualarium"), across the street. In the grocery store, Mexican music is playing softly in the background.

Here—I remember exactly where I was standing on the sidewalk—I stood one day perhaps twenty years ago and overheard two old ladies speaking to each other: *Es hot azoy gebrent*, "It was so hot that day," one of them said, as they pushed their shopping carts along. Thinking of that woman on a hot day and remembering another day when I walked down the same block through a bitter winter rain, I thought of a title for a Yiddish article that I've still never written: *Groyl un mesikes af der hayntiker ist sayd*, "Horror and Sweetness on Today's Lower East Side." On yet a third occasion, perhaps during the same time—I know this one must have been twenty years ago, because Jonah was speaking, but still in a stroller—I walked with Jonah along the same stretch of Grand Street, at a spot where the approach to the Williamsburg Bridge was visible. Jonah looked up at the bridge and shouted excitedly, "Train! Train!"

I leaned over and said gently to Jonah, "I don't think it goes up there."

A young man with a black yarmulke and conservative suit was walking by just then, and without breaking stride or even quite looking directly at us, he corrected me and corroborated Jonah: "It goes up there."

## Day Six of Parshas Badmidbar, May 30, 2008

I don't know why it's so hard to get a minyan on Friday mornings. In the winter, one could at least speculate that it's a short day with a lot to do, and people can't spare the time. But we don't have to light candles until well after 7:30 tonight. Still, it often seems to be the case. We waited for perhaps fifteen minutes, as various shul-related conversations went on: where the second hot plate is, to keep things warm for the shabbes kiddush; a voice mail that Rabbi Pollak had responded to, from someone who wants to be interviewed as a candidate for the position of our new rabbi but didn't want to go through the Yeshiva University placement service (whatever his reasons were, a signal that this probably wasn't someone we want to consider further); Benny Sauerhaft asking young Isaac Maxon, "Get your father [Benny S. himself] a cup of coffee."

Isaac, who had just walked in, goes to get it.

Rabbi Pollak: "Right, get the coffee, then say brokhes."

Isaac: "I said brokhes at home already, but anyway—*mipney sayve* is *midoraysa*, *brokhes* is *miderabonon*": the commandment to honor and serve the elderly is Scriptural, and the blessings are only a Rabbinic commandment, so the former takes precedence anyway.

If it were some regular member of the minyan other than me keeping this journal, he might have noted that I hate sitting and waiting for the tenth (or in this case, the ninth) man to come in. And today I just went ahead and completed the prayers by myself. Meanwhile Dan Cantor was standing outside, Jew hunting. Once Rabbi Pollak had declared that "unfortunately, our streak is over"—it was the first time in a couple of weeks we didn't seem to have a minyan—he went out to bring Dan back in.

As Dan came down the steps and reentered the beis medrash, he said "I didn't see anybody with a beard!"

Rabbi Pollak said, "That's your problem [a suggestion that it's a fallacy to think all male Jews should have a beard]. If you did find somebody with a beard, it could be a Muslim [not wanting to sound bigoted]. On the other hand, then at least he'd be circumcised."

Isaac Maxon: "Yeah, then we'd just have to dunk him in water and we could count him in the minyan."

Rabbi Pollak: "That's what Pinchas and Melech wanted [to attract people to the morning minyan] —a mikva in the shul, so people from Williamsburg could go to the mikva before davening."

I'm nagged by the sense that these fragments have specific resonances for me that I cannot expect a reader to share, at least two of which I can identify as stemming from earlier experiences and writings of mine about the Lower East Side.

One such resonance was evoked by the joke about how easily we could make a Muslim a member of the minyan. It suggests, sotto voce, our awareness of the arbitrary boundaries that declare who can and cannot be counted in our minyan. I heard a similar remark years ago, one forlorn shabbes afternoon when nine men and an elderly woman were sitting and waiting. After a short silence, Benny Sauerhaft spoke up: "Mrs. Wechsler, put on a pair of pants—we'll have a minyan."

I've also described in earlier work the way younger people, often newcomers to the neighborhood and perhaps newcomers to traditional Jewish study and practice, as well, will use fragments of traditional categories to insert themselves into this very particular Jewish world.[1] Here, Rabbi Pollak chose to soften by ironic repetition what might have seemed an inappropriate command by Benny that Isaac serve him, rather than pray, but Isaac turned the situation around with a response that simultaneously acknowledged his appreciation of Benny's presence and his ability to apply the principles of Jewish law to this unique circumstance.

1. See my essay in Boyarin, ed., *The Ethnography of Reading*.

# Week Four

*And the princes brought the dedication-offering of the altar in the day that it was anointed, even the princes brought their offering before the altar. And the Lord said unto Moses: "They shall present their offering, each prince on his day, for the dedication of the Altar."*

—NUMBERS 7:10–11

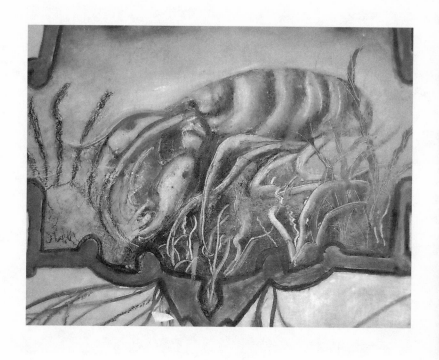

*Upstairs Zodiac Mural, Depicting a Lobster*

*A Jewish summer: seven weeks of counting, three weeks of mourning,*
*four weeks of blowing the shofar, and the summer's over.*

—YIDDISH PROVERB

## Day One of Parshas Naso, June 1, 2008

Shabbes mornings on the Lower East Side, if I wake up early enough and I have no particular reason to daven at Stanton Street, I make my way to the early minyan at the big Bialystoker Shul on Grand Street, which sets off on its weekly journey at 7:00 A.M. I had first found out about that minyan almost fifteen years ago, when our second child, Yeshaya, was a baby, and I couldn't easily leave Elissa home alone with both children for the whole morning. My teacher, Yankl Redelheim, suggested I come daven early, and then I could be home for the rest of the morning. Some time after I started going there, he explained that the reason he likes it is because he has to continue on to two other synagogues, one the shul that's now called the Sixteenth Street Synagogue and the other over on Charles Street in the West Village. At both Sixteenth Street and Charles Street (as at this early Bialystoker minyan), he serves as the Torah reader. "So," he said, "I'm the only guy who comes to this minyan for the original reason. It was started decades ago, when there were a lot of members who couldn't avoid working on Saturday. They would be out by 8:30, and then they could go to work."

The minyan is held in the beis medresh, downstairs from the main shul, but it's a much larger room than at Stanton Street. The Bialystoker Shul, originally built in the nineteenth century as the Willett Street Methodist Church, is much grander than the narrow tenement shuls, of which Stanton Street is one of the last exemplars. Neighborhood notables, stalwarts of the Orthodox community on Grand Street, daven at the early Bialystoker minyan: Rabbi Reuven Feinstein, son of the late

Reb Moshe Feinstein and head of the Staten Island campus of Mesivta Tiferes Yerushalayim; Shelly Silver, who is said to dominate the New York State Assembly with an iron hand.

In this journal, I'm trying to let signals from this summer spark reminiscences spanning the three decades I've lived on the Lower East Side. That's why, yesterday morning at the Bialystoker Shul, I started thinking about the theme of the Levite, the male Jew tracing his descent from the Levite tribe, whose ritual distinctions now are limited to the privilege of reciting the blessings for the second segment of the Torah reading and assisting the kohanim, priests, as the latter prepare to recite the priestly blessing on festivals. They are not quite indispensable to an Orthodox service today; you might have one, two, or none. But back at the old Eighth Street Shul, when Elissa and I went there in the early eighties, a very modest older man named Moshe Dretel was "the Levi," and so of course he always got the second aliyah. For whatever very local historical reason, he also had the regular task of announcing in Yiddish, on the Sabbath before the new moon, the exact time when the crescent moon would make its appearance in the sky, and for years I was under the misapprehension that this, too, had been the special ritual task of a Levite since time immemorial. I thought of him one morning last week at Stanton Street when we were waiting for the tenth—or perhaps the ninth—to arrive, and Benny said, referring to one of the more recent regulars and certainly not to the long-deceased Moshe Dretel, "Is the Levi coming?"

I thought of Levites and "the Levi" again at Bialystok yesterday morning, because one of the regulars at *that* minyan is a middle-aged man, still apparently a bachelor and I believe also a rabbi, whose name is Levi. Levi is not, however, a *levi*, and of course there's no reason to assume that he should be. (Things get more complicated when you find out that people whose last name is Levine aren't Levites, or people whose last name is Cohen aren't priests.)

Like most Jewish males, I and the other males of my family are neither kohanim nor levi'im (Levites), but ordinary *yisroelim*, just plain old Israelites with no particular notion of our tribal origin. We have to wait at least until the third aliyah comes along, and since that one is fairly prestigious as well, it usually goes to someone fairly prominent in the congregation. Yesterday, perhaps because I haven't been at the minyan for a few months, I'm called to the fourth aliyah, and with Reb Reuven Feinstein standing next to me (as a particularly honored member of the congregation, he was called up to recite the blessings for *shlishi*, the coveted third aliyah), I'm careful to pronounce the blessings in the generic Lithuanian Ashkenazi accent that is about all I've tried to retain in memory of my mother's father, raised as the stepson of the head of the yeshiva of Telz. (A couple of years ago, I went to the DC Minyan, a Modern Orthodox minyan made up overwhelmingly of young adults that pushes toward gender egalitarianism about as far as any minyan can and still credibly call itself Orthodox. When I was called up, I pronounced the blessings in my usual way, and a young visiting rabbi said to me afterward: "Oh, so you're a Boyarin. I thought you sounded like a *ben toyre*," someone steeped from childhood in the study of Torah and Rabbinic literature. I thought later that I should have corrected him: "Actually a *ben bas ben toyre*, the son of a daughter of a 'son of the Torah,'" since my mother's father, Yeshaya Weltman, was the last in his line to receive a traditional yeshiva education.) Meanwhile here at Bialystok, after the service, the man who had called me up to the Torah wishes me a *guten sabes*, pronouncing the first consonant in *shabes* with the characteristic sibilant of the northeastern region of the Russian Pale of Settlement, again evoking that lost world of an integrated culture of Lithuanian Yiddishkeit and religious traditionalism. I can't be sure, but I surmise again that he caught the particular tones that I try to convey only when I have the chance to recite these blessings in public.

The Bialystoker Shul's Rabbi Tsvi Romm speaks briefly before the Torah reading. He points out that the list of tribes and families departing from Egypt that takes up much of Parshas Bamidbar reveals the tribe of Levi to be about half the size of the other tribes. He cites first, in explanation, Nahmanides' account, according to which, to spite Pharaoh's attempt to exterminate the Hebrews, God granted to all of the other tribes miraculous increase in the number of live births per pregnancy, while the birthrate among the children of Levi remained natural. But he then provides his own homily: The Levites, who are the smallest in number of all the tribes, are the servants of the Temple. Of all the tribes, they are the closest to *kedusha*, holiness. Elsewhere in the Scriptures, God tells Israel: Not because you are the greatest of the peoples do I love you, for you are the smallest of the peoples. Whether you're doing the right thing or not shouldn't necessarily be determined by how many people agree with you, whether or not you're in the majority.

At the modest kiddush after the service, I take a piece of shmaltz her-ring, with as much onion as I can pile on the cracker to cut the herring's saltiness, and a drop of oil falls onto the lapel of my jacket. I go into the kitchen to dab at it with a piece of wet paper towel, but Levi, seeing me, says "Better clean it after shabbes," since rubbing or sponging falls under one of the specific categories of forbidden Sabbath "work."

I turn to him: "I can't even dab at it?"

He says, "No."

Okay. I didn't get upset. I'm not pretending to be as knowledgeable or as strictly Orthodox as seems to be the norm at the early Bialystoker minyan. Or I am, but not doing everything I can to give that impres-sion—after all, my ponytail reaches halfway down my back, although these people by now have known me since before I became a professor and grew my hair long again. And it wasn't such a big stain anyway.

This same Levi might, I thought for a while yesterday morning, have been the person who passed Jonah and me on the street twenty years ago and confirmed that the train "goes up there," on the Williamsburg Bridge. But then I realized that it was more likely someone else, another regular at the early Bialystoker minyan, around the same age and, I think, also a bachelor, whose name I've never learned.

Back at Stanton Street this morning, Sunday, it takes longer than usual even to get nine. Bob Flantser, who has shown up like clockwork at 7:00 every Sunday for as long as I can remember, complains doggedly to Rabbi Pollak: "If the minyan starts at 7:00, that's when people should be there. It's terribly inconsiderate for people not to come on time."

By now, Rabbi Pollak has a storehouse of responses to such com-plaints (the kind I've voiced myself in the past), but this one struck me as worth recording: "Look, anyplace else in the world, where there's more than one Orthodox shul, on weekdays, people go to the one that's most convenient for them. Nearly everybody here, with the exception of one or two, has someplace else he could go to more easily. So it's a tribute that people come at all—and if they don't come at 7:00 A.M., they get here when they can. And we should be glad that they come at all."

Eventually Isaac Maxon comes in. Benny Sauerhaft looks up at him and says, teasing, "Sleepyhead!" Though old Benny's strength is clearly fail-ing him in major ways, I'm struck by how he continues to identify the new regulars, and even more by his continuing capacity to extend affection.

## Day Two of Parshas Naso, June 2, 2008

Today is Yom Yerushalayim, the anniversary of the entry into the Old City by Israeli soldiers during the Six-Day War in 1967. Yesterday, Rabbi Pollak had announced that, in celebration of the occasion, we would be reciting the full Hallel, a series of psalms recited on festivals and other special days.

I stumbled into shul after sleeping badly: my feet hurt after a long and wonderful city hike several days ago; I was afraid I was coming down with Jonah's cold; I'd left the window open, which gave us a sweet breeze but also the full brunt of the garbage trucks' noise—and Rabbi Pollak greeted me with, *Chag sameach!* "Happy holiday!"

I stared at him blankly for a moment, and then responded in a more or less neutral tone, "Enjoy your holiday": It's not a celebration with which I choose to identify.

He understood my meaning well and responded in turn with an anecdote. Yesterday, he had marched in the Salute to Israel parade with the contingent from Yeshiva Chovevei Torah, where he earned his ordination. He told me the parade was delayed for a couple of hours, partly because of a scuffle involving counterdemonstrators from Neturei Karta, the old-line Hasidic anti-Zionist group. "There were about twenty-five of them, waving one Palestinian flag. So as we were passing them, one of our guys started walking toward them, and the police rushed up to restrain him. But all he wanted to do was say hi to a woman he recognized, a peace activist photographer who was hanging out near the Neturei Karta."

I've never had a sustained conversation about Israel or Zionism with Rabbi Pollak. He's certainly aware that I'm not interested in the additional prayers that the Stanton Street congregation, like many other Orthodox congregations, inserts into the standard service on shabbes mornings—prayers for the welfare of the United States, the State of Israel, and the Israeli Defense Forces. By countering my gently reserved "Enjoy your holiday" with his anecdote about a colleague of his who literally reached out to a friend associated with the fiercely anti-Zionist Neturei Karta, he was making a point that this extension beyond the Orthodox Jewish consensus is *also* part of what Chovevei Torah includes within the realm of "open Orthodoxy."

## Day Three of Parshas Naso, June 3, 2008

A slow Tuesday morning. There are eight of us at 7:15. Dudi Dembitser is out this week because his daughter is sick; others are away as well, though I know of no particular reason. As we chat and wait, Dan Cantor asks the rabbi: "Where you're going in Connecticut—how do they do in the morning minyan? Do they get a minyan every day?"

The rabbi answers, "They don't have a daily minyan, just shabbes and *yontev*," only on the Sabbath and holidays.

And I joke, "That's why he's taking the job there!"

Cantor continues, "My shul doesn't have a minyan during the week, either. That's why I come here."

I joke, "I thought it was because you loved us."

Cantor doesn't miss a beat: "That too!"

The pause and chat give Mendel Trebitsch a chance to share one of his fanciful ideas for making the morning minyan work: homing devices that would allow the rabbi to track each regular's movements early in the morning. A grim thought!

A man named Sam Gelber comes most days, around 7:20. So Benny Sauerhaft asks the rabbi whether Sam is coming today, and the rabbi admits that it's almost annoying to wait ten minutes for someone who comes more than half an hour after the minyan is officially scheduled to begin. We proceed on our own, which I've been doing for the past fifteen minutes anyway. Not Sam, but Melech Goldfeld walks in around 7:20, and thus we have nine, but having proceeded thus far on our own, we finish without the pretense of a minyan.

In any case, neither of our two regulars who need the minyan to say kaddish—Buddy Bardin and Charles Copeland—is present this morning. When they are, it puts extra pressure on us to wait for a tenth or to accept nine plus the open ark. Sometimes, though not recently, the rabbi or Benny Sauerhaft will announce that so-and-so has *yortsayt*, meaning they're observing the anniversary of a relative's death and need a minyan to say kaddish. Indeed, there have been many stable and observant Jewish communities where the holding of a daily minyan, whether someone needed to say kaddish or not, was hardly a sine qua non. One of my professors, Shlomo Noble, who spent some time as an immigrant youth in the town of Beaver Falls, Pennsylvania, in the early 1920s, reminisced once about a member of the Jewish community there who would come around knocking on doors from time to time, announcing: "Yortsayt!" Eventually the other members of the community caught on to the fact that this man couldn't possibly have so many relatives to say yortsayt for: He just enjoyed the chance to lead the congregation in morning prayers.

Why, then, does the maintenance of a daily minyan at Stanton Street remain as vitally important today as it was in Rabbi Singer's time? Clearly *he* believed that the daily minyan was vital to the definition of a functioning congregation, since one of the signs that he referred to as evidence that the shul was inevitably dying was the cessation of his daily combined afternoon-evening service. It's plausible enough to suppose that Rabbi Singer had, in his decades at the shul (which, so<<stet>> far as I can determine, had begun no later than the early 1960s), accumulated enough souls for whom he felt obligated to recite an annual kaddish that he personally needed the minyan every day. And if, in fact, someone is coming to shul with the expectation that he will be able to recite kaddish, it can seem vital not only to the fulfillment of that individual's needs but also to the long-term continuity of the minyan that it be constituted every day. In my quarter-century of more or less regular morning attendance, at Stanton Street, Community, and elsewhere (such as the Beth Israel Abraham and Voliner Shul in Overland Park, Kansas, where I recited kaddish for my father in the spring semester of 2006), I've heard enough mourners complaining that if they can't rely on a minyan, they'll have to go somewhere else. Thus it is at least plausible to imagine that if there is no minyan for a few days, the minyan will die—like a creature deprived of oxygen for just a few minutes. The tension even extends sometimes to those who are not saying kaddish: They might say they come to shul because they want to have the merit of praying with a minyan, and that's more important to them than being at this particular shul, or they might simply say that they want a minyan that starts on time and ends promptly.

At times in the past, Benny Sauerhaft—perhaps because he's the society's nominal president, perhaps just because he knew so many people—had, like the rabbi, agreed to say kaddish for those who had no living descendants who would do the job, but for the past couple of years, Benny has been silent at the time to recite the mourner's kaddish. So he's not the one who needs the minyan now. And, dare I say it—extrapolating here, in fact, from my own experience as a mourner for my father, when there were days I could not get to shul to recite kaddish, yet it was clear to me that I need feel no guilt—that our current mourners, Buddy and Charles, experience no profound existential qualms, no anxious fears for the fate of the souls of those they are mourning, should it be impossible to say kaddish one day. Anyway, both of them travel frequently, one as a journalist and the other as a musician, and surely there is frequently no minyan where they find themselves. I surmise that, like I did, they say kaddish when they can.

It may also be that in the current situation, where we are concerned to retain an aura of legitimacy as an Orthodox congregation on the Lower East Side while reflecting Upper West Side–style "openness," continuing to sustain a daily minyan helps us believe, and believe we are convincing others, that "open" doesn't simply mean casual or convenient Jewishness.

For whatever reasons, continuing the morning minyan seems to be a priority to at least some of us, as evidenced by the fact that participation in it is part of the job description we've prepared as part of our search for a new rabbi. I know that it was a struggle for Yossi to get to Stanton Street promptly every morning as well, especially at the beginning of his tenure, which started just shy of two years ago and is about to end soon. It may seem odd for us to insist on this, especially since the position here at Stanton Street is officially considered part-time, and the pay we offer will continue to reflect that. But we do expect our rabbi to be in shul every morning. Wish us luck.

## Day Five of Parshas Naso, June 5, 2008

Sleepers, awake!

Yesterday morning was rainy. It's not clear to me why that should discourage people from coming—certainly it doesn't keep Benny Sauerhaft away—but for whatever reasons, we were seven in total, and we proceeded by ourselves. It was Rosh Chodesh, the first day of the month and thus a minor holiday, so lacking a minyan meant that one part of the service we could not observe was the Torah reading. As we prayed silently, Rabbi Pollak called out *Ya'ale veyavo!* as a reminder to insert into the shemona esrei the extra paragraph beginning with those words. I rushed through, and thus realized only while listening to the rabbi's quiet prayers that even without a minyan, I could have / should have recited the Hallel psalms, as well as the long psalm recited every Rosh Chodesh, "Bless my soul."

All this week I have not been sleeping well—I haven't been exercising, perhaps because I pushed myself too hard in the gym last week. Feeling sluggish and unrested makes it hard to avoid becoming inured to my surroundings, to lose consciousness of the astonishing variety and immediacy that always strike me when I first return to New York. As I mechanically rushed through the closing prayers yesterday morning, I did at least pause at a phrase that I have long found especially inspiring: "Blessed is He, our God, who created us for His glory." The thought has always helped me to stand up straight, as if I were balanced on one side and on the other: We are to be the best we can (and not just sleepwalk through our days!), but not for our own sake.

Reb Simcha Bunem, the Rebbe of Przysucha in the early nineteenth century, had a saying that works the same way for me: "In one pocket you should carry the words, 'For I am but dust and ash.' In the other, you should carry the words, 'For my sake was the world created.'"

Years ago I spoke to Menachem Dunkel, a Gerer Hasid who for a time came regularly to Stanton Street, about this anecdote and asked him whether he knew a jeweler who might inscribe those words on silver plates that I could hold in my pocket. That particular plan was never realized, but sharing the idea did net me another story from Mr. Dunkel: "There was a certain renowned Talmud scholar in the previous generation. His students noticed that whenever he would share a particularly profound insight, he would pull a tiny box out of his pocket, open it up, peer into it, and then put it away again. After he died, they learned that what he kept in the little box was dirt. He was reminding himself that he was only dust and ash."

I told Mr. Dunkel that wouldn't work for me: I need the other reminder as well. If all I bore in mind was my lowliness, I would collapse to one side.

So perhaps even if it didn't get me writing yesterday, a moment's actual focus on the idea that our purpose is to be the best we can to return glory to the Creator helped me to remember and to want to return to writing today. Yesterday, my experience of shul ended in an uninspiring fashion, the leather straps of the arm tefillin sticking slightly to my skin as I unwound them from my triceps in the muggy air.

Yesterday morning, after I'd returned home from shul, I wasn't in a frame of mind for journal keeping. Instead, I was preoccupied waiting for Jonah to get up so we could drive upstate to Peekskill, where he'd decided he had the best shot at successfully passing the road test to get a New York State driver's license. While I waited, I tried some quick research into a question about recent Hasidic history. I knew that the beloved and elderly Rebbe of Bluzhev—one of the towns whose landsmanshaft, the Bluzhever-Rimenever, came to the Stanton Street Shul decades ago—had passed away within the past decade, but I did not know whether he had a successor. (I have never heard that he had any connection with the Bluzhever-Rymanower society or with the Stanton Street Shul.) I still don't, after a quick and casual Internet search, but I did learn something else: that there is apparently a group called Monastritsh Hasidim, followers of a rabbinic dynasty named Rabinowicz whose founder was the "Holy Jew" of Przysucha, the master and predecessor of Reb Simcha Bunem, whose insight I quoted just above. And this Sunday night, the first night of *Shavuos*, the Feast of Weeks understood to celebrate the giving of the Torah on Mount Sinai, I will be giving a brief talk at Stanton Street about Reb Menachem Mendel of Kotsk, who was Reb Simcha Bunem's successor. This is how much of the learning and experiencing happens, disjointed, not one thing after another: I do not know whether that is more true today than thirty years ago, before the Internet, or a hundred and thirty years ago, before radio, or five hundred years ago, before the newspaper. Like you, reader, I am frustrated and also (I hope, like you) intrigued by these hints of ways that names and the memories they represent ripple through the lives of a group in the present.

After Jonah and I drove to Peekskill (to our mutual relief he passed his test), we drove over the scenic Bear Mountain Bridge to celebrate. Starting back south toward New York City down the Palisades Parkway, we saw signs for the Hasidic community of New Square and debated making a detour to see it, at least briefly. I wasn't sure I wanted to intrude, but I wanted to reward Jonah for getting his license and also to encourage his budding curiosity about the ethnography of Jewish communities. New Square was established decades ago as an enclave of Skver Hasidim (hence its name, which the Internet tells me is the result of a government clerk's scribal error, though I prefer to think of it was a bit of interlinguistic wit). It's entered via a modest turnoff, which Jonah and I made, though a young Hasidic driver in the car behind us honked his horn, evidently to suggest that we were going where we don't belong or perhaps just annoyed that we didn't make the turn fast enough. We just drove up and down the main street, long enough to observe that people were dressed as we would expect, and also (something we had not known) that the sidewalks on one side of the street were designated *mener zayt*, the men's side (with actual signs in Yiddish to make the distinction clear) and the other side for the women. Driving back out, I saw a sign in Hebrew that said: *ad kan ha'eruv*—this is where the boundary marker that allows observant Jews to carry outdoors on the Sabbath stops.

Eruv has been, in fact, one of the major issues facing the Jewish community of the Lower East Side in recent years. New eruvin have been established in the past twenty years in places as varied as South London and Tenafly, New Jersey, partly because they permit Orthodox Jewish families to push baby strollers and otherwise be out and about with small children on the Sabbath. An effort to attract younger families and sustain the neighborhood's Jewish population confronts the legacy of Rabbi Moshe Feinstein, who declared decades ago that, for complex reasons of Jewish law, it is not possible to have an eruv in Manhattan. Attitudes toward the possibility of an eruv will, in fact, quite possibly be among the questions we ask of four applicants for the position of our new rabbi in interviews that begin tonight and will continue a week from tonight, with a view toward inviting two of the four to serve as guest rabbi for a Sabbath. (Zev's template questionnaire for these interviews includes the words: "Please describe your approach to an eruv, bearing in mind that this is a controversial issue within parts of the established Lower East Side community and one in which the shul would prefer to be proactive.")

Here, on the corner of Third Street and Avenue A, I can look out my bedroom window and see a yellow clothesline-type rope, strung from light stantion to light stantion along Avenue A. It is part of a new downtown eruv, created largely at the initiative of Rabbi Yehuda Sarna at New York University, but it encompasses an area that stops at Houston Street, two blocks south of our apartment and one block north of Stanton Street. In effect, therefore, it does not impinge on the Grand Street neighborhood that remains the bastion of the Feinstein family and the Orthodox community that remains most fiercely loyal to the halakhic authority of the late Reb Moshe. But there is an unusual twist here:

Often or usually, creation of an eruv indicates the growing popularity and consolidation of a neighborhood's Orthodox population (though most are not as exclusive or insular as the suburban New Square), but that will not happen here. This new Lower Manhattan eruv encompasses an area that does not have a significant Orthodox population, and its character in terms of housing stock, existing institutions, and the like is such that the presence of the eruv here is not likely to attract a substantial influx of Orthodox Jews. On the contrary, it is, if anything, because the area north of Houston Street is not really considered part of the Jewish Lower East Side that these younger and more liberal Orthodox rabbis have been able to create the eruv north of Houston. This eruv, it may be said with some exaggeration, but with considerable metaphoric validity, draws a boundary unlike nearly every other: The Orthodox community in Lower Manhattan is outside the eruv, not inside it.

Stanton Street, just down from Houston, is also somewhat marginal to the Grand Street community, and as I try to think about this issue of neighborhood boundaries and eruv, I am momentarily overwhelmed by the complex mix of style, housing stock, infrastructure, and other factors that determine what the potential constituency of an "Open Orthodox" congregation in a small tenement shul just south of Houston would be. If I have focused so far on matters as intimate as the proper placement of my tefillin on my forehead, it is partly because any kind of bird's-eye view of these larger demographic questions seems beyond my grasp and energy.

Still, as Nate Hacker leaves shul this morning, I ask him whether he might share with me the membership list. "For my research, I'm interested in seeing where most of our people live." I have a hunch that, for all our "East Village" flavor, the majority of our membership are folks who live in the co-ops along Grand Street, but are looking for something a bit more progressive than the Bialystoker Shul. This hunch might still be colored, more than anything else, by an anecdote I heard from Lenny Rivers—a mainstay of the shul for several years and still active, though he and his wife, Melanie, bought a house across the river in Teaneck, New Jersey, last year. When he first started coming to Stanton Street, Lenny told us that he and Melanie had tried the Bialystoker Shul, but when she went into the women's section, someone looked at Melanie's relatively short sleeves and said, "Oh, you must be cold—do

you want to borrow my shawl?" In context, Melanie was being told in
no uncertain terms that she was not dressed modestly enough.

Maybe someone at Bialystok even suggested that Lenny and Melanie
would be "more comfortable" at Stanton Street: I'm relying on my
memory here, just out of a stubborn purism, when it would be easy
enough to ask Lenny to relate the story to me again. For the record, I
think that Lenny and Melanie's finding their way to Stanton Street also
had much to do with Melech Goldfeld, who had been Lenny's roommate when they were both undergraduates at Yeshiva University and
who welcomed Lenny to the neighborhood. Melech is the cousin of Dr.
Kara Goldfeld, who is in turn married to Zev Gross, the current executive vice president. Zev started coming to Stanton Street after meeting
Elissa about ten years ago at a Saturday afternoon discussion group
called the *shabbes shmues*, which met nearby on Norfolk Street and
which she had started with the express purpose of finding younger Jews
interested in revitalizing the neighborhood. Zev was told about that
discussion group by our old friend Dr. Leah Fogel, a professor of Hebrew at Baruch College who has for years tried to expand the possibil-
ities for women's study and prayer within the Orthodox framework on
the Lower East Side. How Zev and Leah met, I don't know. But I am
quite certain that—even remembering a series of individuals who have
for a time in past years taken up the burden of primary responsibility
for making the shul survive, such as Jack Fish and Lenny Rivers, and certainly Elissa herself—had not Zev come along when he did, it is much
more likely that the shul would have been lost to the Singer family or
that the congregation would not have survived until now. So that moment, when Elissa created a context to bring Zev to the shul and when
Leah knew to send Zev to meet Elissa and the others at the shabbes
shmues, stands out in my personal history of Congregation Anshei
Brzezan as a vital turning point.

Well, that's all history now, if quite recent history by Jewish standards. Today's a Thursday, as ordinary as any Thursday is or isn't. This
morning at about 7:15, a young Hasid walked into the beis medresh.
I'd never seen him before, but I knew why he was there. He was "collecting"—asking for modest donations, possibly for himself, but more
likely (at least nominally) for some communal cause in the Williamsburg Hasidic community, such as funding the marriage of a poor bride.
I used to see his like more regularly at Stanton Street, almost invariably

on Thursday mornings, perhaps because communal charity was expected as part of the long preparations for the Sabbath. I've wondered
why they stopped (though I guess they decided that our minyan was
too small or too miserly to make the trip worth their trouble) and even
more, I wonder what made him give it a try today. Had we been close
to having a minyan at that point, I wonder, too, whether Rabbi Pollak
would have tried to convince him to stay: In my experience, that rarely
works—these collectors have to make their rounds on time.

### Day Six of Parshas Naso, June 6, 2008

Everybody was a bit cranky this morning. No minyan, though if we'd
waited five minutes more, we would have had nine. I sense that Rabbi
Pollak is less inclined than he once was to give those extra five minutes;
perhaps it's because he will not be with us much longer in any case, perhaps he's also swayed somewhat by my own impatience.

While the others are waiting, Benny Sauerhaft, who is obsessed
about the shul's electric bill, asks somewhat querulously a version of a
question I've heard him pose many times before. Usually, as today,
Rabbi Pollak is the addressee, though it's not obviously his responsibility: "Someone was in the shul last night? They left all the lights on in
the bathroom."

I took this a bit personally, since I was the one who made sure all the
other lights in the shul were turned off when we'd finished interviewing
our first two rabbinical candidates last night, and knowing that Benny
probably wouldn't hear me anyway, I said from the back of the beis
medresh, "So what?"

And Rabbi Pollak replied to me, "Now you know what I've been going through the past two years." Though he's learned to deal with the
elderly members with much better grace than when he first started, he's
never become inured to Benny's needling.

But at this, young Isaac Maxon took offense in turn. To Rabbi Pollak:
"You can't rebuke the elderly! The respect you owe them is absolute!"
And to me: "Do you want to pay the electric bill?"

I retorted, "Sure, I'll write a check for the extra thirty-five cents it
cost." (I look: There isn't even a cent sign on this computer's keyboard.)
And later it struck me that I could have said also, "If it comes to that,
kid, I'm a lot older than you, too."

*The Local Journalist*

*Lives in Jersey Now*

*Benny Sauerhaft and Yossi Pollak*

*"Jason Frankel's" Portrait of Benny Sauerhaft*

*Abie Roth,
of Blessed Memory*

*Jonah Sampson Boyarin as Tour Guide*

*Alternative Transportation*

*Rabbi Joseph Singer, of Blessed Memory*

*Kosher Chef and Treasurer*

*Stanton Street Square Dance?*

*Pediatrician and Accountant*

*Abie Roth and a Friend*

*New Music Composer Holding Torah Scroll*

*Now She's the Shul Vice President*

And also while we're waiting, Dan Cantor expresses a garbled version of news headlines, evincing a certain tendency to read politicians' statements as indications of ill will toward Jews: "McCain and Obama both said they would give Jerusalem away to the Arabs!"—the opposite, pretty nearly, of what each of the candidates had said in speeches to AIPAC over the past few days. Benny Sauerhaft responded, "McCain's going to get in."

As it turned out, I was proven at least somewhat wrong in my claim yesterday that the Hasidic collectors come infrequently to Stanton Street, and only on Thursdays. Around 7:15 this morning, just after everybody besides me had decided to proceed separately (I was already doing so), two Hasidim, one middle-aged and one younger, came in and approached each of us in turn. Conveniently, I had a couple of singles, and I handed one to each of them. I was right that they wouldn't stay to complete the minyan, if asked: Gordon Gross did ask them to, but the older one gestures no: Can't stay, got to move on. Later, Gordon insisted he was just doing it to get their goat. Rabbi Pollak was annoyed: He told us that he'd explained several times to these *meshulachim* ("representatives," though I wouldn't be surprised if sometimes the collection was for the "representative's" own family, and also I'm not sure whether it was *these* men the rabbi had seen before, or merely others of their type) that they should come before or after we're davening, not while we're in the middle of prayer. "He sees that I'm saying the *shema*, 'Hear O Israel,' but still he comes right up to me!" And Dan Cantor chimed in: "Did they grow beards just so they could come collecting?"

I understand the annoyance, but I find it exaggerated. I probably retain some of the sentimental attachment to the very idea of being around Jews in traditional dress that moved me when I was a younger man and thus welcome the idea that our shul, as much as it has changed in its makeup, can still be within the circuit of the meshulachim. Today, when they passed through, we were not in fact close to saying one of the prayers that particularly require a minyan. And as to being interrupted in our prayer, five minutes before we had all been chatting as we put on our tefillin, murmured preliminaries, or waited for the ninth man, who came too late in any case.

As I wrote yesterday, keeping the morning minyan limping along, making it more secure, or leading the congregation through the painful process of dropping it will likely be a major responsibility of our next rabbi. Here are a few notes on the two candidates we met with last night.

Josh Yuter, thirtyish or less, single, red-haired, son of a rabbi from Baltimore ("My father believed it was a good thing to learn enough so you could form your own halakhic opinions"), just laid off from a computer job at JP Morgan Chase as a result of its acquisition of Bear Stearns.

*How he would resolve halakhic issues that come up in the community*: There is a process for halakhic decision making. First, does the question involve something that is either obligated or prohibited by halakha? If neither, does it involve something that is permitted, that is optional? If so, does it make sense? I may consult others if I find it useful, but I would never turn to another authority to make the decision for me.

*How he feels about the kinds of women's participation that currently take place at Stanton Street (women's* megillah *reading on Purim, women's Torah reading on Simchas Torah, women dancing with the Torah on Simchas Torah)*: This part doesn't bother him. The question is: What's best for the shul that's halakhically permitted? Since this isn't the only shul in the neighborhood, nobody's being forced to come to Stanton Street if they disagree with its halakhic standards. Also, people have to be educated as to the range of what's actually permissible: "What you're doing is wrong because it's not what we do" is not a legitimate objection to a fellow Jew's behavior.

This I consider very revealing of Josh's intellectual style: He doesn't think women dancing with the *sefer torah* on Simchas Torah is a problem, although he did note that the rabbis of the Talmud were opposed to anyone dancing with a sefer torah, altogether. (See his answer on eruv, immediately following.)

*The eruv question*: Zev, asking Josh his opinions on the eruv controversy, states that this is a question of life and death for the Jewish community of the Lower East Side. (As I've suggested, I'm not quite so sure.) Josh has been involved with this issue in Washington Heights, where his current synagogue, Mt. Sinai, created an eruv despite the opposition of the traditionalist Breuer community there. This he sees as a big problem, not necessarily because Rabbi Feinstein ruled against it, but for another reason: An eruv requires the agreement of everyone, certainly every Jew within it, since it creates the fiction of a shared private domain. Thus, if there are people who object to the eruv, it's halakhically very difficult to create it. Now, in a place like New Square, he adds, it really works, because everyone agrees to the eruv and the place is practically walled to begin with. But if others took the initiative, he would cooperate on the creation and maintenance of an eruv.

*Gay and lesbian members?* Not an issue.

*Think of this position as being handed the keys to the family business. It's largely up to you to keep it going:* I would need feedback: Tell me where the Jews are here, so I can go out to find them. In the end, the best way to grow is to be the best shul we can be.

Jacob Unger. Our second interviewee last night was as eager as the first was deliberate and serious. Jacob Unger's c.v., as shared with us, stated that his objective was "To become the rabbi of the Stanton Street Shul," and he enthused straight out of the starter's box. He told us that he and his wife, a Ph.D. candidate in behavioral psychology, are both eager to live downtown and that he enjoys the avant-garde cultural scene here. He referred more than once to "Tonic *alav hasholem*" (may it rest in peace), the recently closed pioneering club that for years featured the Sunday "klezmer brunch," but he didn't know that before it became Tonic, it had been the Kedem wine store.

He'd prepared for the interview with several conversations with Rabbi Pollak and knew exactly what he wanted to say about attracting new people to the shul. "I liked what someone wrote about the Stanton Street Shul on Facebook: 'Where hip meets hip replacement.' I did a search on Facebook for 'Jewish Lower East Side' and found at least thirty people who didn't seem like they were affiliated with a shul yet. I'd contact all those people and invite them to join a Stanton Street Facebook group. And if they did come to the shul, my wife and I would invite them for a Friday night dinner to our home. You say you get large crowds for Purim and High Holidays? I'd want somehow to get e-mail addresses for all those people, and, over time, I'd want to extend hospitality to them, as well. One way to build community for the people who are already coming regularly is round-robin Friday night dinners, where people are assigned randomly as guests at each other's homes." (None of us said it to him, but this idea, which might work well on the Upper West Side, would need serious adjustment in our neighborhood, where it's not safe to assume that most members' households are set up to accommodate guests easily. Still, though I also didn't say this to him, I think that developing hospitality is indeed essential and is not just the rabbi's job.)

Gordon Gross asked a question that it took Rabbi Unger some time to digest: Where do you place yourself between Rav Kook (as the most spiritual) and Rabbi Soloveichik (as the most halakhically rationalist)? A: I'm not a "halakhic man." In my current position (as associate rabbi? intern? at Kehillat—on the Upper West Side), when I give a *droshe*, sermon, I tend to quote the later Hasidic masters—the Izhbitser, the Sfas Emes, Reb Tsadok Hadohen. So I guess you'd say I'm more on the Rav Kook side.

*How do you approach decisions on halakhic questions?* Halakha is an art, not a science, and values are always a large part of the process. If I needed to consult an authority, I might turn to Rabbi Boruch Simon at YU, or to Rabbi Mintz (at Rayim Ahuvim).

*Women's participation?* Unger knows that Stanton Street is the only shul on the Lower East Side that emphasizes expanding the range of women's participation and would not compromise on anything we've been doing until now. Yet he would want to maintain good relations with other shuls in the neighborhood insofar as possible. He knows Rabbi Romm from YU and would want to hold joint events where possible with the Bialystoker Shul. (He's also heard about joint programming between Stanton Street, Community, and the Sixteenth Street Synagogue and would like that to continue.)

*Openly gay and lesbian members?* Not a problem.

*Eruv?* Is familiar with the issue; knows Rabbi Sarna, who created the downtown eruv, and also Rabbi Mintz, who was instrumental in setting up the West Side eruv. Would like to work toward its establishment here. (A couple of us tried to impress upon Rabbi Unger the degree of opposition he would find in doing so, but he professed to be undaunted. It's not clear he appreciates how much of a challenge he would face if he tried to create an eruv including Grand Street.)

We are scheduled to have preliminary interviews with two more candidates next Thursday and then plan to invite two of the four to be with us for a shabbes. The consensus was that, had the two we met last night been our only applicants, both of them would have been invited for a shabbes. More to come, God willing . . .

Post Scriptum: Zev Gross just circulated to those who were at the meeting last night the following e-mail message from Rabbi Pollak (I had almost written Rabbi Unger: If it comes to that, red-haired Josh Yuter looks more like blond Rabbi Pollak than does thin, dark-haired Rabbi Unger):

To: Zev Gross; Nate Hacker; Dudi Dembitser; Jason Frankel
Subject: Lights

Please make sure that when there are meetings in the shul that ALL lights (including the bathrooms) are turned off when you leave. It upsets Benny greatly (and leads to arguments at the minyan, which are very distressing).

Thank you,
Yossi

*Upstairs, View from the Front of the Women's Gallery*

# Week Five

*And the children of Israel also wept on their part, and said: "'Would that we were given flesh to eat! We remember the fish, which we were wont to eat in Egypt for nought; the cucumbers, and the melons, and the leeks, and the onions and the garlic; but now our soul is died away; there is nothing at all; we have nought save this manna to look to."*

—NUMBERS 11: 4–6

*Radiator, Upstairs Sanctuary*

## Day 1 of Parshas Behaaloscha, June 8, 2008

Erev Shavuos: A Sunday tucked in between shabbes and a two-day festival. I spend much of the morning in a vague funk, not trying too hard to rationalize it, but wishing, as I sometimes do, that I once again had a job where someone would just give me orders and pay me. I don't want to work too hard, but I have trouble successfully managing long stretches of "time off." I don't want to be lost in the summer in the city; I've experienced that, and it's just too terrifying.

I know that the Torah portion for this coming shabbes is Behaaloscha because late one evening last week, I got a phone call from Bernard Pittman, the president of the Janina Shul on Broome Street, asking whether I could come read the Torah for them yesterday. I told Bernard I couldn't make it yesterday, since I was giving a kiddush lunch in honor of Jonah's graduation, but that next week I'd be happy to. And then I glanced at the *khumesh* to see what I'd committed myself to. I've been a regular Torah reader in various places on the Lower East Side in the past, and in fact, my longest stint was at Janina, where I enjoyed getting to know the congregation but also felt lingering sadness that, with my watered-down and improvised Ashkenazi chant, I was contributing to the cultural extinction of the ancient synagogue ritual of the Greek Jews known as Romaniote. Clearly, though, the members were happy to have me and were sorry when I left them because I had taken an academic job in Kansas.

This is the menu I'd arranged with Lenny Rivers for the kiddush lunch yesterday: potato kugel, noodle kugel (sweet—I wasn't paying attention, or I would have switched that to Litvak-style salt and pepper, which I grew up with and greatly prefer), cholent (bean and meat stew), grilled chicken strips (they turned out to be delicious), potato salad, cole slaw. The service required a bit of special coordination, because the

electrical connection for the already-inadequate air conditioning upstairs was no good, and in the sudden hot spell, we had decided to
hold services downstairs and then rearrange the room for lunch. But
it all worked out smoothly: By the end of the service, there were forty-
five or fifty people present, as many women as men (one of the inno-
vations we've made in the past few years, both upstairs and down, is
to move the *mechitza* barrier between the men's and women's areas
forward, to give the women more room and allow them to be closer
to the action in the men's section, as well). The old pews that are usually lined up against the walls of the narrow beis medresh had been
swung out into the room, and the six school benches in front that
were preserved (after a long fight led by Elissa) through the renovation were utilized, as well. Seating was thus a comfortable and somehow nicely blended mix of the old school benches, the old pews, and
folding chairs.

The room hadn't been cleaned for several weeks. Several weeks
ago—as I gather, shortly before I returned from North Carolina for
the summer and started keeping this journal—Mr. Jose Rodriguez,
whom Pinchas Duber knew from Stuyvesant Town north of Fourteenth
Street, where both of them had apartments, stopped coming on Fridays
to clean up and on Saturday mornings to set up the kiddush, and no
one knew where he was. I hadn't gotten to know Mr. Rodriguez well,
since I was away most of the time he was here, but I understood that he
was an articulate, gentle, and thoughtful man, who volunteered at the
shul because of his Noahide beliefs[1] and general respect for observant
Jews. In one of the few private conversations I ever had with him, he
told me: "I know you're a professor, but you should consider becoming
a rabbi, too."

There's been considerable speculation and some worry and certainly
regret that we don't see Mr. Rodriguez anymore. He hasn't been answer-
ing his phone in Manhattan. As best Pinchas has been able to determine, he gave up his apartment in Stuyvesant Town and moved to East
New York. This morning, I overheard a snatch of conversation between Rabbi Pollak and Sol Decker, who were speculating that perhaps

---

1. Adherents of the idea that, in conformity with the Torah, there are seven divine
commandments incumbent upon non-Jews.

Mr. Rodriguez had been the prophet Elijah in disguise: "He comes, he helps, you don't know where he came from, and you don't know where he's going."

Yesterday, late in the long summer shabbes afternoon, having slept off the substantial kiddush lunch and exhausted the half of the Sunday *New York Times* that is delivered to our door on Saturday morning and is the easiest way to while away the times on shabbes when I'm not in shul, eating, or sleeping, I turned to my Yiddish library and picked up a volume from 1943, a volume in a series of annual of anthologies edited by Joseph Opatashu. I read through Mani Leib's story "How the Prophet Elijah Saved the Jews of Vilna from Snow." The coincidence—Elijah appearing twice in one journal entry—seems both strained and artificial, and I won't say more about that story. But here, in my translation, is the explanatory footnote the author provided:

> I wrote this story about the Prophet Elijah saving Vilna from snow for the children of the fifth grade in the Folk Shul in the Vilna Real-Gymnasium, where Mire Bernshteyn was the teacher. Thirty-two children from that class sent me thirty-two letters in 1938, containing very interesting questions about my life. In my reply to the children, I promised them that, instead of answering their questions about my life, I would write down for them a story that my grandmother from Vilna had told us, her grandchildren. But the children had to help me out, by describing Vilna and all of its important places, because I myself hadn't been to Vilna or seen it. In exchange, I promised them that the story would be *theirs*.
>
> In 1939 sixteen of the children sent me wonderful descriptions of the city of Vilna—and this story is *theirs*.
>
> Where are these precious children now? Are they at least still alive? Has the hand of the German murderer spared at least them?

This Friday, anyway, it wasn't Elijah, but Sol Decker himself who came in and mopped the floors, helping to make the long, narrow room comfortable and festive for the celebration of Jonah's graduation. As I reminded a few of the people there, it was the same room where we had, a little over twenty-two years ago, observed the ritual of *pidyon haben*, redeeming our firstborn from the kohen Irving Gruenfeld, a fellow shabbes morning congregant at the old Eighth Street Shul.[2] (The Torah prescribes that, like the firstborn of various domestic animals, a firstborn Jewish male whose birth "opens his mother's womb" is sanctified for holy service, but the Torah also prescribes "your firstborn son you shall redeem" from such lifetime dedication.)

At the kiddush, the potato kugel went very fast, but some of the noodle kugel, a few of the chicken strips, and most of the cholent were left over. So after Sunday morning services, Gordon Gross brought his car around and we delivered the leftovers to Mary House, the soup kitchen run by the Catholic Worker on East Third Street near Second Avenue, just down the block from the headquarters of the New York Hell's Angels.

Walking back to shul around 11:00 to put in a solidarity appearance at our first-ever bake sale, organized by Kara Lemberger (Sam's niece and a professional cook in her own right), I was annoyed by a high-pitched vehicle bell. I couldn't tell quite where it was coming from, though I'm used to the phenomenon of cars far down the block, seeing that the light has changed and unable to bear the thought that the traffic doesn't start moving immediately, impatiently and irrationally honking. But this time, I realized, the bell was from a bicycle being ridden down Clinton Street against the traffic by a young man with a long black coat and a helmet, with large green plants precariously balanced on the back of the bicycle. He said hi to me, I said hi to him, and though I can't be sure, I'm surmising that he was ringing his bell to be friendly to the black yarmulke and ponytail he saw of me from the back, and that he was taking the plants to decorate a synagogue as part of the traditional greenery associated with Shavuos.

With the holiday starting this evening, that's probably it until Day Four, after the holiday is over.

---

2. The redemption ceremony fulfills the commandment of Exodus 3:13: "and every firstborn of man among your sons you shall redeem." Participating in such a redemption ceremony is one of the few ritual functions that remain to a kohen, a descendant, through the male line, of a member of the priestly clan in the days of the Holy Temple in Jerusalem. Another is the recitation, before the entire congregation, of the formulaic priestly blessing on certain holidays. A kohen, if one is present, will also traditionally be honored by being called to recite the blessings over the first section of the day's Torah reading. In addition, a kohen is forbidden to marry a widow or divorcee, and is enjoined to avoid contracting certain forms of ritual impurity.

## Day Four of Parshas Behaaloscha, June 11, 2008

A Jewish holiday on the Lower East Side is, for us, always partially and powerfully out of the rhythm of the daily round. The newspapers are delivered, and I, at least, read them more avidly than at most other times. The telephone rings only to deliver the random message from a caller who is unaware or unconcerned that we will not be picking it up that day, but I use the telephone relatively little in any case, so that is not such a great change for me. Such work as I do on the days I work this summer (much of it the keeping of this journal) I do at home, so being here is in itself not such a great change. Forty-eight hours without e-mail communication is certainly a big change.

Another, on Shavuos in particular, is staying up hours later than I usually do. This Sunday evening, not for the first time, the shul held a communal dairy dinner (primarily meaning, in this instance, nonmeat, since most of the meal consisted of vegetables, although there was the traditional cheesecake for dessert), catered by the same Teaneck place where Lenny Rivers had gotten the food for the kiddush lunch I sponsored on Saturday. The forty places available for the dinner were sold out days before, some to people I see in shul every day or at least every week, others to people I've known for a long time, but rarely see in shul, some to members whom I've never met before. One young woman to whom I introduced myself, dressed modestly with her head carefully covered, told me that she and her husband are members, but come to Stanton Street only "for special occasions."

Around 6:00 P.M., two hours before the davening was scheduled to begin, Rabbi Pollak sent out an e-mail announcing that the woman hired to set up the dinner wasn't going to be able to show, so a few of us went to shul early to do the setup. We weren't sure when to light the sternos under the aluminum trays of rice, green beans, pasta, and salmon, so we took our best guess and kept an eye on the food during the davening to make sure it didn't burn. Somehow, it seems, I had elected myself head of the serving and cleanup committee; Jason Frankel, Gordon Gross, Jonah, and Isaac Maxon helped out cheerfully, as well.

Setup was complicated somewhat by our being obliged to move the davening downstairs into the beis medresh, due to a combination of bad wiring upstairs, which prevented use of the inadequate air conditioner, and a record heat wave, which began on shabbes and broke only last night, four days later. Everyone cooperated cheerfully, and we started dinner a bit before 9:30.

At dinner, Jonah and I ended up sitting with Sol Decker and his wife, along with a young man named Ethan, who attends on Friday nights from time to time. I remembered Ethan as being in law school and committed the faux pas of asking him how close he was to finishing: as he reminded me (and I had in fact learned this from him before), he's in his third year of doing criminal defense at the Legal Aid Society. No matter: Ethan (a Brown University alumnus) and Jonah seemed to get along fine with each other.

Though many congregations sponsor actual all-night study sessions on the first night of Shavuos, followed by morning services that begin the first minute halakhically permissible and are wrapped up quickly, at Stanton Street we aimed to study only until about midnight. We weren't quite that efficient, though. Three *shiurim*, lessons or lectures, were scheduled: Dudi Dembitser, drawing on an eclectic mix of texts, but especially *midrashim*, purported to show how famous episodes of incest and harlotry—Lot's daughters' coitus with their father and Judah's recourse to his daughter-in-law Tamar, posing as a prostitute—were predestined to lead to the Davidic lineage and thus connected to the promised arrival of Messiah. Well, Dudi likes to work sex into the material he chooses to teach.

When I got up to give the second lesson, I had to admit that Dudi was a tough act to follow and joked that my talk might be called "No Sex, Please, We're Kotskers." I drew, in fact, on the same material I've been using for years when asked to speak to a synagogue audience—my draft translation of Abraham Joshua Heschel's monumental study of the fierce and enigmatic Rebbe of Kotsk, who lived in Central Poland in the first half of the nineteenth century. Since Shavuos is regarded as the time of the giving of Torah, I focused on excerpts that demonstrated how the particular approach to Hasidism of the Kotsker Rebbe reintegrated study of Torah as a central value. It seemed apt to me for a congregation with Hasidic origins, but with some orientation now toward the Modern Orthodoxy that traces its origins in part to the Lithuanian, anti-Hasidic yeshiva world.

Finally, Rabbi Pollak spoke at some length about the Talmudic dictum that anyone who recites Psalm 145 three times a day is assured of membership in the World to Come, elaborating his discussion with study of Rabbi Kook's commentary on this point. I didn't pay close attention. It was after 12:30 by then, and the lesson was extended by a complicated debate between Dudi and the rabbi about whether we're supposed to ignore the distractions of the world or encompass them. Moreover, it was time to take Elissa home. Weakened by arthritis, she rarely walks to shul, especially on shabbes or holidays, when she would have to walk back as well—but she had very much wanted to hear my talk and stayed for most of Yossi's, as well. With Jonah supporting Elissa on one arm and me on the other, we slowly made it home and got to sleep around 1:00 A.M.

Monday morning, we had a minyan reasonably close to starting time. Jonah, a habitual late riser, had agreed to join me as a guest for lunch at the home of the Jewish journalist Simon L. Roth and his wife, a dancer named Ruth. Simon and Ruth are members of Stanton Street, though they rarely seem to attend these days. Jonah showed up just as we were finishing our davening. We made our way through the brutal midday heat to their home at 577 Grand Street, the next-to-last co-op building before the East River. We were pleased to see that the other guests at the lunch were Henry and Rachel Wiener, also Stanton Street members. Henry is Mayor Bloomberg's press secretary, and Rachel until a couple of years ago was a staff member in the office of local Assemblyman Sheldon Silver, whom I've mentioned as a regular at the early shabbes morning minyan at Bialystok.

Rachel has been out and about quite a bit lately, despite being a week past her due date for giving birth: As she explained to me at lunch, once she had the baby (which, I just learned, finally happened early yesterday morning, during the holiday), she would not be able to go to shul on shabbes, since there is no eruv. In fact, Rachel admitted that eventually, though not right away, she and Henry will leave the neighborhood, not only because they want an eruv, but because they want a house with a backyard. Neither eruv nor backyard is to be had on the Lower East Side.

The thought of their leaving brought home to me again that any attempt at Stanton Street to model our growth on the assumption that our congregation will ever remain put for decades, raising its children and growing old as members of the Stanton Street Shul, is both illusory and demoralizing. New children in the community are always a blessing and are usually counted as a sign of the community's growth, but here, their arrival often seems, on the contrary, to start the clock ticking on their parents' inevitable departure. (I turn to discuss this dilemma with Jonah, who responds: "Well, an eruv would definitely help that.") But what other models for participatory Jewish community do we have? After all, this is a neighborhood, not a college campus.

On Monday night, the second night of the holiday, I had invited Rabbi Charlie Buckholtz from the Community Synagogue and his girlfriend Tamar, a trade-book editor, to come for dinner. I left Stanton Street early because I remembered I'd left cauliflower steaming on the stove, but before I left I stopped to invite an older single man named Aaron to dinner. We've known this Aaron for perhaps twenty years; he moved into the block on Eighth Street across from the shul when a seniors' building was first put up there and sometimes came to Eighth Street while it was still a functioning synagogue. He's one of the few people I see regularly who understands and is willing to fulfill the traditional role of the Sabbath guest, helping his hosts to fulfill the obligation of hospitality.

In the end, the evening worked fine. Aaron was visibly tired after dinner, so I suggested that we recite the blessings after meals and let him go home, and then Charlie and Tamar stayed for another hour or so, Tamar quizzing Jonah about his rather vague plans now that he's graduated from college, Charlie looking over the few Hasidic books I have on my desk in the dining room, Jonah telling Charlie about his experiences at Chulent, the Thursday night gathering of young men at the margins of the Hasidic community that's found a provisional home in the Community Synagogue. Charlie made an obvious point that I hadn't considered when talking to Jonah about Chulent until now: It is in fact traditional in many Orthodox communities for men to try to stay up all night studying every Thursday night, so in fact, Thursday night was the obvious time for this marginally Hasidic event.

Once again we had a minyan, without trouble, Tuesday morning, though it seems I've started going into one of my periods when I really don't have the patience for extending communal prayer. At such times, having the option of focusing instead on setting up the kiddush is a blessing. One social note caught my interest in particular: A middle-aged man in blue jeans, whom I'd never seen before, walked in and explained that he had been taken to the shul by his grandfather when he was a boy and this was the first time he'd been back since. It turned out that he was a kohen, so unexpectedly we had the chance to include the priestly blessing—recited only on holidays, here in the Diaspora—as part of the musaf additional service. There was some hurried instruction in the back of the room, as this was, I gather, perhaps the first time he had ever recited the priestly blessing, but with the prompting of Dudi, who was leading the additional service, he got nearly every word right.[3]

I awoke from a long, but fitful and not especially restorative afternoon nap to find Elissa in a stupor; it seems that, venturing out to the Community Synagogue for *yizkor*, the memorial service to commemorate the dead, she had managed to become dehydrated, even though it's only a few blocks and she'd seemed fine when she sat with Jonah and me at lunch. Gradually she came round, and eventually (the word keeps appearing: these are, after all, very long days) it was time for me and Jonah to return to shul once more, for the last afternoon service of the holiday. Jonah had the happy thought of bringing two copies of Shimon Petrushka's edition of the Mishnah with Yiddish translation, and as we waited for the . . . ninth, as it turned out . . . and then between the afternoon prayers of mincha and the evening service of maariv, Jonah and I, joined by Jason Frankel, studied the first chapter of the Mishnaic tractate of Zevachim, sacrifices—the same tractate I've been struggling through in the Talmud, so I was able to parse some of the telegraphic text without reading through the commentary in much detail. At the table next to us, Isaac Maxon and the young, but not quite as young man I now also know only as "the Levi"[4] sat studying Talmud, and across the narrow room Mendel Trebitsch was glancing at another Talmud volume. It may have been the first time in years that three separate study sessions were going on in that room at once. It's fitting that it happened in the waning moments of Shevuos, which is entirely devoted to

---

3. If you look in an ArtScroll prayer book, you will see that the leader of the service is in fact supposed to prompt the kohen (or kohanim, if there is more than one) before each word of his blessing, a practice universally followed and, I would guess with some confidence, originally instituted because there were plenty of kohanim who needed such instruction.

4. Male descendants, through the male line, of the tribe of Levi retain few vestiges of the special social and ritual roles they possessed in the times of the Temple. They are, however, traditionally honored by being called to recite the blessings over the second section of the day's Torah portion, right after the kohen.

the giving and study of Torah, and fitting too because the room we were in is called beis medresh, the study house.

After the quick evening prayer, Rabbi Pollak asked us to move plastic garbage bags from the metal cans to the curb so that they would be picked up by the garbage trucks in the morning. But Gordon Gross pointed out that the wind was blowing so hard it would be better to do it in the morning. Jonah and I stepped outside, and indeed it seemed that a storm of grit was blowing down Stanton Street, accompanied by nearby lightning. Rather than run into the storm, we turned east to Attorney Street and went north toward Houston, running to try to beat the rain. I left Jonah with the two Mishnah volumes to run home quickly and made my way along at the best pace I could. Just as I was turning into our building, I heard a loud crack and saw that a large tree kitty-corner from us, on the southeast corner of Avenue A and East Third Street, had split at its base and fallen onto the street. I stood under the awning of our building and waited with our doorman Thomas from the Bronx until the rain started sweeping down in torrents. Just before it did, Rabbi Charlie turned the corner on his way back from Community Synagogue, having beaten the downpour by less than a minute.

Elissa slept badly, perhaps because she'd had coffee late yesterday afternoon to rouse herself, and I slept fitfully, as well, having had little exercise and too much sleep during the day. On such mornings, I wait for the passing of waves of despair, and even when they're gone, they leave me with the sense that any synthetic account of this transient community, and of my transient life within it, is well beyond my powers and would certainly be illusory in any case. Still, as Jonah said when we were both safely home and waiting for the rain to come, "It *was* a nice yontev at Stanton Street. And it didn't have the same sense of desperation it had, say, six years ago, when you felt like you didn't know how much longer it was going to last."

Good news this morning in shul, about Rachel having finally given birth. In fact, the most recent issue of the shul newsletter has an impressive list of *mazal tovs*: an engagement, two weddings (one groom among them being Benny Sauerhaft's "actual" grandson), and no fewer than five new babies. Some of the members and member families blessed with such *simchas*, such joyous occasions, live in the neighborhood but don't regularly come; some live elsewhere and are "members" really as gestures of solidarity (family membership being available for just $200 a year). Who knows where these babies are going to grow up?

## Day Five of Parshas Behaaloscha, June 12, 2008

Rabbi Pollak had announced several days ago that he would not be in shul this morning. He had two brisn to attend, conveniently a few blocks from each other about half an hour apart, both on the Upper East Side. The father of one of the little boys is Rabbi Zach Geller, who, as a rabbinical student at Chovevei Torah, was our first rabbinic intern, following the departure of Rabbi Singer. The second, for two years before Rabbi Pollak was hired, was Meir Goldfeld, Melech's younger brother, who is now living in Boston and serving part time as the Orthodox rabbi of Portland, Maine.

Despite the rabbi's absence, we had no trouble getting a minyan on this second lovely morning after Tuesday night's storm broke the heat spell. Based on attendance over the past month, I'm beginning to wonder whether finally, morning after morning, we're getting a minyan more solidly than in the last few years Rabbi Singer was here. One of the newest attendee's presence may be especially significant: Kobi, an Israeli whom I would guess to be in his early thirties, who has come regularly on shabbes morning for a couple of years now, and who is the first of the neighborhood's many young adult Israelis to attend Stanton Street regularly. Perhaps Kobi is coming more often now because he is engaged to be married: I saw an e-mail note announcing that he will be giving a hot kiddush (presumably including cholent and kugel, but not the chicken strips I sprang for last week to turn it into a "lunch") this shabbes in celebration of his engagement.

I had slept better and concentrated a bit more on the davening than I've been able to for some time. I looked at the end of the strap of the arm tefillin wound around my hand, as Rabbi Singer taught me, thus: first, three extensions across the back of the hand from the wrist to the ends of the fingers, the three extensions one on top of the other at the outside of the hand away from the thumb, then stretched outward from each other toward the thumb side, thus forming the Hebrew letter *shin*; next, over the ring and middle finger near the end, and then once around the middle finger only, to form a *dalet*; last, once around the middle finger between the first and second joint to form a *yud*. Thus I wear on my hand each morning the Hebrew word *shaday*, one of the most sacred names of the Divine, as Rabbi Singer taught me. As I discretely look around the minyan, it seems no one else has his tefillin wrapped around his hand in quite this way. Surely a study could be made of the different techniques for this very end of the mitzvah of tefillin. Presumably we will arrive at this topic soon in our daily study of Mishna Berura.

I continue to dwell on a particular point in Dudi Dembitser's shiur, his lesson on the first night of Shavuot. His complex argument about "Ruth and the foreign lineage of Messiah" began with a point captioned "the spirit of Messiah was created before the world," and he cited a statement from the ancient rabbinic collection Midrash Rabbah, commenting on Genesis 1:2: "Now the earth was unformed and void, and darkness was upon the face of the deep." Reb Shimon ben Lakish said, "'and the spirit of God hovered on the waters,' this refers to the spirit of King Messiah."

I had occasion to cite this gem yesterday when struggling to draft a portion of a commentary on Jacques Derrida's *Specters of Marx*, and realized I wanted to see the full quote in its context in Midrash Rabbah. That is one of the basic texts of rabbinic literature that I do not possess. I did once: a magnificent, large-format edition, printed in Berlin in the late nineteenth century, which I had taken for safekeeping from the ruins of the old Eighth Street Shul but left behind, along with a few similarly large old European volumes, as long ago as 1990, in one of our several successive moves to larger apartments here at 141 East Third Street. I remember the sight of those volumes, on the floor of an otherwise empty living room as we moved out, and I'm sure they were just discarded by the superintendent when he came in to clean for the next owners. They haunt me as though they were the abandoned graves of ancestors.

Jonah has, however, brought home substitutes, if not replacements for them: several large, old volumes of the Babylonian Talmud—nearly complete, though heavily used and badly rebound, in a 1912 edition published by the famous Romm publishing house in Vilna—and the Shulchan Aruch, in four volumes with identical binding, though printed by two different publishers at four different dates, and with inscriptions indicating that they once belonged to a congregation in El Paso, Texas. Of the four Shulchan Aruch volumes, the most recent, published in 1904, seems the most worn, and no wonder: It is the volume

Orach Chayim, which deals with the rules for conduct of everyday life, the very subject of the Mishna Berurah we study with Rabbi Pollak after services each morning. Jonah acquired these volumes two summers ago, when he was an intern at the National Yiddish Book Center. The center isn't interested in the Hebrew religious books that occasionally come in, like dolphins caught in tuna nets, along with the Yiddish books they collect, and they are quite willing to dispose of them to their occasional intern, such as Jonah, who is interested in religious Judaism as well as secular Yiddish culture.

For several days I was torn over what to plan to do tonight, after receiving an invitation to a benefit for the National Foundation for Jewish Culture that will honor, among others, my mentor Barbara Kirshenblatt-Gimblett with a Jewish Cultural Achievement Award at the nearby Center for Jewish Culture. I have left her a message expressing my pride and regret that I will not be there, choosing instead to attend the second round of rabbinical candidate interviews at Stanton Street. I hated the idea of not going tonight, partly because I felt confident that I could not express an opinion as to which two candidates to invite back for full shabbes visits without hearing all four interviews and partly, I confess, because I am intrigued by the fact that one of tonight's interviewees is an African American (or perhaps Afro Latino) convert to Judaism. What finally made up my mind, however, was that Jonah, who attended last week's interviews, will be unable to go tonight, since he's taking the GREs as preparation for application to Ph.D. programs in Jewish Studies.

## Day Six of Parshas Behaaloscha, June 13, 2008

Six in shul this morning, including the rabbi; no question of a minyan.

My notes from last night's two interviews of rabbinical candidates, transcribed more or less verbatim.

### RABBI ISAIAH PORTER

Porter: Do we want to grow the shul? Do we want to make it the leading shul on the Lower East Side?

Zev: Actually, my family is moving. But I'm still interested in understanding the factors that can make the Lower East Side a more attractive place for young Jews to move to and stay.

Porter (re his background): Inner-city Detroit (later: pharmacist father, social worker mother), started at Brown and transferred after one year to Yeshiva University. After receiving ordination, twenty-three years in Israel. Wouldn't do it again, given the difficulty of being an African American at YU in the late 1970s.

Porter (responding to the question about women's issues): This stuff is all gimmicks of Chovevei Torah, who lack real halakhic authority. You might say that you don't want me to be your rabbi, but I have to say that clearly. I would have to find out: Who are the women who want this? Is it just another gimmick to boost numbers? I wouldn't say it's *asur*, forbidden, but I think the halakhic grounds for a women's minyan are very weak.

Elissa: Would you give an aliyah to an openly gay member?

Porter: That's a real problem. If they're open, we're giving our approval to a lifestyle the Torah absolutely forbids. The person yes—the lifestyle no.

Zev: How do you approach resolution of halakhic issues generally?

Porter: It depends. Is the person genuinely interested in the answer, whatever it is, or just looking for somebody to sign off for him? In any case, I would look at the books first, then if necessary call Rabbi Bleich at Yeshiva University or Rabbi Blau in Jerusalem or Rabbi Zimmerman in Gateshead.[5] I would not automatically accept their ruling; and the answer might not be the same depending on who asked.

Nate: What about working with multidenominational groups such as the Downtown Kehilla?

Porter: We can't be ghettoized, even though the Grand Street community is. We can belong to the Orthodox Union and our rabbi can be a member of the Rabbinical Council of America, but more open than that "inside." You don't want to have a shul that calls itself Orthodox but doesn't fit into any communal definitions.

Elissa: What about the eruv question?

Porter: So we make our own eruv. (Extended discussion of this question continues while I run out to look for Pinchas, who has meanwhile walked out. I find Pinchas and confirm he is not angry at the committee for continuing this interview and will return for the second interview.)

5. Gateshead, England, is the site of the leading Orthodox yeshiva in Great Britain.

Gordon, Nate, Zev: The lack of an eruv discourages young families from moving in.

Zev: You have fifteen shuls on the Lower East Side—why should anyone come to this one?

Porter: Personal connection—warm and serious and accepting. As far as his strategies for growing the shul, he would want to get face time with organizations. You can make a business plan for this sort of thing. (Porter is currently studying for an MBA.)

Zev: What would you teach?

Porter: Bible, if that's what people want; women should study *Gemara*, Talmud, so they can tutor their sons, because fathers really aren't at home.

Andrew: We have a unique niche—we are the most open, least religious group in the neighborhood. People come here wearing shorts, short dresses, etc. How do you feel about that?

Porter: That doesn't bother me. I view this as a communal synagogue with a strong outreach focus.

Zev: Do you see this as a shabbes add-on to a full-time job?

Porter: Yes.

Zev: We're not paying full-time salary, but the rabbi's the only employee.

Porter: Wouldn't want to spend an hour on the phone every day to make sure the cake is there for the kiddush.

Zev: Fundraising?

Porter: Love it. I thrive on rejection. (At this point Rabbi Porter made comments about approaching a gay funders' bureau that by their tenor, if we were not certain before, made it altogether clear that he would not be considered further.)

## RABBI MARTIN TELLER

(Martin is a new graduate of Chovevei Torah, whose day job this year is a one-year residency in hospital chaplaincy, which he plans to make his permanent career.)

Martin: What do you people like about the shul and how do you want to grow here?

Zev: Likes the davening, needs more learning, shul has served him better than his family.

Sari: This is the only shul where I can be religious without being closed minded.

Me: It's a crossroads where you never know what's going to happen, and I'd like to see that contingency continued.

Zev: So what's your style? What would you do here?

Martin: Want to meet the people first and see where they're going.

Zev: What kind of learning would you foster? What would you want to teach?

Martin: Likes to organize classes around emotions and character traits. Fascinated by Rebbe Nachman's book,[6] though teaching it would be a challenge to him.

Zev: How are you at Torah reading and leading services?

Martin: Not really his strength—not musically skilled. Could work with congregants on meaning and structure of the prayer service, etc.

Martin says what means most to him is the one-on-one contact with people, hence his attraction to chaplaincy. But the congregation would give him the chance for larger relationship building.

Zev: This is a family business—it needs someone who's going to grab it and make it his own. Is that you?

Martin: I can do a version of it. Two evenings a week, shabbes, and part of Sunday would be available for the shul. Would like to do community holiday programs—last year he served as the first rabbi of the Educational Alliance.

Andrew: We're sort of the black sheep shul—more open, some people ride to shul, etc. How do you feel about that?

Martin: Whatever, you gotta do what you gotta do.

Pinchas: Megillah reading[7] for women a big draw here. How would you build on women's participation?

Sari: I like the participation at women's services the way it is—maybe we can make them more regular.

Martin: Wants to encourage women's services where women want it—but even more so, wants to encourage women teaching.

6. Rabbi Nachman of Braslov, a great-grandson of the Baal Shem Tov, founder of the modern Hasidic movement. Though Rabbi Nachman had no successor, the Braslover Hasidim are one of the liveliest and fastest-growing Hasidic groups today.

7. Here, the Book of Esther, read on the evening and morning of the holiday of Purim.

Elissa: Are you comfortable with the policy of welcoming "whoever comes through the door"?

Martin: Not just comfortable with it—it's a requirement.

Andrew : How do you feel about being the ultimate day-to-day manager?

Martin: Has experience coordinating volunteers. You have to encourage people and make sure they're going to get things done. (He said this more convincingly than I've summarized it here.)

(Somewhat extended discussion of the daily minyan. I don't recall Martin committing to attending.)

Zev: How prepared are you, if necessary, to go your own way in the context of this neighborhood?

Martin: Would want to be able to work with those people (e.g., the other rabbis) if possible. What is the view of the shul concerning Reb Dovid Feinstein?

Zev (diplomatically): He's viewed on Grand Street as the *mara d'asra*, the rabbinical authority of the community. Our shul doesn't have a view—people have different opinions.

Martin: I wish and hope that I could work on an eruv, as I'm doing in Washington Heights. If Reb Moshe were still here, I certainly wouldn't build an eruv in his neighborhood (since he had declared it couldn't be done).

Zev: What's your approach to resolution of halakhic issues?

Martin: I haven't been asked too many, but—you need to talk to the person first and find out why it matters, then, trying to make it work for the person, look in the *sforim*, the authoritative rabbinical texts, and if necessary ask some of the rabbis at YCT (Chovevei Torah), or Rabbi Klapper in Cambridge, or Rabbi Dov Brisman, *av beis din*, head of the rabbinical court of Philadelphia.

Andrew: How to grow the shul?

My notes end there; the question remains.

*Memorial to the Victims of the Nazis in Bluzhov*

# Week Six

*Speak unto the children of Israel, and bid them that they make them throughout their generations fringes in the corners of their garments, and that they put with the fringe of each corner a thread of blue. And it shall be unto you for a fringe, that ye may look upon it, and remember all the commandments of the Lord, and do them; and that ye go not about after your own heart and your own eyes, after which ye use to go astray.*

—NUMBERS 15:38–39

*Upstairs Zodiac Mural, Depicting a Pair of Birds*

## Day Three of Parshas Shelach, June 17, 2008

This is the dream from which I awoke around 5:00 A.M., shortly after daybreak: I was somewhere in the country. (I am often somewhere in the country in my dreams.) I had been walking with the owner of the land, who wanted to show me his far pasture. Then I was praying with a small crowd and pleased at how quickly the service and the day were going, since (as I realized during the dream) it was Yom Kippur. (The evening before, I had been reading to Elissa passages from Alfred Kazin's memoir *A Walker in the City*, where he cites at some length the Yom Kippur liturgy.) We took a break, and I was to lead the portion of the services after the break. I was thinking of this portion to come as musaf, the additional service, though actually on a Lower East Side Yom Kippur the break would usually come after musaf and before mincha. In fact (and not in dream), for the last few years, when I have helped out leading the High Holiday prayers at Rabbi Ackerman's synagogue, I have been responsible for mincha and not the more prominent and longer musaf, which the rabbi leads himself. During the dream's break from services, I gratefully sipped a glass of lemonade, then realized I was supposed to be fasting and wondered whether I could lead the prayers anyway. I tried to get up from where I was resting, but my feet were tangled, and floodwaters began to rise. (Dreadful flooding in the Midwest this month may, God forbid, cause starvation for poor people around the world as well as the terrible suffering in the flooded areas themselves.) I awoke, my calves tense, perhaps from the strain of a hike the day before and the lack of exercise and stretching yesterday.

No minyan this morning. Jokes instead. Weak suggestions about counting in the minyan the ants that have invaded the beis medrash. The old line about how the rabbi can make rats leave the shul: Give them all bar mitzvahs. (It's a famous phenomenon, especially in the more liberal congregations and in the suburbs, I'd say, that kids stop coming to services shortly or immediately after their bar mitzvahs). With that, Rabbi Pollak is on a bit of a joke-telling jag. (He and a couple of others are waiting to see if there will be a minyan; I'm going ahead on my own.) Benny Sauerhaft, who doesn't hear everything, catches what's going on and asks Isaac, "Do you smoke?" Isaac is startled, but Benny was really just leading into a story about the chimney that told the other chimney, "You're too young to smoke." It's not very funny, but it's something that happened in shul this morning.

Tuesday morning, and unlike last week, no Jewish holiday interrupted my daily journal entries. Sunday I left the city early, skipping both the later than usual morning minyan and the congregation's annual meeting, for a long-planned day hike at the Delaware Water Gap with a couple of family members. Yesterday I was too exhausted from the hike to focus on my note taking, though I did make it to the morning minyan. So just now I had to look at a Hebrew Bible to remember what the parasha was, although once I did, I remembered a *vort*, a saying of the Kotsker Rebbe, that came to mind when I heard Pete Silver chanting the first words of that parasha during yesterday morning's Torah reading: *shelach lecha anashim*—literally, something like "send out for yourself men." In context it surely indicates God's instruction to Moses to send out spies to reconnoiter the land of Canaan. But the Kotsker Rebbe read these words as "send away people's image of you"—expel from yourself the worry that other people will think about whether you're a *mentsh* or not, look inward rather than outward. Our transitory community at Stanton Street is perhaps not bounded or solid enough yet to focus on its own internal development, rather than its image and, indeed, its "market."

The term *hashkofe*, which has come up several times in the course of the rabbinical search, overlaps a bit awkwardly with "image" and "market." I first came across the term in Israeli Hebrew, where it is pronounced *hashkafa* (with the last syllable accented), and I understood it there to mean something like philosophy or spiritual perspective within Judaism. In the context of this search, it has been used—for example, by members of the search committee in their dealings with the representatives of Yeshiva University who have forwarded various candidates' applications to us—to mean something more like the religious outlook and the halakhic profile of the congregation, as in "We are only sending you candidates whom we believe appropriate for your shul's hashkofe." It seems to me that what distinguishes our congregation's hashkofe from, let me say, the middle range of congregations that Yeshiva University would be likely to supply with rabbis, are the issues, already documented in my interview notes, of women's participation, openly gay and lesbian members, and, more ambiguously, the desire to have an eruv in a neighborhood where Reb Moshe Feinstein's ruling against the eruv still holds. By labeling this complex of issues a matter of philosophy or outlook, everyone can sidestep the risk of openly recognizing that some of our fundamental practices are at the margins of, or even outside, what would be considered halakhically normative at Yeshiva University. The concept is not infinitely plastic, however, since it's clear that one of the candidates that YU sent us, and whom we chose to interview, is no match at all for the hashkofe of the Stanton Street Shul.

I am sorry I missed the annual meeting Sunday morning, and if this were dissertation research—mine or that of a student of mine—I never would have permitted skipping it for the hike. Elissa gave me a brief report, highlighted by an account of an eloquent speech Sol Decker gave urging active involvement by members, which, Elissa said, elicited concrete volunteer offers as well as intelligent questioning from members about how the shul's annual budget is met. (Unlike, perhaps, the standard congregational model, membership dues at Stanton Street are kept low, if not quite nominal, and are not intended to cover the shul's operating budget. Rabbi Pollak's salary for the past two years has largely been met through pledges by a handful of member individuals and families.) There is one member who runs for the board each year, and the entire standing board unites to make sure he is not elected, since he has been found obstreperous in the past and, this year, announced that his goal is "social justice" for a former member who was expelled a few years back after threatening violence against two other members. His candidacy was once again unsuccessful, so there's another item of business taken care of.

The search committee met briefly after the board elections, and Elissa listened in on their discussion while she was counting votes in the board election. Despite Jason Frankel's spirited argument that we should bring all three of the candidates not eliminated in the interviews in for a shabbes, and Elissa's chimed-in agreement on behalf of herself and me, only Rabbi Yuter and Rabbi Unger will be invited back: Gordon Gross, in particular, was adamant in refusing to consider hiring a rabbi for just one year again, as would presumably be the case with Martin Teller, who intends to look for a permanent chaplaincy job, probably outside of New York, after this year. The first visit will be Rabbi Unger's, this coming shabbes; Elissa and I have agreed to host him and his wife for lunch, along with at least a few members of the search committee.

Intriguingly, Josh Yuter's father, Rabbi Alan Yuter of Baltimore, has a brief article in *Conversations: Orthodoxy and Kelal Israel*, a volume published by the Institute for Jewish Ideas and Ideals (I don't know what that is!), that bears closely on the "hashkofe" of different types of rabbinic leaders. Rather brusquely, if not crudely, he divides Orthodox rabbis into three types. The first is the "charismatic commander": "this person was called a *gadol*, or great one, by [the medieval commentators] Tosafot and Raabad, whose stature and office command authority." The chief example of this type that Rabbi Yuter identifies—and certainly criticizes as such—is "Rabbi Moses Feinstein." The second type is the "cookie cutter charismatic rabbi." It is not clear exactly whom Rabbi Yuter has in mind here, because he seems to waiver between describing the traditionalism of the "charismatic commanders" themselves and the supposed lack of independence of their followers. The third type—obviously Rabbi Yuter's ideal—is the "covenant creator modern Orthodox leader." "For this Covenant Maker rabbi, creed trumps culture, principle controls and is not controlled by persons, and respect for God and God's image that is invested in every human being overwhelms the forces of confusion, intimidation, and injustice." It appears that, for Rabbi Yuter, a covenant maker includes a "rabbi who would restore the daily recitation of the priestly blessing, challenge the validity and legitimacy of community *eruvim*, or outlaw women's wigs on the Sabbath"—but since this clause appears in the midst of a discussion of cookie cutters, there is some ambiguity. I do sense here, at least, an echo of the statement of his son Josh about concern for the possibility of an eruv where not everyone inside its boundaries concurs.

More broadly, looking at other brief entries in *Conversations*, I see at least two references to Reb Moshe Feinstein as an authority on whom more inclusive Orthodox rabbis may rely and take heart. One reference concerns the issue of women reciting kaddish for a parent, the propriety of which Rabbi Feinstein is claimed to assume in an article by Rabbi J. Simcha Cohen of West Palm Beach. The second, in an article on intellectual openness in Orthodoxy by Rabbi Marc D. Angel of the Spanish and Portuguese Synagogue on West Seventieth Street, cites Rabbi Feinstein's comment when he rejected an opinion of the sage Reb Shelomo Kluger: "one must love truth more than anything."

I am reminded of something Rabbi Avi Berkowitz, sometime rabbi at the Community Synagogue, now resident of the West Bank and an assertive Modern Orthodox Jew, said more than once in my presence: "*Haredi* Jews are people who accept all of Reb Moshe Feinstein's stringent opinions and none of his leniencies. Modern Orthodox Jews are people who accept all of Reb Moshe's leniencies and none of his stringencies." Hashkofe, indeed! But in any case, it may be said that Reb Moshe's legacy looms, not only over the East Side, but over a broader range of North American Orthodox Jewry, as well.

Just two personal notes, for the record: Sometime in the mid-eighties, when I was studying with Rabbi Yankl Redelheim at Mesivtha Tifereth Jerusalem, he took me to the home of the aged Reb Moshe for a blessing. Yankl explained to Reb Moshe that I was new to observance and Torah study (not entirely true, but close enough). Reb Moshe blessed me in Yiddish: *Zolst hobn kinder talmidey khakhomim un zolst aleyn vern a lamdan*, "May you have children who are outstanding Torah scholars and may you become learned yourself." I was brought to his wife Rebbetzin Feinstein as well, who more simply and pragmatically wished me: *Zolst matsliyekh zayn in ale inyonim*, "May you succeed in all your affairs."

And this: I remain convinced, as I wrote years ago, that part of what drew me to the Jewish community on the Lower East Side was an attitude of inclusiveness toward "different" Jews that was clearly part of Reb Moshe's heritage, especially at his yeshiva. Oddly, this contrasts sharply now with the stereotyped image of the remains of the Orthodox community he once led. And I remember specifically, at a memorial meeting thirty days after his death, one of the speakers citing a halakhic ruling that Reb Moshe had justified on the grounds that to rule otherwise would violate the principle that the pathways of the Torah are *darkhey noam*, ways of pleasantness—precisely the verse Rabbi Alan Yuter cites in the last paragraph of his polemic.

An e-mail from Zev Gross informs the search committee that Alan— whoops, Josh—Yuter wants to come for the shabbes beginning Friday July 11. Why so late? I'm impatient for his visit!

A walk to the kosher butcher on Grand Street, half a block east of the grocery store I mentioned in Week 3. I decided to walk from our apartment at Third Street and Avenue A as far east as I could along East Second Street, which ends at the intersection of Houston Street and Avenue D, after passing, among many other sites to whose historical interest I remain oblivious, the site of the former Rabbi Shlomo Kliger (that's how the Galicianers pronounced the name) Yeshiva. South of Houston Street, Avenue D becomes Columbia Street and passes the city housing projects named respectively for Samuel Gompers, Bernard Baruch, and Jan Masaryk. When the projects were built, there were a fair number of Jews in them, but no longer. Just before Columbia Street goes under the Williamsburg Bridge overpass, at the corner of Columbia and Delancey, stands a plain brick building from the early 1960s, the Lutowisker Shul, built by the Housing Authority to replace an older synagogue they tore down when the projects were built, with a continuing active congregation, led by Rabbi Horowitz. That's Dan Cantor's shul, when he's not with us in the morning, and when he asks halakhic questions at Stanton Street, he refers to Rabbi Horowitz as "my rabbi."

Outside the butcher store, where I stop to buy a couple of quarts of chicken broth for Elissa, a hand-lettered, photocopied sign solicits men who are willing to attend, for pay, a 9:30 daily minyan at the Home of the Sages of Israel, on East Broadway. I am surprised: I had always understood that a minyan of elderly men were bussed in daily from Williamsburg, to pray and study Mishnah there for the souls of the dead. Maybe it's hard to get a minyan to come from Williamsburg now. Maybe I should stop by some morning.

Inside the butcher store, a young man in a simple yarmulke serves me and then attends to a young black man who inquires, "Second Avenue Deli called in an order?" Another surprise: why would the Second Avenue Deli be getting meat from Grand Street?

## Day Five of Parshas Shelach, June 19, 2008

Obviously I'm slacking off my discipline of writing each day: I am drained, not sleeping well, worried about Elissa's prolonged weakness and loss of weight, with little enthusiasm even for hosting Rabbi Unger and his wife, Hannah Golden, for lunch this shabbes.

Yesterday afternoon, to clear my head and get some exercise, I took another one of my long walks, this one more reminiscent than ever of the days in the early nineties when I still had no academic position but hadn't yet started law school. If I had taken detailed notes of what I saw on those walks, I would have a catalogue of things that are not there now: stores, ethnic populations, entire buildings have disappeared. I remember one evening, during some rush of gentrification in a period of financial flash during the early 1990s, when I walked down Avenue A and saw several restaurants that simply hadn't been there two weeks earlier. I thought to myself, "This isn't a neighborhood—it's a *set*." (Contrast the evening, several years before that, when an old friend of Elissa's stopped by to visit and suggested we walk up to the block of Eleventh Street between Avenue A and Avenue B, where a set had been created for scenes of the movie of E. L. Doctorow's *Ragtime*. As we passed through the quiet block late in the evening with no film crews around, I had the eerie feeling that I was actually stopping by the place, not merely as it had been in the 1920s, but *in* the 1920s.)

But yesterday I was trying to ask myself instead: What is it we are trying so desperately to hold on to, and why assume at all that it should still be there? Consider Italo Calvino's marvelous book *Invisible Cities*, which, in my opinion, should be the opening text of any course in urban anthropology. Calvino's fable leads us to understand not only that the city is a place of impermanence but that many cities can be superimposed on the same place, leading to the idea that all of the new construction I saw yesterday is better understood as signs of the emergence of a new city, not merely a place flattened, but essentially the same because called "New York." Consider also: but for the advent of the Great Depression, vastly more of the tenement blocks on the Lower East Side would have been demolished decades ago in favor of Robert Moses's plan for a Lower Manhattan of broad boulevards and modern apartment houses à la Corbusier. Consider, finally (for this list; you are of course free to mediate on anything else my ruminations evoke in your mind), that, insofar as I create an account of the neighborhood that focuses almost exclusively on its Jewishness (whether present or lost), I am obliterating a vast amount of what is there now: primarily Chinese immigrants and Chinese-Americans, a Latino remnant that is larger than the Jewish remnant, and financial-fashion young adults.

All the same, here are just a few highlights of that walk I took yesterday.

On Houston Street, walking toward Eldridge, the Crown Delicatessen, kosher, with a sign that spelled out in Hebrew letters "strictly kosher delicatessen," gone; Ben's Cheese Shop, kosher, with its specialty baked farmer cheeses (pineapple, blueberry, plain . . .), gone; an outlet of Moishe's Bakery, kosher, gone (both of the last victims of a building renovation about a decade ago); Ershowsky Provisions, wholesale, not kosher, in a building that must have been a theater originally, gone to make way for the Sunshine Cinemas, thus a theater again; Russ & Daughters, not especially kosher (although most of their products are traditional Jewish foods, they sell chopped liver along with all the fish and dairy, thus violating at minimum the prohibition against mixing meat and dairy), one of the great smoked fish emporia of New York City, still very much there. On the other side of Houston Street, actually on the easternmost block of East First Street, facing Russ & Daughters, the building of the old Podhajcer Synagogue, no longer a shul, but lovingly preserved by new residents, with, still, an iron gate topped by a semicircle bearing the letters in Hebrew: *presentirt fun podaytser leydis akzileri*, "presented by the Ladies' Auxiliary of the Podhajce Society."

On Eldridge Street, just about everything Jewish gone, but what comes to my mind immediately as missing are the Zion Tallis store and J. Levine's Bookstore. Further down Eldridge, practically under the Manhattan Bridge overpass, the Eldridge Street Synagogue, preserved and restored through a massive, decades-long effort and now primarily a museum and space for educational and cultural programs. The signboard outside says that religious services are still held, and I'm glad to hear that's the case. Other than this, and some traces that a more carefully trained architectural historian's eye might detect, Eldridge Street is simply part of Chinatown now. I guess that's okay. There are a lot more Chinese people than Jews.

If, at the corner of Eldridge and East Broadway, I had turned left instead of right, I would have passed (among others) the Munkaczer Tallis Factory, gone, and the Feldheim Book Store, gone, before, of course, proceeding a couple more blocks to pass Mesivta Tifereth Jerusalem, Rabbi Feinstein's yeshiva, still there—but a quarter-century ago I was already referring to it as the Yeshiva of Chinatown.

Where I did continue, south and west of the Manhattan Bridge along Henry Street, then under the Brooklyn Bridge overpass almost to the Battery, there is little Jewish trace of which I'm aware. If the headquarters of the Orthodox Union are still on William Street, as they were years ago, I passed them, but they seem little connected to Jewish life in lower Manhattan. I stopped my walk at the old Fraunces Tavern, haunt of George Washington and his Revolutionary cohort, deserving of mention here only because after my return, when I report to Elissa on what I'd seen, she says: "Fraunces Tavern—sometimes when we do tours for the Lower East Side Conservancy, we start there, because it's the closest we come to anything dating from the original Jewish presence. Asser Levy's butcher shop, from Dutch days, is long gone."

I walk back uptown by way of Chatham Square, so that I can stop at our favorite Chinese vegetarian restaurant and pick up some dim sum to tempt Elissa's appetite, and thus I pass the first cemetery of the Spanish and Portuguese Synagogue, the congregation now on West Seventieth Street, where Rabbi Marc Angel has his pulpit. As far as I know, the cemetery is the oldest institution of European settlement in Manhattan still serving its original function. I've been inside the cemetery at least twice. The more recent was a few years ago, during the annual Memorial Day ceremony with Rabbi Angel presiding, attended by army veteran members of his congregation dressed in Revolutionary uniforms as a color guard. The first was in the mid-eighties, when I was a regular participant in a Talmud and Bible study session at Tifereth Jerusalem. On Tisha B'Av, when we fast in mourning for the destroyed Temple, when even Torah study is strictly limited to certain pertinent topics, and when it is (as I learned that day) customary to visit Jewish cemeteries, Rabbi Berl Feinstein—Red Dovid's son, Reb Moshe's grandson— led a group of us down East Broadway to Chatham Square to pay respects to these Sephardic dead.

Prior to the walk today, I was toying with the idea of dipping into a selection of recent e-mails related to the shul. It seemed a bit like cheating, for several reasons: It's not my own writing; it will still be there a

year from now, unlike my immediate impressions of what goes on in
shul and what I see in the neighborhood; and others do not write e-
mails thinking they will end up in my notes. But later a message came
in that I will copy here verbatim, since it articulates standing issues
about the shul's direction, as a congregation and as part of the Lower
East Side Jewish community (as to the third of the reasons listed above
for not copying e-mails, it raises precisely the same confidentiality question that I will have to address before I publish almost any of the material in these journals).[1]

So: On Wednesday, June 18, 2008 2:56 P.M. Sari Zuker-Frankel wrote:

Hi all,

Obviously we're moving ahead with having both Rabbis Unger and
Yuter for shabbatot, but I wanted to let you all know about another option, rather un-Orthodox but possibly very exciting, that has just presented itself, which I think we should consider if we're not happy with
the other choices.

Bear with me while I explain:

Katherine Taub, a Drisha scholar who spoke a few months ago on
Shabbos morning (she's very small and very smart, with red hair if that
rings a bell), and who I think most people were impressed by, is getting
married this fall to Rabbi Jason Maltz, a friend of mine from college.
He has smicha [rabbinical ordination] from a well-respected, RCA
[Rabbinical Council of America]-approved program that's not YU or
YCT, he's very smart and very dynamic and interesting, has worked as
a community organizer, and is, I think, a very good fit for Stanton
Street in many ways.

Both he and Katherine will be working (part-time?) this coming
year (Katherine teaching, Jason will be at NYU hillel) and are interested in the possibility of working as a team to lead the Stanton Street
shul. Jason would be the official Rabbi but Katherine would be more
than just the Rebbetzin. We'd have to come up with a good title.

They understand that the salary is only meant for one part-time person and seem okay with that. Both of their resumes are attached.

1. I have solved this issue, as best I could, primarily through the use of pseudonyms.

Keep in mind, this is just an idea, with several considerations that need to be considered. But if people are open to it, let's discuss.

Sari

I am of at least two minds about this proposal, well, at least three. On the one hand, Jason and Sari (like, for example, Henry and Rachel Wiener, who have been around less in the past couple of weeks since their baby was born) seem to represent the next phase of best continuity—relative youth combined with having been around for a few years—that the shul will need to survive, and hence I think that anything they propose should be considered. On the second hand, this sounds like a potentially make-or-break proposition for the shul: Hiring this couple could highlight the strengths of the new congregation, bring it more attention, and galvanize in particular the population of Jewish women downtown who want to be fully involved in a congregation that defines itself as halakhically observant—but the more this strength is played up, the sharper and nastier the ostracization of our congregation by the rest of the Lower East Side community is likely to be (even if we just call Katherine the "educational director"). On the third hand, I'm tempted to stand back and let others, especially the younger people, figure this one out, to invoke, most selectively and adventitiously (arguably, in overtly cowardly fashion) the Star Trek Prime Directive of noninterference in another culture's development. But that doesn't seem a good-faith stance in this case: How am I "other" to the future of the shul, except insofar as I take refuge in the stance of the participant observer?

Melech Goldfeld showed up to make the minyan this morning, but he didn't actually put on tallis and tefillin until I teased him: "You've davened already, I suppose?" He had some stories he wanted to tell me, and after he'd finished all of them, he wanted to review them with me. All the same, I don't care to record all of them here, just these two, certainly to be taken with a grain of salt, both meant to illustrate Melech's wise-guy participation in the Hasidic community as well as his notoriety there.

*Shtreimlekh*, the round fur hat made of beaver tails worn by Hasidim on shabbes, holidays, and to celebrations: He's scheming with a friend of his in Williamsburg, an animal rights activist, to have shtreimlekh banned. Melech claims he's not particularly concerned about animal rights, he just likes to stir up the Hasidim. Recently he was driving past a Hasid wearing a shtreiml and called out: "Sir! That's a beautiful hat! Tell me, what kind of dog do you make it out of? A poodle? A collie? A German shepherd?" And the Hasid, with whom Melech wasn't acquainted, replied, "Well, I don't know the answer to that question, but tell me—how's [Melech's wife] Tsippi?"

Melech also tells me about his friend Jimmy Justice, and Wikipedia confirms Jimmy Justice's existence: "Jimmy Justice is a famous *vigilante* in New York City. He became well-known after posting a video on *YouTube* of several NYC traffic cops parking in front of *fire hydrants*. Since then, he has posted further videos of cops breaking regulations." Melech has discussed with Jimmy Justice his dispute in the beis din with his erstwhile partner, who has meanwhile come under investigation by the Federal Trade Commission for deceiving phone card customers on the number of minutes they have left on cards they purchase. His partner has a newborn son, and the bris will be Monday, so Jimmy Justice proposed attending and calling out, "Are you going to do the bris with one of your dirty phone cards?" This will, fortunately, not actually happen, though the event may be videotaped by the vigilante.

## *Day Six of Parshas Shelach, June 20, 2008*

After writing yesterday's notes, and after seeing the positive response of several other search committee and board members to Sari and Jason's proposal, I did send my own reply, suggesting we set up a preliminary interview and adding:

> If we do have a preliminary meeting with them, I believe it should concentrate frankly on the particular challenges a spousal team would face in our neighborhood, which is an issue of great concern to me—indeed, one that in my view might ultimately preclude our hiring them—and one I think we should all be carefully thinking about in relation to their potential candidacy, and again, an issue they should fully understand as well (as some of our preliminary interviews revealed, not all candidates understand how the Lower East Side differs from the Upper West Side).

Among pertinent responses, Sari said she understood my concerns; Sol Decker asked me, privately, for clarification; Dudi wrote to the whole group, inter alia, that "I'm not eager to pick fights with Grand Street, but I don't think we should run our business with our head constantly turned back in fear. This couple sounds great, and if the only reason to reject them is that the wife is a woman, then we may be having a serious disagreement over the shul's mission"; and Pinchas wrote to me, privately, "I am sorry to report but the Frum LES [Lower East Side] is disappearing and what those few people think about us should have no bearing on our decision making." Dudi's and Pinchas's remarks hurt me and made me want just to observe the process, as I wrote of being tempted to do yesterday. But this is too interesting. Anyway, we now have an interview with Rabbi Maltz and Katherine Taub for next Thursday.

In his e-mail to me, Pinchas also reiterated a claim I've heard him make before, that most of our members no longer live on Grand Street. I suspect he's exaggerating, and I had asked Nate Hacker to send me the membership list, which he did a couple of weeks ago. Checking it now, I see that it lists only the city in which members live, not their street address, so further illumination of this point will have to wait. Meanwhile, arranging hospitality for the visits of Rabbi Unger (tonight and tomorrow) and Rabbi Yuter (in three weeks) hasn't been so easy, a confirmation of my sense that, in major ways, the congregation is not a "community" but, more precisely, an occasional gathering of mostly young adults who are less prone to have formal shabbes meals to which they can readily invite guests and simultaneously more prone to go away on beautiful weekends in the early summer. (Among those from the congregation we had invited are our friends Charles Copeland and Jean Fox, both avant-garde composers and impresarios: Charles just wrote back that he's in Amsterdam and Jean has been out of town, as well.) We are hosting Jacob and Hannah for lunch tomorrow, and so far, most of those we have invited to join us are either going away, invited elsewhere, or haven't replied, so the group won't be so big. Good thing Jonah will be around, to represent the real youth contingent. I suppose that now he's out of college, he's "graduating" from being a child of members to a young adult member in his own right.

*Pew in Memory of "Avraham ben Yeshayohu"*

# Week Seven

*And the Lord spoke unto Moses and Aaron, saying: "Separate yourselves from among this congregation, that I may consume them in a moment." And they fell upon their faces, and said: "O God, the God of the spirits of all flesh, shall one man sin, and wilt Thou be wroth with all the congregation?"*

—NUMBERS 16:20–22

*Flourescent Light and Rose Window, Back of Upstairs Sanctuary*

## Day Two of Parshas Korach, June 23, 2008

Dov Ber, our regular young Lubavitcher shabbes afternoon visitor for the past couple of years, used and explained to me the meaning of a Yiddish proverb I had heard decades ago and never understood before: *a gast af a vayl / zet af a mayl*, "a guest for a while sees for a mile." I had always tried to read it as a sardonic comment about unwelcome guests, reading in words that weren't there so as to indicate something like "Even a guest who's supposed to be coming for a short visit, you can see coming a long way before he arrives." The words don't support that reading, and Dov Ber's explanation makes much more sense: A stranger who comes for a short visit perceives a great deal that those more familiar might miss. The sentiment should be heartening to a participant-observer anthropologist, but in my case, since I'm trying to "see for a mile" but am not really "a guest for a while," it's less than encouraging. Not, that is, unless I do what I know I must in any case: remind myself that we are all here only as "guests for a while" and that I will see more if I try to retain that consciousness, as perhaps I did better even the first week or two that I kept this journal.

The proverb also suggests that it might be extremely revealing to hear the reactions of Rabbi Jacob Unger and his wife, Hannah Golden (eventually to be Hannah Golden, Ph.D., God willing), to their visit to Stanton Street this shabbes. Once again, we stayed downstairs in the beis medresh for the davening Friday night and Saturday morning, even though, before discretely disappearing for shabbes, Rabbi Pollak had said that, with the cooler weather, we could go upstairs to the un-air-conditioned shul for the morning prayers. So this, perhaps, is how Jacob (or more likely Hannah, with more time in the women's section by herself Friday night and fewer performance obligations than Jacob in any case) might have described the beis medresh as they saw it, assuming they were not too nervous and preoccupied with making a good impression on the congregation to notice such details.

A glass door, with in cursive script the Hebrew words *beis medresh tsvi borekh ben yekusiel vebrayndl,* "The Tsvi Boruch son of Yekusiel and Brayndl Beis Medresh," and additional decorations of flowers and deer (*tsvi* means "deer" in Hebrew), leads into the startlingly long and narrow room itself. The walls are plain white, and so far unadorned. (When Jonah mentioned to Isaac Schoenfeld, the director of Chulent, the possibility of bringing Chulent to Stanton Street if the Community Shul becomes unavailable due to neighborhood opposition, Isaac said, "No, it's too plain vanilla." An ironic comment for any of us who, like Jonah, remembers how the beis medresh looked when the place was Rabbi Singer's shul.) The new wooden-plank floors are already well scuffed and due for a good polishing. A low, semi-transparent mechitza hangs about four feet from the floor, dividing the length of the room about half and half into men's and women's sections. It is suspended with strips of the same cloth from metal poles that, if necessary, can be moved farther back to change the proportion of space between the men's section and the women's. Six old school benches with inkwell holes, from the old beis medresh and thoroughly redone as part of the renovation, stand in two rows toward the front of the room, on runners so that they can be pushed out of the way to allow more room for social events. Another relic, four smaller wooden pews, similarly refurbished, line the left wall of the room toward its middle, placed on hinges so they can be made to face forward as part of the seating (for men or women) during prayer services. The same modest, time-beaten wooden *aron kodesh*[1] as in Rabbi Singer's day still holds our Torah scrolls; now it is ensconced in a framework in the front wall, on a wooden platform raised just about six inches. The pressed-tin ceiling has been preserved, as well.

The back third or quarter of the room—the part that you step into first when entering from the street—is the "library," lined with bookshelves on both sides and marked off by retractable glass doors that, however, do not reach all the way to the ceiling. These glass doors are

1. The usual English term for this item of synagogue furniture is "ark," but that word always makes me think of Noah. "Sacred trunk" might be a more precise (and evocative) translation.

also etched, with natural and deer scenes and appropriate verses from the Sabbath liturgy: *Vehu yehiye li la'ateres tsvi*, literally, "and He shall be for me [an adornment] like the crown of a deer." On the right side, two stained-glass windows repeat the art nouveau deer-in-the-woods motif, adding what appear to me to be cherry blossoms, which would recall Pinchas's love of Japan. I haven't mentioned: Tsvi Baruch was the name of Pinchas Duber's deceased brother, and the renovation of the beis medrash was largely financed by Pinchas and his parents in his brother's memory.

Of course, Jacob and Hannah would not have—do not in fact have—any mental image of what the room looked like before the renovation, and I have not now the courage to face the melancholy of trying to recall it in full. (Walter Benjamin quotes Flaubert: *Peu de gens devineront combien il a fallu être triste pour ressusciter Carthage*, "Few people will guess how sad one had to be in order to recall Carthage to life.") But one image does present itself to my memory: an annual membership meeting, most likely just around two years ago, when the plan for renovation was first being presented. Dudi Dembitser, sitting at one of the old, long, heavy wooden tables with the matching long, heavy wooden benches toward the back of the beis medresh, complained, "But I don't want to have to sit at a chair in the front when I'm part of the morning minyan. And Jonathan doesn't want to have to be regimented, either. We like to be able to sit at one of the school benches, then wander back here to a big table at the back." Dudi was reassured that (as has turned out to be the case) the room could be fully open any time we wanted it to be. I'm tempted to add that, as became clear only in retrospect, what he was really complaining about was whether there would be room for the room's ghosts after the renovation.

Meanwhile, Pinchas himself... this is a stretch (somewhere the Yiddish writer Sholem Aleichem writes, *A smikhes-haparshe?* "What does this have to do with what came before?"—a sarcastic reference back to the rabbinic interpretive tool of explaining, pragmatically or homiletically, the pertinence of a given weekly Sabbath reading from the Prophets or Writings to the Torah portion that it follows) ... Pinchas wants to hear the accents and tones of those ghosts in the young leadership we hire today. More prosaically and more accurately, one of the areas of gossip that he has concentrated on, at least with me, is the extent to which any young rabbi (and for the past two years it has, of course,

been Rabbi Pollak) can sustain the traditional Ashkenazic pronunciation of liturgical or other religious Hebrew. Since Pinchas is, of all our
members, the most vigilant in insisting that the shul countenance no
homophobia, stressing such traditionalist features permits him, by contrast, to indulge his "conservative" side.

The two most signal features of this distinction between Ashkenazi
and modern Israeli (so-called "Sefardi") Hebrew would be maintaining
the distinction between the letters *tof* and *sof* (rather than, as in Israeli
Hebrew, collapsing both into a *t* sound) and maintaining the distinction
between the vowel sounds *komets* (*aw* as in "pawpaw") and *pasek* (*ah* as
in "papa"). Yossi Pollak has, it seems, spent a good deal of time learning
to speak Hebrew like an Israeli. When he first came to Stanton Street
and I semi-jokingly reported Pinchas's preference, he modestly replied
back that he was having a hard enough time getting used to our "Sefardi" (meaning: Hasidic) version of the regular prayer service. But over
the course of Yossi's two years with us, I have noticed that he has slipped
back into the Ashkenazi pronunciation, if not when praying, then at
least in conversation. He is as likely to wish a congregant *gut shabbes* as
*shabbat shalom* and more likely to refer to a *bris* than to a *brit milah*. If
I am not mistaken, he is not merely acknowledging the preferences of
part of the community here but allowing himself the luxury of a more
*heymish*, dare I say, a more Jewish self-expression.

So we were very interested to hear how Rabbi Unger would speak.
I hardly paid close enough attention to his phonetics to satisfy the
sociolinguist in me, but I can say this: He has a noticeable "New York
accent," whatever traits may mark that (indeed, in his preliminary interview he mentioned that he had lived in Manhattan virtually his entire life), and when leading the congregation in prayer, he maintained
the *tof-sof* distinction, but did not maintain the *komets-pasek* distinction. I suppose this is the way he was taught at the Orthodox Manhattan
Day School on the Upper West Side, where he had his presecondary
education.

We got to hear Rabbi Unger speak at greater length over lunch in our
dining room. Nine of us ended up sitting around the large wooden mis-
sion-style table that had more or less come with the apartment when we
moved into it (our fourth apartment in the Ageloff Towers, where we've
lived for almost thirty years now) just under four years ago. At one end
Elissa, in the ergonomic chair that we roll in from her work desk in the

living room at mealtimes, so that she will be somewhat more comfortable despite her arthritis; at the other end, me. I didn't intend it consciously, but it turned out to be boys at one end, girls at the other: at my
right Jonah, with Jacob (Unger) next to him; at my left Boas Cohen,
son, roughly Jonah's age, of former congregants, who appeared quite unexpectedly with his mother and sister for the first time in years and who
is about to start a Ph.D. program in intellectual history at Yale; to Jacob's right, Hannah and then a middle-aged woman named Terri, a new
congregant whom Pinchas has befriended and whom Pinchas asked us
to invite; to Boas's left, a young but longtime congregant, architect
Sarah Stein and her roommate Eve, a graduate of (or still student at?)
NYU's Stern Business School.

   We had advance notice that Hannah had several allergies, including
dairy, and since Elissa's a vegetarian, I decided to make an all-*parve* meal.
This is what we ate (ethnography should be *concrete*, at least sometimes): melons from California, available for the excellent price of $2.99
from the new Whole Foods on Houston Street, part of the so-called
Avalon development that, on the south side of Houston Street, replaced
a parking lot and, on the north side (facing the Bowery), replaced various older buildings, including Gloria Steinem's home; then an assort-
ment of Tofurkey sausages, not as good as real meat, but substantial; a
green salad with the first Jersey tomatoes of the season, from the Union
Square market; rice pilaf with grilled vegetables (again, Whole Foods
is the only place I know where I can get the "original" long-grain and
wild-rice variety, without orzo pasta, for the sake of those on gluten-free
diets); beets and asparagus, again from Union Square (and isn't where
we get our food an important part of our "culture"?). We drank a bottle
of Chianti (it seemed to me excellent, but what do I know about wine?)
that Jacob and Hannah had dropped off before shabbes. In a neighborhood without an eruv, they could not have brought it to us on
shabbes—even if they didn't share the halakhic concern that giving a
gift on shabbes is a forbidden form of transaction, and I have no idea
whether they do or not. The conversation at our end of the table, as I
recall it, revolved largely around Jonah's research on the Thursday night
Cholent gatherings and Jacob's enthusiasm for my brother Daniel's
book *Carnal Israel*: academically respectable, liberal, Jewishly knowledgeable conversation. And Jacob's brief Talmud lesson between the
afternoon and evening prayers, focusing on the midrashic description

of God roaring at the destruction of Jerusalem in Tractate Berachot 3, flirted with the possibility of a rabbinic understanding of a "corporeal" God, which is consistent with much in Daniel's work and much else in progressive rabbinic studies today. Still, I find I have difficulty writing lucidly about Jacob and Hannah's visit, or more generally, about the prospect of Jacob's becoming the rabbi of our shul. He is young enough to be my graduate student. And how could my student be my rabbi?

## Day Three of Parshas Korach, June 24, 2008

I am thinking today of what I'm tempted to call the synagogue's "acephalous" period. The term is an allusion to some notions of the French surrealist and social critic Georges Bataille that I never studied first-hand but have read about only indirectly, yet nevertheless inspired some of my earlier musings about whether the shul would survive without Rabbi Singer, who locked the doors and attempted to close the shul entirely several years ago. Around the time the controversy over the sale of the shul first broke, there was an article about it in the *Village Voice*, accompanied by a photograph of Andrew Pearl putting on tefillin for the morning minyan. (The Singer family's court papers had claimed that there was no longer a daily minyan.) One of Rabbi Singer's sons-in-law was quoted in defense of the need to close the shul because it was no longer viable: "It can't survive as a shul. Maybe it can continue for another six months or a year. But long term, it can't survive." It has—not forever yet, but for a lot longer than a year.

Some days (like today, when there was once again no minyan—but that in itself is hardly a sign of "decline"), I think that the acephalous period, when we continued without the aid of even an interim "spiritual leader," was the most interesting, that I am keeping this journal *too late*. But the barest sketch of brief memories of that time may be better than nothing at all. This, then, going backward. Yossi Pollak has been our rabbi now for the past two years, since August 2006. A year before that, we had taken the momentous step of searching to hire our first rabbi since Rabbi Singer left. All of the five candidates we interviewed back in the spring of 2005 were new graduates of Chovevei Torah; four of the five were acceptable to us, and we were bitterly disappointed that our first choice eventually turned us down in favor of another position at Columbia University's Hillel, presumably better paid and more stable, and certainly on the Upper West Side. We ended up failing to hire a rabbi that year and kept on, as very part-time rabbinic intern mostly paid by Melech Goldfeld, his older brother Meir, who had already been serving as rabbinic intern for the previous year. (Meir was thus our rabbinic intern for two years, from 2004 to 2006.) Prior to Meir, we had our first rabbinic intern, Zach Geller, from 2003 to 2004. Getting rabbinical students from Chovevei Torah to serve as our interns was the idea of Sura Ziskind, Andrew Pearl's wife, and though Sura and Andrew are hardly regulars at Stanton Street anymore, this is a particular legacy of theirs that has left a shaping mark on the shul and doubtless contributed to the possibility of the congregation's continuing until now.

That leaves a period of three or four years during which there was no regular rabbinic authority at all in the shul, followed by another three years when there was no rabbi per se, but only a rabbinical student intern (in addition to having lessened halakhic authority, both Zach Geller and Meir Goldfeld were responsible only for being present or conducting services every other shabbes). Moreover, as vital as the presence of these two interns was, I do not recall a sudden or sharp change in the tone of overall interactions upon their arrival. (Meir did attempt, with some success, to curtail the habit of congregants' taking a shot or two of scotch or bourbon prior to *kabboles shabbes* on Friday night.)

There should a psychological or ethnographic explanation for this, but irresistibly, when I try to recall the variety of persons and interactions at the shul during the acephalous period, what comes first to mind is Hasidim from Williamsburg, and particularly a young Satmar Hasid named Velvl. He came fairly regularly, sometimes with an older man named Rabbi Yidl Stein, whom I'd known for a lot longer: Decades ago, when the young man from my building who was studying to convert to Judaism came with me to Rabbi Singer's shul and Rabbi Singer chose to include him in the minyan, rather than embarrass him by publicly identifying him as a non-Jew, that young man was studying for conversion with none other than Yidl Stein. Yidl at that time worked at the H & M Skullcap Company on Hester Street, just off Essex and across from both Kadouri Provisions (fruits, nuts, spices, Middle Eastern foods) and Gertel's Bakery. H & M Skullcap: long gone. Kadouri: left the neighborhood about four or five years ago. Gertel's: closed more recently, and just yesterday, when Jonah and I were walking by, we noticed that the building it was in is being demolished.

About Velvl what do I remember? The very effort makes it seem as though, God forbid, he were no longer among us, when the truth is, more simply, that I haven't seen him for a few years, and so he seems to me like someone "from the past." Two things, most immediately, one kinder than the other, though certainly there would be more if I sat still for a few moments to, as they say, "think back." First, this: that one day he told me he was involved in real estate, and ever since I've wondered whether all of the times he, and Yidl Stein, and occasionally other Williamsburg colleagues of theirs came to Stanton Street or also, sometimes, to Rabbi Ackerman's shul what they were most interested in was the synagogues as the subject of potential real-estate transactions. But this is a mean thought, and I have no solid grounds to think it. Second: an image of a Purim night, perhaps in 2003 or 2004, when Velvl sang together with members of the Village Klezmer Band a song called *shnirele perl*, "A String of Pearls." I later learned from Jonah that this was not necessarily a traditional Hasidic song, as I first supposed, but had been popularized by a Klezmatics record: *oy, oy, dos iz vor, meshiekh vet kumen hayntiks yor*, "Oh, this is true: Messiah will come this very year." And a third thing: Velvl was deeply involved in a lawsuit his aunt, a Holocaust survivor, had brought against the Conference on Jewish Material Claims against Germany, arguing (if I recall correctly) that she had been denied just benefits.

I think I just found it cool to have Williamsburg Hasidim as part of the Stanton Street mix, whatever their motives: It's something, at any rate, that's not likely to happen again soon.

## Day Five of Parshas Korach, June 26, 2008

Dudi's back, after a long ordeal with his daughter's health; Nate came back after a brief vacation; Dan Cantor's grandson came to shul this morning; and Rabbi Unger came, to meet and be interviewed by Benny Sauerhaft. We all overheard the brief meeting between the two: Benny was tough and very straightforward, exclusively concerned with the practicalities of Rabbi Unger's ability to help run services.

"Can you *layen* [read the Torah]?"

"With preparation."

"Can you *layen megillah* [read from the Scroll of Esther]?"

"I could learn it."

"You know, or you don't know?"

                ...

"You live where?"

"On Seventieth Street."

"You'd come down here every morning?"

"No, I'd move down here."

                ...

"You're working for the OU?

"Yes."

"You're a *mashgiach* [a kashrut supervisor]?"

"No, I answer questions on the telephone." (The word for "questions" that Jacob Unger used here was *shaylos*, pronounced with a long *o* at the end, like "Shiloh." It was another confirmation that his Hebrew pronunciation is not Yiddish/Ashkenazic, certainly not modern Israeli, but an amalgam American Orthodox that points in the direction of tradition without betraying any trace of Yiddish as a native language.) "Like if someone calls and says they dropped the meat spoon into the dairy pot, I tell them what to do."

"They pay you for this?"

Benny was not being sarcastic: I think he wanted to make sure that Rabbi Unger didn't expect the salary from the shul to be a full-time income. He properly told Rabbi Unger, "We'll have to have a meeting and discuss it," and he ordered Nate: "Take a pen and paper and write down his name and telephone number and address."

Nate, who handles Benny very well, replied, "We already have it, but I'll be happy to write it down again."

Afterward I commiserated with Rabbi Unger, "That was a tough interview—he's a *shtarker* [a tough character]."

He confirmed it: "You guys were a pushover compared to him."

Some notes from an impromptu Lower East Side tour I gave yesterday morning to my colleague Timothy Reynolds, visiting New York from Chapel Hill.

I saw, for the first time, every level of the Orensanz Center for the Arts, the former Anshei Slonim, from the basement, which now contains the Torah ark and several pews from the old Eighth Street Shul, up to the attic, where you can see the naked bent wooden ribs of the false Gothic-arch ceiling under the actual, steep-sloped roof. The director of the center explained, "That's why this building survived when so many others fell down. If they had a flat roof, they suffered from a century of heavy snows that didn't slide off, but just melted on the roof. Like the Rumanian Synagogue on Rivington Street. That building was built by people from Scotland [originally as a church, of course]. They didn't know about snow. The people who built this building were from Germany." He was pleased as I rehearsed, this time for his, but also for Timothy's benefit, my appreciation of the way he and his artist brother Angel Orensanz have gone about the "restoration" of the synagogue, in a creative and not literalistic way, but even more important, in a way that doesn't efface the effects and ravages of time. "Yes, it encourages me to hear you say that, because sometimes I look at the Eldridge Street Synagogue or the Oranienburger Strasse Temple in Berlin, where they got so much money and restored it exactly as it was, down to the very chemical makeup of the original paint. That way, they create the effect that it's 'real,' that you're really there way back then, and nothing has happened in the meantime. We want this to retain the traces of Anshei Slonim, the East European congregation that came in here after the German Jews, and not try to skip over time and live in an eternal 1849."

Chasam Sopher happened to be open, and a young Orthodox woman whom I didn't recognize readily permitted Timothy and me to go upstairs: so here I was able to show him a renovation that had made no attempt to be aesthetically distinctive or exactly faithful to the "original," but nevertheless, as we agreed, had created or retained a beautiful space. What caught my eye upstairs were the plaques commemorating donors' gifts *lebedek habayis*, "for the maintenance of the building," indicating a significant renovation decades ago. Since the names were, for the most part, engraved in English and I recognized a few of them, my guess is that the plaque was from the 1950s or 1960s. Among them, listed as vice president, were M [for Moshe] Weiser, who by the time I came along in the early 1980s was the president and who really ran the building by himself. Another board member whose name caught my eye was Harold Gleicher—"Cheap Heshy"—whom I knew from both Saturdays and weekday mornings at Stanton Street from the time I started going until his death. There's a suggestion, then, that at one time Heshy Gleicher had been associated primarily with the Chasam Sopher shul and then switched his allegiances to Rabbi Singer. Just a suggestion, I don't recall ever hearing anything about it while Heshy was still alive, but certainly a plausible one given what I remember of his cantankerous personality and the difficult relations between the two congregations going back as far as I remember.

Streit's matzoh factory, at Rivington and Clinton: Timothy and I stand outside the window, watching the Rube Goldberg machinery that patiently expels sheets of baked matzoh and the workers who break it up and place it onto slowly moving racks to be boxed. A middle-aged man with a short gray beard and yarmulke passed us by on the street and said, "It's Mediterranean today—with garlic and herbs."

I asked him, "How much longer are you going to be baking?" because I'd heard they were selling the building and would only be there for a few more months.

He replied, "Well, there's a lot of family members with interests in the business, and it's hard to get them to agree. It looked like they were going to sell, but now prices have dropped in real estate anyway, so as far as I know we're going to keep baking for years—as long as this antique equipment lasts, anyway."

We noticed that the workers were discarding the broken sheets, and I joked with one of them, "Give those to me, I'll make *matzoh brei*." I'm not sure he understood what I was referring to—a pancake or scramble of softened matzoh and eggs—but he smiled and handed each of us an unbroken Mediterranean matzoh, hot out of the oven. As the Second Avenue Deli menu says: "Dah-licious!"

At the reading room of the Center for Jewish History, to meet a woman named Amanda Abelson, who's collaborating with Elissa on the research on the mazoles, the zodiac signs. Amanda wants to look at (is looking at) the records of the congregation that were donated to YIVO decades ago and attempt to determine more precisely when the mazoles were painted, on the strength of a mention, in the report that architectural historian Tony Robbins prepared in connection with an earlier grant application, of a notation of money spent for restoration of the mazoles in 1939. What I want to look at is the Brzezany memorial book, to see whether it has an article about the landsmanshaft and/or shul in New York; some memorial books do that, most don't.

Meanwhile, I find in Shimon Redlich's recent *Together and Apart in Brzezany: Poles, Jews, and Ukrainians, 1919–1945*, the following: "Menachem Katz, or Munio Huber, as he was known in Brzezany, is an architect. He remains the 'living memory' of our town. He was editor of the Brzezany Yizkor Book and has published his Holocaust memoirs. Menachem drew designs of all the Brzezany synagogues from memory." I will try to contact Menachem Katz to ask about mazoles in Brzezany.

The map of Tarnopol Wojewodztwa at the beginning of the memorial book reveals the proximity of Chodorow, famous for its synagogue decorations, to Brzezany. One clue at least to the history of the mazoles on the walls at Stanton Street.

The memorial book does indeed contain wonderful architects' sketches of the Large Synagogue and others in Brzezany, but with my limited Hebrew, I do not see anything about mazoles in the text. The brief English introduction to the volume is adorned by two small photographs of the shul on Stanton Street, one of the façade and the other a shot of the main shul from the back of the women's section—miscaptioned as "The Brzezaner Synagogue in Brooklyn, New York."

Included in the old cash book that Miriam is reviewing for clues to the dating of the mazoles are notations in English from 1956 of donations from "Mrs. Don." I didn't know her, but I did know an elderly man whom I guess to have been her widower: a very poor man, quite literate in Hebrew, whom Rabbi Singer, at least, just called "Don." Another congregant, Mr. Berger, would always mis-recite the first phrase that introduces the Psalm of the Day: Rather than *hayom yom rishon* (or *sheyni*, etc.), "Today is the first day," Berger would say, *hayom yom yom*. Finally Don couldn't take it anymore and cried out in Yiddish, *Ir zugt az haynt iz yedn tog*! "You're saying that today is every day!"

Other entries for miscellaneous expenses from 1956 seemed to me to be in Rabbi Singer's handwriting, though I would not have guessed he was involved with the shul that early; words like "cakes" and "soda" spelled in Hebrew. I can't positively identify the handwriting, but they certainly reminded me of the shopping list that Rabbi Singer wrote out for me for a shabbes kiddush some thirty years later.

The young couple who caused a bit of a stir with their potential candidacy as a "two for the price of one" synagogue leadership team have pulled out of consideration; they've "decided that it's not the right time in [their] lives to take on a congregation."

# Week Eight

*And Moses sent messengers from Kadesh unto the king of Edom: "Thus saith thy brother Israel: Thou knowest all the travail that hath befallen us; how our fathers went down into Egypt, and we dwelt in Egypt a long time; and the Egyptians dealt ill with us, and our fathers; and when we cried unto the Lord, he heard our voice, and sent an angel, and brought us forth out of Egypt; and, behold, we are in Kadesh, a city in the uttermost of thy border."*

—NUMBERS 20:14–16

*Talleisim and Charity Box, Downstairs*

*Day Four (already!) of Parshas Chukas, July 1, 2008*

As you may have noticed, I've refrained almost entirely from attempting to draw allegories between the title or major theme of the weekly parasha and whatever observations or ruminations I happen to record during that week. It would, in many cases, be easy enough to do so. A *parshat hashevua* sheet—a free circular with notes and commentaries on the weekly Torah reading—that I saw this past Saturday morning at the early minyan at Bialystok focused on this custom of linking events of the day to the text of the week. It pointed out that speakers intending to reprimand their audience often have to strain to connect their message to the text of the weekly parasha, but that by contrast, last week's Korach, with its tale of rebellion against the family of Moses and Aaron, was always pertinent, since Jewish communities are always experiencing internal disputes.

This week, for personal reasons that, like some latter-day Victorian anthropologist, I wish to keep separate from this journal, I've been having a hard time keeping up the journal, which makes the temptation of starting with a *smikhes haparsha*, a connection to the parasha, almost irresistible. "God spoke to Moses and to Aaron, saying: 'This is the decree of the Torah, which Hashem has commanded, saying: Speak to the Children of Israel, and they shall take to you a completely red cow, which is without blemish, and upon which a yoke has not come." Rabbinic commentary articulates a distinction between *chok*, translated here as "decree," and *mishpat*, "judgment" or "ruling." *Chok* is the kind of rule for which we have no explanation in terms of simple human logic or interest; *mishpat* is the kind of rule a rational and just order of purely human origin would also establish. Perhaps there's some value in seeing a similar tension in the work of anthropologists between the recording of *chok*, things just as they are, without any particular rationale, and *mishpat*, the reflective ordering of things in the world consequent on the human work of analysis. In this journal, I'm trying to dance between those raindrops, a metaphor itself inspired by the heavy thunderstorms that came for several afternoons a row this week, especially on shabbes Korach.

Korach is also the maiden name of my sister-in-law Chava, born in Czechoslovakia in the years immediately after World War II. She and my brother Dan were visiting with us this past shabbes, while accompanying our eighty-nine-year-old mother on her first trip back East after moving to California to be closer to Dan and Chava about a year ago. So I got to repeat what apparently is an old joke, congratulating Chava on "her" shabbes. She responded that while her father, Latsi Korach, was still alive, he used to insist that his family was distinct from that of the biblical Korach. The proof: the biblical Korach family had died, while he was still alive.

Though that's not so simple, either. Latsi, like Chava's mother Magda, had lost much of his family during the war. And the midrash, basing itself on the biblical account of Korach and his assembly being swallowed up alive by the earth, says that they are still somehow "alive" down there. Dan Cantor reminded Rabbi Pollak about this midrash this morning, while we were waiting for a minyan that never came. (I think we ended up with eight: the young Levi has left the neighborhood to return to Israel, which I gather is or was his more permanent home; Charles Copeland is in Miami visiting his ailing father and then off to the Berkshires for several weeks, where he and Jean run an annual composition and new-music workshop; Dudi is not back on an everyday basis yet.) And Rabbi Pollak responded in his accustomed fashion, which boiled down to: "How do I know? What it could mean that the earth swallowed them up, and that's where they are now—we don't even say that dead people go under the earth, but how do I know?"

This question from Dan Cantor came after a discussion lasting several minutes, which Dan initiated by reporting back the response of Rabbi Horowitz, from the Lutowisker Shul, to a claim that Dudi had made yesterday morning. Dudi was then responding to a hypothetical question Dan had posed linking our daily study topic of tefillin to the question of *tume*, ritual uncleanliness, which today for practical terms applies only to those Jewish males who are kohanim, primarily (exclusively?) in regard to defilement by contact with a corpse. Evidently there had been a prior discussion—I don't even know where now—in which

it was established that, if one happened to be driving through a cemetery wearing tefillin (which must not be worn in the presence of items,
such as corpses, that can convey tume), there would not be a problem
of tume contamination so long as the windows were closed. What, Dan
wanted to know, if the windows of the car were open? Rabbi Pollak, if
I recall correctly, demurred from expressing an opinion, but Dudi spoke
up: "Tume spreads vertically [its contamination extends indefinitely
toward the heavens], not horizontally [proximity to tume, short of
touching it, does not convey impurity]."

This morning, then, after Dan had recited the preliminary prayers
up to *yishtabach*[1] and while we were waiting for the minyan that never
came, he said to Rabbi Pollak: "I told Rabbi Horowitz what Dudi said,
and he said he had no idea where Dudi got that, and there's no source
for it."

That is as much of this odd halakhic discussion (many halakhic discussions are equally odd) as I can readily reproduce now, a few hours
later. A tape or video recorder would have created a fuller record that,
in any case, would have had to be abstracted somehow, according to
some principle of mishpat. Isaac Maxon, who had not been present yesterday, didn't understand what the issue being argued about was and
made that clear, but he was absolutely tickled that for once we weren't
arguing about contemporary hot-button issues such as women's prayer
but about "real" halakhic issues, *torah leshmah*, in this case meaning (in
my words, not his), the kind of debate that is purely hypothetical and
never likely to come up in real life, and hence a pure exercise in the
working through of Torah. I sense that Isaac's stance in a situation like
this is the product of a long and perhaps complex process of acquiring
a view of Torah and its authority, a view that is not merely inherited
from whatever community raised him. But so far I am reluctant to break
the surface of the water by broaching the possibility of an actual interview, with Isaac or anyone else at Stanton Street.

What made me, nevertheless, recognize this odd conversation as
worthy of note, at a time when (as has become my own habit the past
couple of weeks) I was not waiting for a minyan but just going ahead

1. One of many prayers of praise to God in the daily morning service, *yishtabach*
("May your Name be praised") immediately precedes the recitation of kaddish, which
cannot be done without a minyan.

and rather mechanically and distractedly praying on my own? Was it that, some other outside blocks having been eased or removed, I knew I was ready to write in the journal again today and thus was hunting for new material? In any case, it seemed like a bit of a revelation to note, in at least minimal detail, something like this, and I was brought back once again to Professor David Lipset's challenge, when I presented a talk about Stanton Street to the Anthropology Department at the University of Minnesota. Lipset wanted to know how I handled the ethical challenges of working with my own people. In that context, I found myself unable to learn exactly what lay behind his question, but I've since thought from time to time about it. The question implies complex dilemmas of ethnographic practice and writing: not merely what it means to refer to "one's own" people (an old and difficult question, and one that's hardly been resolved once and for all) but how the challenges of writing about a familiar context compare with the challenges of writing about a strange context. One thing I might say now is that familiarity breeds an odd kind of blindness or preselection of what is noteworthy and what is not. A hypothetical debate about wearing tefillin while driving through a cemetery seems the sort of item I've been tempted to preselect out as either insignificant or untranslatable, and Isaac Maxon's enthusiasm for precisely that question cured me from at least that moment of blindness.

One morning—perhaps Monday of this week—the halakhic issue Rabbi Pollak taught in the Mishna Berura was very simple. He didn't even read through the text in Hebrew, but just said, "Basically, it says that we don't make a brokhe when we take our tefillin off." Then he went on to the next substantial issue in the halakha of tefillin. As Rabbi Pollak is getting ready to leave us, here are a few "brokhes" we've been saying.

A birthday cake that accompanied the generous kiddush given this past shabbes by the Levi to mark his return to Israel. I didn't share that kiddush, having gone to the early minyan at Bialystok instead. Later, when I returned for mincha at eight o'clock, Zev Gross reported that I'd missed a very big crowd. Evidently the White Street Shul in Tribeca closes altogether for shabbes twice a year, once in the summer and once in the winter, and this shabbes a number of folks from White Street had come to Stanton Street instead.

An article by Dudi Dembitser in the *Grand Street News*, which Dudi edits, about "Stanton's Music Rabbi," focusing especially on the free Purim performance by Sway Machinery, when the shul was " 'packed to the gills,' as Pollak puts it, with hundreds of the band's fans, many of whom had never been inside a shul before." Nor, I might add, likely will ever see the inside of a shul again.

Two ads in the same issue of the *Grand Street News*. One, full page and paid for by several Stanton Street members, but in the name of the entire congregation, with a photograph of Yossi in tallis and tefillin, playing a guitar at a microphone (I imagine at a Chanukah "musical hallel" that I might have missed), thanking Yossi and Brooke "for their work and commitment over the past two years" and inviting the community to a "deluxe Kiddush in their honor Saturday, July 26." The second, half a page and, I must say, with a more flattering photograph of Yossi, teaching Mishnah Berurah and bearing the following remarkable text:

> Dear Rabbi Yossi, Your presence affected many in the short time you were here. You and Rebetzin Brooke accomplished a lot and forced us all to think about the community as a whole. We thank you for all that you have taught us and wish you the best of luck in your new position. We are sure that the community you both will help build will be one filled with love and understanding, enabling each individual to feel a special connection with Yahdous ["Jewishness"], no matter what stage they are at.
>
> Our community was privileged to have you as one of its leaders, we will miss you dearly.
>
> Your friends from "the other shul."

Elissa showed it to me, saying "Look what Charlie did," assuming "the other shul" was the Community Synagogue. But my strong hunch is that it was from a relatively friendly group at Bialystok. When Dudi comes back, maybe I'll ask him.

## Day Five of Parshas Chukas, July 2, 2008

Dudi confirms that "the other shul" is Bialystok and credits the initiative for the ad in honor of Yossi Pollak to someone named Max Zimmerman, a "real mentsh" according to Dudi, but not someone whose name I recognize.

At 7:00, I tell Yossi that I have to leave at 7:23, to meet my brother and visiting mother in front of the building and lend them my car for the day. It's Rosh Chodesh, and with me there are nine, so Yossi asks Dudi to lead an express davening, which Dudi promptly does. At 7:20, the fellow whose name escapes me now (though I think I've written it earlier in these notes), who shows up at 7:20 when he does show up but hasn't been in shul for the past couple of weeks, shows up. I'm taking my tefillin off by then, and as a joke, I call out fairly loudly at Dudi, "Slow down a little bit!"—obviously a joke on myself, since my imminent departure was what made him go faster. Buddy Bardin (whom Benny Sauerhaft has taken to calling "Louie" for some reason) gets the joke, though the rabbi shushes me as though I were being genuinely rude.

Dan Cantor, seeing a tenth man walk in, moves forward to close the ark, but the rabbi stops him: "Don't close it, Jonathan has to go out in a minute and we'll just have to open it again. We don't need to keep closing and opening it like a crazy person." As I head out, Nate and I give each other a look, as if to say: "What other way is there to keep closing and opening the ark?"

Rabbi Pollak, overheard Monday morning leaving a voice mail for Isaac Maxon: "Isaac, there's eight of us here, and I'm wondering if you're coming. If you're on your way, we'll wait for you. If you're not, we won't wait for you. We'll wait for someone else." Then the rabbi gets off the phone and adds, to the room in general, "I don't even know what I'm saying with these early morning minyan voice mails."

## Day Six of Parshas Chukas, July 4, 2008

Sometimes in this kind of project you get the intimation that you don't know the half of it, which is okay, more or less, except when you're tempted to write as if that unknown half wasn't there. Because of Elissa's physical limitations, which keep us close to our own home on shabbes, and because we don't live on Grand Street, and also I suppose because we're older than the younger couples, we don't—for example— necessarily know what kinds of social support networks members really have been creating for themselves. Thus I probably see the congregation as even more fragmentary a community than it might look to others. The occasion for this suspicion today is a casual remark by Rabbi Pollak that he and Brooke expect to watch the fireworks tonight from Henry and Rachel's apartment: "It was our turn to cook [shabbes dinner] for them" (as the parents of a newborn), "and they invited us to eat with them and to watch the fireworks." On previous occasions—when Elissa was stronger and, perhaps more pertinently, when Lenny Rivers was still living in the neighborhood and running (single-handedly constituting, really) the "life-cycles committee," we've helped out with groceries for parents of newborns, but for Henry and Rachel, we're completely out of the loop. I don't even know who's organizing the rotation of supplying meals for them. Elissa has a nice baby present for them that I'll take over sometime in the next few days.

Part of the reason I've been slacking off on this journal is that the fresh eyes with which I was seeing the neighborhood after a semester's absence have started to glaze over. As I've noted, my prayer as well has tended to be completely mechanical for the past two months. Which leads to one other reason why I've been slacking off: an old project, a translation from Yiddish of Abraham Joshua Heschel's book about the Kotsker Rebbe, is back on the fire, and I need to finish it over the next few months. One of the things the Kotsker struggled against was precisely praying by rote: "Anyone who performs commandments by rote becomes chilled and forgets that there is a Creator" (from chapter 8, near the end). I've been finding it very hard to think about God at all this summer. But not hard to get to shul.

*Detail of Cover for Torah Ark*

# Week Nine

*And [Balaam] took up his parable, and said . . .*

> *Who hath counted the dust of Jacob,*
> *Or numbered the stock of Israel?*
> *Let me die the death of the righteous,*
> *And let mine end be like his!*

*And Balak said unto Balaam: "What hast thou done unto me: I took thee to curse mine enemies, and, behold, thou has blessed them altogether."*

—NUMBERS 23:7, 10–11

*Memorial Plaque with Liquor Bottles, Downstairs*

*If you're looking for a hotel bar plunked down in the midst of a bustling, hip neighborhood, it is really rather impossible to beat Hotel on Rivington's Thor, a lounge (and in the back, a restaurant) on a particularly happening stretch of Rivington Street in the 21st-century playground known as the Lower East Side.*

—SETH KUGEL, "High on the View as Much as the Cocktails," *New York Times*, Sunday, July 6, 2008

## *Day One of Parshas Balak, July 6, 2008*

This time I knew without looking which weekly portion is coming up, even without looking in the ArtScroll khumesh, but how I knew requires a bit of explanation. The Jewish calendar is lunar; each month is one cycle of the moon. Twelve lunar months are eleven days shorter than a solar year. To keep the Jewish ritual year roughly synchronized with the natural cycle of the solar year, the rabbis instituted regular "leap years," in which one of the lunar months is double, so there are a "first Adar" and a "second Adar," both toward the end of winter and the beginning of spring. Years without a second Adar have a smaller total number of Sabbaths, and as a result, a few of the weekly Torah portions are doubled, so that the entire Pentateuch can be completed in the course of the year. One of those doubled portions is Chukas Balak, but this year *is* a leap year, so I knew that Balak would actually come the week after Chukas. And yes, twice yesterday—once in the morning at the Community Synagogue and once in the evening at Stanton Street—I heard brief homilies from visiting Chabad rabbis, members of the Lubavitch Hasidic community, about the significance of chok, the category of commandment that has no basis in human logic and that we would not have arrived at left to our own devices.

Much of the distinctive thrust of Chovevei Torah and the "Open Orthodoxy" that it promotes and that is given some allegiance, at least by
many other rabbis who are not Chovevei Torah graduates, has to do
with emphasis on the importance within Judaism of the broad range of
commandments and ethical directives that seem consistent with hu-
manist ethics or even a nonreligious "reverence for life." This is most
clearly evident in the protest against the currently dominant kosher
slaughterhouse in the United States, run by the Rubashkin family.
The Rubashkins, whose main operation is in Postville, Iowa, are ac-
cused of hiring (and mistreating?) illegal immigrant workers. There are
also allegations of ill-treatment of animals (a video of a shackled animal
being badly misslaughtered by Rubashkin's was circulated a couple of
years ago by People for the Ethical Treatment of Animals) and even—
rumor has it, I didn't even read the articles—a methamphetamine lab
in the slaughterhouse. I'm not sure why I haven't taken the trouble to
inform myself better about the case, but it might have something to do
with my multiform ambivalence about being a consumer of kosher meat
altogether. On the one hand, consuming meat isn't quite the mark of
family conviviality I remember from my childhood anymore, since
Elissa has been a vegetarian for almost twenty years now. On the other
hand, I'm not convinced that kosher meat is either divinely ordained
for me or "better" in any mundane way, and am less than perfectly consistent in my avoidance of nonkosher meat outside the home. But still,
it's an issue, one that Elissa, at least, has taken very seriously, though she
buys no meat at all.

My brother Daniel enjoys going to the better kosher restaurants
when he visits New York. Last Thursday, Daniel arranged a family gathering at Mike's Bistro, on West Seventy-Second Street, next to the ven-
erable (and to me, more tempting) Fisher Brothers & Leslie butchers
and kosher barbecue take-out. At Mike's, I had the wonderful short ribs.
Quite by coincidence, at Stanton Street the next day, on Friday at mincha, Rabbi Pollak reported that he'd had a long phone call the day before with Mike Gershkowitz, the owner of Mike's Bistro, as a result of
which Mike's will be placed on the "acceptable" list of Uri L'Tzedek, the
organization sponsoring the protests against Rubashkin's. The one thing
Mike's serves that comes from Rubashkin, according to Rabbi Pollak,
is the short ribs—but they come from Rubashkin's slaughterhouse in
South America, not from the one in Postville, Iowa, that was raided by

the federal government recently. "Oh, the short ribs," I said. "That's what I had. They're delicious."

At Mike's on Thursday, while some ten or so of us were looking at the menu, Sam Lemberger strolled over to say hello. Sam said to my brother, "You were at the deli last night. And I know what you had— the corned beef hash." Daniel: "How do you know?" Sam: "That's what you always have at the deli."

And to me Sam said, "When are you coming to [the Community] shul?" I told him I would come shabbes morning, and I did. It was July Fourth weekend; Rabbi Buckholtz was away; and the crowd was small. I arrived shortly after 10:00 A.M. (Community starts promptly at nine, unlike, for example, Stanton Street, which officially starts at 9:30 and actually gets going closer to 10:00) to find the Torah service over. Sam saw me walk in and immediately called from the podium to the back of the big room, "Jonathan—come up and I'll give you *gelila*," the task of wrapping the Torah and placing its cover back on.

After the Torah reading, I started to tell Sam, "Rabbi Pollak says the only thing at Mike's that comes from Rubashkin is the short ribs. So guess what I had last night?"

But I didn't even get to my punch line; Sam was clearly annoyed at the whole protest against Rubashkin's, which he presented as being solely based on the fact that there were illegal immigrant workers there. "If Rabbi Pollak is upset about patronizing businesses that hire immigrant workers, then he shouldn't just boycott Rubashkin's—he can't even shop at the local supermarket."

After the service at Community, I moved on to Rabbi Ackerman's shul: I haven't been there as much this summer as in the past. There the service was wrapping up, and I was greeted by a youngish Hasid, perhaps in his late thirties, whom I recognized from previous visits. The young man, whose name I've never learned, but who also remembered me as one of the prayer leaders at Rabbi Ackerman's from last Rosh Hashanah, was eager to chat, both during the end of the service and later, as the small group sat around a table over shots of whiskey and slices of *potatonik*, a sort of mix between potato kugel and bread that is, apparently, found only on the Lower East Side. These bits I remember.

"Is it raining now? Last week I was walking back over the bridge around 6:00 P.M., when it started pouring. There was no place to get shelter there. My shoes were full of water. Yeah, so I walk over the bridge. Williamsburg is very quiet now—everybody goes away weekends in the summer. Me, I don't go to the country. I come here, to the Lower East Side. For me, this is the country.

"Why don't people like Obama? Is it just because he's colored? You know, now that Hillary gave up and she's supporting Obama, people in Williamsburg are supporting him, too. They don't like him so much, but you have to do—how do you say it in English—*khanife* ["flattery"].

"There's a shul on East Fifty Fifth Street, between First and Second, what is it? Yeah, the Sutton Place Synagogue. You know they have a woman rabbi there? The rebbetzin is a rabbi! I drive the *bikkur cholim* bus,[1] and one day there was nobody on the bus, so my friend and I decided to see the shul. We walk in and we see this woman's name, she's listed as the rabbi. I guess she puts on tefillin and she layens the Torah! I really have to see that some day." This was all said without sarcasm, sort of in an "isn't America amazing" tone of voice.

After shabbes, Elissa tells me that Brooke Pollak is the one who's been organizing the meals for Henry and Rachel.

This Friday night, at last, Josh Yuter comes for his shabbes visit. Since Elissa is not able to come to shul, she decided that we should host him for lunch, as we did with Rabbi Unger and Hannah Golden; that way, Elissa will at least have a chance to meet him properly.

## Day Four of Parshas Balak, July 10, 2008

On Monday morning, Pete Silver showed up with a couple of dozen bagels, several packages of lox, cream cheese, cookies and cake, and orange juice. It was a yortsayt breakfast for sure. When the Torah reading was over and we were about to put the scroll back, Benny Sauerhaft stopped Rabbi Pollak to indicate that he should recite the memorial prayer *El mole rakhamim* for whomever it was that Pete was remembering. But Pete just nodded from the back of the room, "No, it's not a relative."

1. The Yiddish phrase *bikkur cholim* designates the righteous deed of visiting the sick, which is facilitated for members of Hasidic communities in Brooklyn by the provision of buses to take them to the hospitals on the East Side of Manhattan.

To me he had confided—and eventually he told the rabbi as well—
that he had given the kiddush in honor of the sixty-first anniversary of
the death of Bugsy Siegel.

That would be a nice punctuation anecdote, a combination of deep
neighborhood memory, popular culture, and the irony of mourning a
notorious gangster. But, aside from the fact that we still have a rabbi to
choose, other things come up that cast an intriguing light on aspects of
the shul's uncertain future. Elissa, as I may have mentioned, has been doing intense research with a group of collaborators—some from the shul,
such as Jason Frankel, and others just interested students or scholars—
on the history of zodiac symbols in synagogue art and on Stanton Street's
mazoles in particular. I'm on the group's list, but usually skip through the
communications back and forth pretty quickly; about the only contri-
bution I've made is to ascertain that the Brzezan memorial book doesn't
say anything about zodiac paintings in the shul there. This morning,
Elissa reported to me that she'd sent a notice to the shul board indicating
that, once the rabbi question has been dealt with, she would like to make
a presentation to the board about preservation of the mazoles. To her
obvious distress, she got replies from Pinchas Duber, Lenny Rivers, and
Andrew Gold that she described as "flaming." I'm not privy to the board
communications (and don't know why Lenny is, since he's not on the
board anymore) and don't know exactly what they wrote or whether I
would evaluate their tone as she did. But I do know that some members
find the mazoles undistinguished even as folk art, and I surmise that for
some members, what's important is that we have a building of our own
and can do with it as we like, not the preservation of its particular character. There's nothing startling or unique in that kind of dispute, and I
can sort of go either way. But I suppose as a matter of loyalty to Elissa
and the work she's done, I've told her—but not others—that if the mazoles are obliterated, I won't be entering the shul again.

## Day Five of Parshas Balak, July 10, 2008

Two bits of morning minyan humor.

—Yesterday, because there were perhaps just a total of five or maybe
six of us, Rabbi Pollak checks in with Isaac Maxon to see if he's coming.
Isaac is usually utterly reliable, but he's spending several weeks living in
Tribeca at Charles Copeland's place, while Charles and Jean are running

their summer composing workshop in the Berkshires. It was clear yesterday that there was no sense making him rush to shul just to be the
sixth or seventh. Yossi got off the phone and announced, "Isaac's not
going to make it—he's running late."

Buddy, who's not the one from whom we expect the insider
"frummy" wisecracks, immediately responded with perfect timing and
straight-man tone, "Why—is he still in the mikva?" suggesting the un-
likely possibility that Isaac was observing the unusual ascetic practice of
daily immersion in a ritual bath.

—Today the minyan very slowly came together, and eventually it was
actually composed of ten of us. When Pete Silver showed up around
7:20 (it's a Thursday, and he's quite reliable on the days he's expected to
do the Torah reading), he announced: "It's the late Pete Silver." Ptu ptu
ptu, may he live for many years!

# *Week Ten*

*And Moses spoke unto the Lord, saying: "Let the Lord, the God of the spirits of all flesh, set a man over the congregation, who may go out before them, and who may lead them out, and who may bring them in; that the congregation of the Lord be not as sheep which have no shepherd."*

—NUMBERS 27:15–17

*Upstairs Zodiac Mural, Depicting Scales*

## Day One of Parshas Pinchas, July 13, 2008

I'm cheating: here's Elissa's report to Zev (who has been on vacation in Israel with his family for the past few weeks and hence missed Josh Yuter's shabbes visit). Elissa, who is not currently strong enough to attend shul, agreed that we should host Josh for lunch so that we could meet him. We ended up inviting (well, we ended up hosting; there were others we invited who couldn't attend) these others, in addition to Rabbi Yuter: Cal Pinsker, a graduate student in anthropology at the University of Michigan who wanted to consult with me about a project on Jewish hipster culture; a woman named Esther, with whom Elissa was acquainted, a regular at the White Street Shul who, as Elissa later explained to me, started coming occasionally to Stanton Street after Stanton Street made it clear that occasional women's Torah readings were genuinely welcome, as opposed to being barely tolerated by the rabbi at White Street; Zeke Goldenberg and his wife, Molly Pritchard, a couple in their thirties who've been coming to Stanton Street for about five or six years, during which time Molly completed her conversion to Judaism and their son Avi, now two years old, was born; Rosie Prager, just out of college and working her first full-time job, with her boyfriend Hank (although I didn't really get to talk to him, I'm guessing he isn't Jewish, since he made no effort to put on a yarmulke at lunch); and Tsvi Vilner, who may have been mentioned in these notes before—a quiet, reserved young man whose manner is somewhat traditionally Orthodox and who, on the High Holy Days, serves wonderfully as one of the *baalei tefila*, the leaders of communal prayer, at Stanton Street, yet who is also comfortable with the skeptical and not necessarily pious conversation that, for example, flows around our shabbes lunch table. (Tsvi had seen my brother on CNN this week, talking about the import of an ancient tablet, recently analyzed by Israel Knohl, that talks about a Jewish messiah figure who was expected

to die and be resurrected after three days, and I was able to explain to
Tsvi my brother's notion that most of the major themes of the Gospel
narrative of Jesus' career were current in varieties of Jewish belief at the
time, even though much of the population obviously did not believe
Jesus' messiahship: Tsvi's reply: "I wonder what Chabad is going to
make of all this").[1]

The ten of us sat comfortably around the dining-room table. I had
spent most of Friday shopping and cooking, and for the ethnographic
record, this is what the Jews at Third Street and Avenue A ate for their
Sabbath lunch: "Ariel" melon (more like a large, ribbed cantaloupe)
from California, $2.99 at either the Houston Street or the Fourteenth
Street Whole Foods; broiled chicken, marinated in tamari, maple syrup,
and fresh garlic; Swiss chard, sautéed and seasoned with balsamic vine-
gar; Near East brand long-grain and wild rice (good for Elissa because
it's gluten free); rainbow cookies, cinnamon strudel, and rooibos tea for
dessert. Elissa opened our best kosher bottle, a Barkan Pinot Noir 2004,
and I used it for kiddush, but in the end it wasn't even finished.

Josh Yuter started to set off back to Grand Street with Molly and
Zeke, but on learning that Elissa would not be able to come to his shiur
between mincha and maariv, returned to give her a brief summary in
our living room. In its short form, as I took it, the moral of this shiur is
that it is, on the one hand, wrong to treat *minhag* (custom) with the
sanctity of halakha and, on the other, that the principle barring innovation, *chadash asur min hatorah*, "Innovation is forbidden by the
Torah," is itself a dramatic innovation. The punchline, both in the version Josh shared with me and Elissa and in his longer talk at the shul
later on, was Maimonides' following retort, in a responsum (no. 263)
to an argument for following a custom with which he disagreed: "And
that which this other 'Sage' argued, that 'in Baghdad and other cities
they do this [stand for the reading of the Ten Commandments],' this is
no proof at all. For if there were sick people in these places, a healthy
person would not contaminate himself from them just so that they
should be the equal. Rather, he would attempt to heal them as best as
he could."

1. Tsvi was referring to the fact that, following the death of the last Rebbe of Lubavitch (whose Hasidim also are known as Chabad Hasidim), many of his followers continue to believe that the Rebbe was/is the Messiah.

Cute, sure, like my mother-in-law's "And would you jump off the Brooklyn Bridge just because your best friend told you to?" But: I do understand that what motivates Rabbi Yuter here is a concern for distinguishing between the requirements of halakha, on the one hand, and the supposed dead weight of custom, on the other. And I understand how this distinction between Jewish law and Jewish custom can be practically useful in bridging, with less agony and more satisfaction, the pull toward something that can be felt as authentic Jewishness and the various other pulls that may be molding selves that are also known as Jewish. I tried to suggest to Josh that, when minhag is forgotten or abandoned, this can nevertheless be cause for mourning. It recalls, in any case, that famous line from Lampedusa's *The Leopard*: "If things are going to remain the same, things are going to have to change."

Oh, here's Elissa's report:

Zev,

   The shabbes lunch with R. Yuter was one of the best times I have ever had on shabbes; we had a very diverse group of people including a grad student named Cal Pinsker whose father is a reform rabbi in Durham, who is in NY and attended Stanton St for the first time that morning; Molly, Zeke and Avi (age 2); Esther Coleman with parents who are holocaust survivors and who had just spent 3 months dealing with her mother's stroke etc., Rosie Prager and her indie film maker boyfriend; and Tsvi Vilner.

   Unlike the lunch when the Ungers were here, I didn't have to play hostess to move the conversation along; it was fluid, fun, Jewish, and just worked and I regretted when we *benched* [recited the grace after meals] and people left. I knew from the interview that R. Yuter has a quiet mature self-confidence and is a good listener; the surprise was that he was a natural conversationalist who put people at ease and could deal in a natural fun way with the diversity of the group. This guy has both depth and social skills that are a total pleasure. There was no nervousness and there was no arrogance; just fun in talking. This may be in part because he is the son of a Baltimore rabbi and used to such situations; hard to know. A pretty poignant moment was when the son of the reform rabbi asked how do you learn enough to be able to deal with an orthodox world and shul, and Molly explained she was a convert and had to learn everything and the conversation took off again from there.

And of course everyone dealt well with the usual stuff when you have a 2 year old around.

When everyone was leaving I walked people to the stairs; he realized something was wrong with my walking and asked if I was coming to hear the shiur and I had to tell him regrettably no. He just turned around, came back (I knew he was heading to the Pollaks' to nap and had wanted him to walk with Zeke et al), and conversationally talked to me about his notion of how minhag works and where it does and doesn't run into trouble at shuls in terms of a halakhic approach. He is very flexible; even when something is asur [forbidden by Jewish law], he explained a smart rabbi then figures out where to pick his battles.

Your father called after shabbes for a blow by blow description and wanting in particular to know about women's issues and the eruv; my sense is that we would be lucky on both given our hashkafa and the con- clusions that he has come to because these are topics that he has re- searched in depth due to where he has lived (Washington Heights, Chicago, etc.), and can hold his own on and will tell us where there are issues he believes that we will need to deal with. We knew he wasn't an intellectual light weight—the surprise is how socially fluent he is and how savvy about how a shul should run.

I will send notes to the guests asking if they are comfortable giving feedback and copying you. I know that negotiating with him might be harder and there will be people who will not be comfortable with the fact he is not married and how will we work *parnassa* [his in- come] and housing; I am fully confident that you are the best possible negotiator the shul could have and that if these issues can be addressed, you are the one to do it. But yes, I believe he can get people through the door and more importantly, respectfully engage and keep them and that he is the genuine article and that he is as hungry as R. Unger for the shul because he really likes the diversity. He also mentioned that he really liked the intergenerational aspects and that we had artists and professionals. We are very lucky.

—Elissa


Evidently I've been operating under a false assumption about the pro- jected schedule for concluding the rabbinic search. Though both can- didates have visited now, there doesn't seem to be general urgency for another meeting of the search committee, especially as Zev is just about now returning from a trip to Israel. When I mentioned to Nate the idea of consulting soon, he told me that some of our deliberations might depend on the outcome of Melech's *din torah* (a hearing in a rabbinical court), which will determine in turn the size of a promised donation from Melech, which would influence in turn the amount we can offer to a rabbi and, conceivably, even our choice of to whom to make the offer. Moreover, in the current issue of the shul newsletter there's an item about the rabbinical search, presumably written by Zev, though I'm not sure, that states our goal as having a "competent rabbi" in place by the time of the High Holidays . . . in late September, long after Elissa and I will have returned to North Carolina.

About Melech: Yesterday morning in shul, I introduced him to Cal Pinsker, saying, "Cal wants to write a dissertation about Jewish hipster culture." Melech said, "I'm your man. I'll tell you everything you need to know." I left them alone to chat at the kiddush, and at lunch Cal told me that Melech had proposed taking him on a tour of the "trouble spots" of Hasidic Williamsburg, with the proviso that Cal would tape it and give Melech a transcript. Cal asked me quietly, as if *glat in der velt arayn*, "apropos of nothing," a very general sort of question about ethnographic practice, how one determines the proper quid pro quo for the value one gets from a key informant. "If it's Melech you have in mind," I said, "don't give it a second thought. He can take care of himself."

I've been wrong about one thing for years, and I should have known it: While it was true that, when we moved into this building thirty years ago, it was easy to see the Forward Building on East Broadway, it could not have been true even then that there was nothing taller in between our Ageloff Towers and the Forward Building: the Seward Park Extension housing project, twenty-three stories tall (I counted it this afternoon) at Broome and Essex must have been there all this time.

## Day Four of Parshas Pinchas, July 16, 2008

Monday around noon, I saw a text message on my cell phone that Lenny Rivers had obviously sent out to a number of members: "Can anyone be at the shul to receive the refrigerator at 3:30 today?" I didn't respond; I was by then well up the Hudson Valley in Columbia County, where I'd gone overnight to visit friends from Kansas.

This morning, as I opened the door and began to head down the short flight of steps to the beis medrash, I barely noticed a rat scurrying up the narrow, gated stairway to the upstairs shul. Not common, but not unheard of, either; the last time I remember rats was while the beis medresh was being renovated, but still, it's midsummer (smelly, hot midsummer in New York), so if there's going to be one, it's likely to be now.

The tile floor outside the beis medrash seemed like it had been washed, though, and even inside, the wooden floorboards seemed cleaner; a damp mop leaned next to the sink in the narrow food-service "staging area" in the corridor that flanks the beis medrash, but a sour smell lingered there, as well. Rabbi Pollak came in a minute or two after me, and I suggested to him that we place the garbage by the sidewalk for pickup. Easier said than done (we'd done this together Monday morning as well, in pouring rain, complaining already then about the party next door on Saturday that had filled our two cans with their garbage): One of the bags in the staging-area floor was heavy and leaking, and we had to rebag it before we could take it outside. I wondered aloud where all this new garbage had come from in the middle of the week (surely not from the morning minyan, and there's not much else that goes on at the shul during the week), and Yossi explained, "They came to take out the old refrigerator on Monday, so they threw out everything in it. They brought a new one, but it wasn't the right size, so they had to take it back."

As to the garbage in our cans, Yossi insists that it's not our responsibility: "We'll have to tell the people at 176 Stanton that they need to get their garbage out of there."

We go back inside, and as has become a bit of a pattern, I start davening on my own while Yossi shmoozes, waiting to see if there will be a minyan. Melech comes in, and then Buddy, but that's still just eight of us (in addition, Ben, Benny, Mendel Trebitsch, and Dan Cantor are present). Melech agrees that garbage is a big problem. (Part of the reason Yossi deals with the garbage and that lately I've been helpful, as well, is that the next-door neighbor to the shul on the other side has complained for months about the filth we end up leaving out on the sidewalk.) But that's not what Melech wants to talk about: instead, he's chatting with Yossi about the cover of the current *New York* magazine, which apparently features a friend of Melech's, a young woman who's left the Satmar Hasidic community in Kiryas Joel, upstate. Someone— Melech? Yossi? mentions the organization Footsteps, which helps people from the Hasidic community who have "left the *derech*," the path, strayed from strict community norms, and are beginning to try to find their way outside the Hasidic communities. Yossi, at Isaac's probing, suggests that he approves of the organization's work, but Isaac is having none of it: "They encourage people to break the laws of the Torah! They give them treif [nonkosher] food! You can laugh at the laws of the Torah, but there's nothing funny about it." Yossi responds: "They've left the derech"—which I interpret to mean, this is not an organization that's taking people away from the Torah, this is an organization that's helping people in need. Yossi, in any case, isn't the one who raised the issue of Footsteps: He's trying, among other things, to make sure there continues to be room for both Melech and Isaac in the beis medresh.

I finish davening a few minutes after Mendel Trebitsch, who wonders aloud why he had just recited the psalm beginning with the Hebrew word *ashrey* for the third time. I tell him it's because he heard me reciting that prayer, and he concurs: "It's the power of suggestion. Oh well, this is a nonsequetarian minyan."

I take off my tefillin, not before discretely and undramatically, but also unthinkingly, passing gas (I would not mention it except that Monday's halakhah of the day stated that one should not put on tefillin if he believes he will be unable to restrain himself from flatulence while he is wearing them; it is considered disgusting and a mark of disrespect to these holy "signs," the tefillin of the arm and head). And I step outside, only to see more garbage strewn on the sidewalk in front of the shul, most dramatically including several jars of herring, all previously unopened, but some now broken. (They may not have been all previously unbroken, since they were probably the source of the sour smell that came from this bag when it was still inside the shul.) Clearly, this is the contents of the leaky bag Yossi and I had rebagged twenty minutes earlier; how it had become ripped and its contents strewn in the meantime, I don't know. I'm thinking to myself how half-assed this all is, and how amazing it is that any institution, even one as modest as the Stanton Street Shul, can keep running in half-assed fashion for so long.

I can't leave it like that. I go back in, and call in Melech, who by this time has stopped pretending to daven, and he comes back out to help me bag the herring for the third time, but not before I take photos of one pile of garbage on the sidewalk and another of Melech standing next to a jar of herring in front of the rear end of Benny's old Dodge. I tell Melech if it comes out well, I may use it for the cover of my book about the shul. Melech wants to know what I'm going to call the book, and I tell him *The Eventual Minyan*. He says, "You should call it *The Dwindling Minyan*," but I reject the suggestion: "That's an old story already."

I go back inside, where what I feared might have happened by now— Isaac Maxon finally deciding he can't pray together with these scoffers— has not, in fact, happened. Rather, Isaac and Yossi are continuing a conversation about whether to approve or disapprove of certain unspecified organizations, while I'm still listening to the conversation. They may have still been talking about Footsteps, but there was something else in the mix for comparison: quite possibly an organization that doesn't exist at all, but that one of them had hypothecated to make a rhetorical point.

I need to send an e-mail to Lenny, who, according to Yossi, has the keys to the chain that locks the garbage-can lids to the fence in front of the shul: If the cans were inside the fence, it would be harder for neighbors or passersby to dump their garbage in our cans. I owe Lenny a message anyway, since he'd sent me one last week suggesting, as is his communitarian wont, that he introduce me to a family friend from Montreal who's here teaching Yiddish for the summer. I didn't reply then because Elissa was so annoyed at Lenny's scurrilous response (which I still haven't seen) to her communication about the mazoles issue.

I don't know if I would have taken the trouble to record these things—food, somehow, which has quite intentionally been featured in these notes already, is a rather more obvious topic for ethnography than garbage, which is usually the province of archaeologists, instead—but for the receipt of an expression of interest in my proposal for a book about the shul that Beth Kressel of Rutgers University Press sent me by e-mail while I was admiring the organic cows upstate.

Nor do I know if this book is going to work, since the editor, quite reasonably, expects a certain measure of coherence that I don't know if I'm able or willing to provide. This garbage stuff is great for the ethnographer, not so great for the congregant, both of whom are inside my body. That's the point—well, that and the difficulty of writing about the shul without treating it as a living being with a life cycle (sickness, recoveries, infirmities and the like)—and I don't want to belabor it with a lot of recycled jargon about fragmented postmodern selves.

The rabbinic search committee is in fact going ahead with a prompt meeting to evaluate our responses to the two candidates, and Nate Hacker will present a report on the resources we can expect to be able to spend on hiring a rabbi. As of this morning, the meeting was called for tomorrow evening, which would have been fine for me, but since Jason and Sari's anniversary is tomorrow, they asked to hold the meeting tonight. Elissa can go, but I have other plans I don't want to break. She and I agreed that our response to the committee is, in essence: of the two, we would (other things being equal) prefer Josh Yuter as our rabbi; Jacob Unger is more likely to do the work of "growing the shul" (a phrase I still find obnoxious), and it will be difficult to hire Josh unless we can offer him a full-time salary. Elissa added, and I agreed, that the committee should rank order the two candidates and then (assuming both are acceptable) authorize negotiations with both of them, since it's not clear we'll ultimately be able to hire either.

## Day Five of Parshas Pinchas, July 17, 2008

Elissa reports that Josh Yuter was determined to be the search committee's first choice, not unanimously, but by a majority vote. One of the board members is unhappy about the outcome and complaining about the process; others may also be unhappy about the outcome, but aren't complaining, at least not by group e-mail. There were no strict rules about who was eligible to vote, but certainly the search committee was open, all along, to any interested member. Any recommendations the search committee or the board may make must, according to the Religious Corporations Law of New York State, be voted on by the congregation—you can't hire a rabbi in New York without a vote of the congregation. Now, as I wrote above, we'll have to see how interested Josh really is in becoming our rabbi.

Yesterday afternoon, as I stepped out of the building, our neighbor Bea (lifelong Lower East Side resident, daughter of a survivor of the

Triangle Shirtwaist Factory fire) was sitting in a beach chair in front of
the building with her affable Polish home health-care aide. She looked
at me and quoted a Yiddish phrase: "*A groyse hamimeh*, whatever that
means." I said: "I think it means it's pretty hot." Truth is, I've never
heard the word *hamimeh* in Yiddish or in any other language, but in
context I guessed (and would lay odds on being right) that it's from the
Hebrew *kham*, which means "hot." How it got into her Yiddish I'll
never know.

I noticed for the first time—though it may have been there for years—
a large billboard on the side of a building at the north end of Orchard
Street, facing north toward Houston. It was clearly done by the de-
signer Marco, because it features his trademark cartoonish sea animals,
and it bears the slogan "Gateway to the Lower East Side." My guess that
it's been there for years, even though I never noticed it, is supported by
the fact that even Marco's store has been pushed out of Orchard Street
by higher rents.

About a year ago, Jonah reported to me that, briefly, the American
Apparel billboard at Allen Street and Houston had borne a photograph
of Woody Allen with the legend, *der heyliker rebbe*, "the holy rebbe." It
came down after just a few days, apparently because of complaints by
Woody Allen's lawyers. Thinking about this today put me in mind of
the very idea that there is some *thing* called holiness, *kedusha*, that someone like a Hasidic rebbe possesses. Certainly it's not something we included in the job description for the new rabbi at Stanton Street. And
yet . . . I will never forget one morning, in the "old" beis medresh, perhaps twenty years ago, when I looked up in the middle of davening to
see Rabbi Singer's face positively aglow.

Two new refrigerators, which apparently fit, have now been installed.

# Week Eleven

*Build you cities for your little ones, and folds for your sheep.*

—NUMBERS 32:24

*Flourescent Lamp, Upstairs Sanctuary*

## Day One of Parshas Mattos, July 20, 2008

Four weeks from today, my summer in New York will end, and I will drive to North Carolina to begin my fall semester.

Friday was a distracted and stressful day for me. The first great heat spell since Shavuos set in. I was draggy and anxious about serving lunch to thirteen family members on shabbes, including my nephew, his wife, and their two little boys just flown in from Victoria, British Columbia, for a long weekend. What seemed to have been a consensus at the end of Wednesday night's search committee meeting that Rabbi Yuter should be approached first to see if the shul could reach an agreement with him on terms for his service as our rabbi turned into accusations by a disgruntled member of the search committee (and the shul board) that the meeting had been manipulated and the final consensus unrepresentative of the shul's membership. Some of the charges this member made seemed impertinent or scurrilous, such as the suggestion that Elissa (who cannot walk to shul) or Gordon Gross (who didn't, last shabbes, because of the accident he'd just been in) shouldn't have had a say in ranking the candidates because they had not seen both of them at actual shul services. Other claims he made might have reflected some real demographic differences (between younger and older, or more recent and long-standing members?) between those who preferred Yuter and those who preferred Unger, but it's not clear. A long series of e-mails ensued, by turns intemperate, overly conciliatory, and judicious. By midafternoon, Lenny Rivers had apparently placed a call to the unhappy member and mollified him, but not before the consensus threatened to crack. (Indeed, it seems clear that, given their druthers, several members would still have made the offer to Rabbi Unger first, but were willing to cooperate with the majority that favored Yuter as the first choice.) The last e-mail in the series came from Zev, still nominally leading the process, though, since the most recent elections, he is no longer officially "executive vice president" (no one has been named to that position, or any other office on the new board yet), suggesting that the issue was over for now. When I saw him Friday evening in shul, I got the impression that he is in fact ready to start talking to Rabbi Yuter.

Whether the process and the discourse were productive or not, they reflect a shared concern that neither of these candidates can or will do everything that needs doing—as Dudi Dembitser put it in a list of alternate priorities, increasing membership, courting donors, and providing a meaningful religious experience—combined with anxiety that, even among those actively concerned with the shul, we won't cohere enough to provide what the rabbi doesn't. And we still don't know whether, on the salary we'll be able to offer, we'll be able to hire either of these candidates.

Anyway, I had a break from Stanton Street yesterday morning, since I'd agreed to read the Torah at Anshe Janina again. I turned out to be the ninth man (enough for Janina, with the ark of the Torah open), did my Torah reading, left immediately afterward, then stopped in at Stanton Street for the kiddush. Naomi Weiss, a sometime attendee who still seems more associated either with the White Street Shul or with the Town and Village Conservative synagogue on Fourteenth Street, stopped me to ask about my quote, in a *New Yorker* article a few months ago, supporting the tenure case of Nadia Abu el-Haj, an old friend and colleague who'd been attacked for her book on the ideological contexts of Israeli archaeology. Nadia's book evidently makes the general claim that Israeli archaeology tends to suppress the remains of Palestinian residence, and she diagnoses this suppression as evidence of Zionist self-doubt concerning the exclusive Jewish claim to the land. I think three times in a row Naomi said to me, "But I grew up Zionist, and I never thought we had any anxiety about our right to be in that land." I stayed civil as I always do in such a situation, but felt terribly awkward about the conversation. On the one hand, I felt my inadequacy at explaining, in a conversation like that, the idea of the politics of historical knowledge. To say that Israeli archaeology is driven by the need to establish the Jewish claim to Palestine is not to say that it is based on falsification; to say that Zionism entails a cultural construction of the national past is not necessarily to distinguish it from any other national movement. On the other hand, I'm troubled, not so much by my marginality in the congregation as a non-Zionist (I'm quite used to that) as, almost, by a sneaking suspicion that my failure to feel the passions of my fellow congregants on this issue might reflect some pathology in *me*. Or maybe I was more sensitive to this kind of moment than usual because of Friday's series of antagonistic e-mails and because it was so brutally hot.

Late in the afternoon, Zev and Kara and their two daughters paid us a visit, and Kara shared with us a rather detailed description (which I had solicited and which I enjoyed) of their recent tour of Israel as part of a group sponsored by the religious Zionist Eretz Israel movement. Though I wouldn't dream of going on such a tour other than as a professional ethnographer, the things she and Zev described as fascinating (such as an excavated town from Talmudic times called Susya, near Hebron on the West Bank) sounded fascinating to me, as well. Maybe listening to that account didn't make me feel defensive because it wasn't in such a crowd, or maybe it was because I wasn't being asked to defend my publicly stated opinion.

News flash: Just this minute (5:30 P.M. on Sunday), Disgruntled Member has sent out the following message to the search committee:

> It [is] very clear that this election was flawed and could be done better in the future as a few other board and committee members agreed. With 12 people on the committee and 6 family votes and only one person bringing in proxies.
>
> However, even with the flawed process there still appears to be one front runner which is Rabbi Yuter.
>
> Let us move on with Rabbi Yuter at the helm.

Well, we'll see.

## Day Five of Parshas Mattos, July 24, 2008

A heavy rain this morning. I walk in, and Isaac Maxon is looking around for a pair of tefillin to borrow; he's forgotten his. He approaches me and asks, "Are these yours?" I indicate no, and tease him: "What, you think you can just pick up anybody's tefillin and borrow them?" As both of us know, that is, in fact, the halakha: If you need a pair of tefillin, you can just pick up anybody's and borrow them.

Later, after the rabbi arrives and settles down, he proposes that Isaac wear Melech's tefillin instead: "They're in much better shape than the other pair you picked up, and besides, whenever I lend somebody Melech's tefillin, Melech shows up."

I start "praying through," as has become my habit, rather than waiting in impatience for the minyan, but the rest are waiting for the ninth man. Yesterday, I was at the *amud* ("lectern") leading the prayers because I was saying kaddish for Elissa's grandmother. The ark was open to stand in for the tenth, and when a living, breathing tenth man walked in and the rabbi was closing the ark, I gave it a shy little placatory wave: suddenly it seemed to me not nice that we shut the ark and hide the Torah scrolls away as soon as we don't need them anymore.

Today, as we're waiting for the ninth, Yossi says, "Who knows?" (Maybe we'll get a minyan.) "You guys came. I mean you're all crazy, but . . ."

"Crazy for the Stanton Street Shul," I responded.

"Crazy for Hashem"—crazy for God—Yossi urged me, a bit mock-shocked, but this time it was Isaac Maxon who gave the nonpietistic, parodic paraphrase, here substituting our shul for the Land of Israel: "As the Zohar says, the Torah, the Stanton Street Shul, and God are one."

The ninth man this morning is Pete Silver. I was confident he'd show up, as he always does on the Mondays and Thursdays when we count on him to read the Torah for us. He arrived at 7:18, obviously in pain, soaking wet, and muttering drily, "It might rain today."

During the Torah reading I'm called up for an aliyah and say self-mockingly, as I walk toward the bima, the table on which the Torah is placed at the front of the beis medresh, "All the way from the back of the beis medresh!" This elicits from Yossi the old line, already long associated with weekday aliyes, "Come on down!" But today was somehow special, because he added for the first time another, more obscure line from the television show *The Price Is Right*: "Make your best bid without going over." *That* impressed me. Maybe Yossi is realizing he may not get to use this kind of line in Westport.

Yesterday, Rachel Wiener stopped by, and she and Elissa went down to the gift shop in our building to buy the shul's going-away present for Yossi and Brooke, a fancy shabbes challah board. Rachel's been to their house for dinner and knew they don't have one yet.

An exchange of brief e-mails about another aspect of the going-away doings for Yossi and Brooke:

BOARD MEMBER A: also ordered a Proclamation from the City Council's office. I hope they complete it in time and that they can present it.

ZEV: If not, make sure we have the text and we can read it.

DUDI: And while we're at it, why not change Stanton Street to Yossi Pollak Alley? [A sardonic reference to a block on Rivington Street where a street sign honors the name of a synagogue on that block, once grand, now defunct and demolished.]

Meanwhile, Zev has approached Josh Yuter with our offer. He reports, inter alia:

> He is interested, but is very concerned about his ability to do this while also having another job (I told him our previous salary was $35,000 and we were thinking about something comparable—I hope that was correct). One concern was financial and especially housing. He was very concerned with having an apartment in which he would be able to cook and entertain guests from the shul. The other concern was time. If he had another real job, he wouldn't be able to guaranty availability 9–5 during the week and was concerned about how the shul would feel about that, e.g., funerals or other emergent needs. I told him to think about it but that we needed to hear from him very soon.

Sounds like Rabbi Yuter has his head on straight.

*Downstairs Old School Benches*

# Week Twelve

*These are the stages of the children of Israel, by which they went forth out of the land of Egypt by their hosts under the hand of Moses and Aaron. And Moses wrote their goings forth, stage by stage, by the commandment of the Lord; and these are their stages at their goings forth.*

—NUMBERS 33:1–2

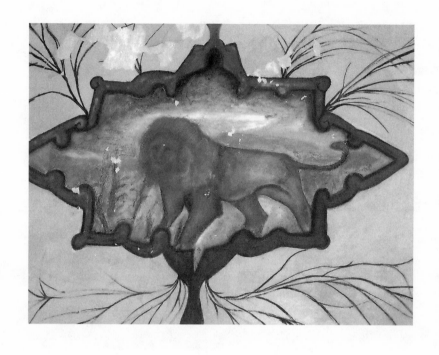

*Upstairs Zodiac Mural, Depicting Lion*

*Yet as is so often the case in memoirs like this one, he never shows us the moment—which one imagines must have happened—when he realized: "I am so going to get a book out of this."*

—JAMES PONIEWOZIK, in the
*New York Times Book Review*, July 27, 2008


## Day One of Parshas Masai, July 27, 2008

Of course, this epigraph is not from a review of some book that might grow out of *this* journal. As I will likely have expressed in that book's introduction, the journal is, rather, the result of my realization that it might offer me a way out of my frustration at being unable to write a synthetic ethnography of such a transient and persistent institution as the Stanton Street Shul. And maybe that a journal might be a way to a book. But never a realization that I am "*so* going to get a book out of this." I don't talk that way, anyway.

Still, with the end of the summer arriving (I'll head back to Chapel Hill three weeks from yesterday), and with Yossi Pollak leaving very soon (his last morning minyan will be Tuesday, the day after tomorrow—I won't be there myself that day, but I'll try to write about where I was instead), I'm in an elegiac mood.

It was a big shabbes at Stanton Street. (In the past I've made fun, gently, of the Hillel Jewish student organization staff at the University of Kansas, where I used to teach, for sending out e-mails with the announcement, "No Shabbat this week!" Of course what they mean is that there will be no Sabbath festivities at Hillel, but I've sent them reminders that, whether they observe it or no, shabbes will come. But here I am referring to our own observance as "shabbes." There's a long Hasidic story about precisely this tension—whether we experience shabbes

because it is, in some cosmic sense, "present" or because of the preparations and ceremonies with which we mark it—and perhaps someday I'll
have the opportunity to publish that story. Or come see me and I'll tell
it to you.)

It was *such* a big shabbes on Stanton Street (that's maybe how I talk,
not all the time, but when I'm talking Jewish, anyway),Yossi and Brooke
Pollak's last, and to mark it, the most elaborate kiddush I've ever seen
at the shul. On Friday night, the crowd was maybe a little bigger than
it's been the last few weeks, which have, as I've already noted, been en-
riched by several folks who would be at the White Street Shul in
Tribeca, which doesn't hold services on Friday nights in the summer.

But the big surprise for me was the presence that Friday night of Stan
Grodner, an old friend from the days I studied at Mesivta Tifereth
Jerusalem, and a crowd of avant-garde musicians and artists.[1] Stan lived
practically around the corner from the shul, on Norfolk Street, down
the block from what later became the Orensanz Center, in the early and
mid-1980s, but he was never a member of Rabbi Singer's minyan: He's
a jazz musician and could never get up that early. And on shabbes mornings he was a regular at the Boyaner Kloyz, one of the last Hasidic
*shtiblech* (modest houses of prayer) still left on the Lower East Side.
Back then—or maybe a few years later, after Stan had already moved to
Jerusalem—I used to think I was clever when I'd say: "There's one shul
I go to where I like the rabbi, one shul where I like the prayers, one shul
where I like the congregation, and one shul where I like the building."
Boyan was the one where I especially liked the prayers: straightforward,
old-fashioned, not too fast, but with a reasonable and not ostentatious
amount of fervor.

Stan had come to Stanton Street not particularly to see me, and not
because of any sentimental attachment of his own to the shul, but because he was staying with another old friend, Eli, one of the "summer
regulars" (there, I've just coined a phrase) from White Street. Seeing
him, apart from being a delight, made me realize that this journal has
turned out to be less a memoir than I thought it might. In passages I
have attempted (whether I've succeeded, I'm not sure) in taking off
from points in the present to recall persons or images from my own past

1. See my "Voices Around the Text: The Ethnography of Reading a Mesivta Tifereth
Jerusalem," in my *The Ethnography of Reading.*

on the Lower East Side, but the journal's inevitable inadequacy as an account of my decades exploring Jewishness in this place still seems almost crushing. Stan came back to Stanton Street with Eli the next morning, in time for the big kiddush, after he and Eli had made the minyan at Boyan, and was quite amazed at the contrast.

Well, it wasn't a typical shabbes. It was a really big one. This morning Yossi said there were a hundred people, and I muttered sotto voce to Buddy Bardin, "Yeah, it was like elephants in a Volkswagen." I don't think that many people could squeeze into the beis medresh, but yeah, I'd say seventy-five or eighty, and as I said to Jason Frankel, it felt like a reunion. There were a number of neighborhood people who are sympathetic to the shul, but not regulars. There were all the regulars who are in town, and maybe, I'm not sure, this was another weekend when there was no morning minyan at White Street either, so we got some extras there.

For the life of me, I can't reconstruct how Rabbi Pollak managed to tie the theme of his sermon—which was basically how wonderful it had been to be on the Lower East Side for the past two years and how we need to think about the entire community, not just our shul—to the weekly Torah reading. He was kind enough to work into his comments a mention of Elissa and me (though in truth, it was Elissa only) as having helped him to figure out where his own grandfather had been born on the Lower East Side (and also, though he did not mention this, that the father of that grandfather had been from Rymanow, Gedalia Getsler's home town, thus providing another link to the shul because the Bluzhever-Rimenever Society has "been davening" at Stanton Street for decades).

I couldn't believe the kiddush, and I'm embarrassed to say that I don't even know who arranged it, though I do know a number of "member units" contributed toward that expense, as well as the going away gift for Yossi and Brooke that Elissa had helped pick out. In the past, Lenny Rivers made arrangements for delivery of "de luxe" kiddush food from a caterer in Teaneck, so maybe that's where these came from, too. Sol Decker, in the absence of Gordon Gross (away visiting family in Boston), took care of the heating and setup, with some help from Pinchas and Jason Frankel, and I stayed on the cleanup crew until the end. (I realize that's a boring sentence. I'm sorry. Somebody has to clean up. Another quote from the book review I cite as an epigraph for this chapter: "The more [the book] becomes about [the author's] personal life, the more mundane and less interesting it is.") There was noodle kugel (salt and pepper, Litvak style, the way I like it; I ate too much of it at the kiddush and then later at *shales-sudes*, the ritual "third meal" on shabbes afternoon, and didn't have such a great night), potato kugel, cholent (didn't touch the stuff), some deli, some fried-onion pastries (too much!), maybe even some fruit.

I got inspired, and at one point after Zev had presented the gift and after the local city councilman, Alan Gerson, had presented and read aloud (only in part) the official New York City proclamation with blah-blah-blah about Rabbi Pollak's contributions to the community (I have to agree with Dudi: two years' service is not long enough for an official proclamation), I spoke briefly to the crowd: "It's wonderful to see all of you here, and not just that, but you're all beautiful. It's true that Yossi and Brooke are going to be blessing a different community next week. But we'll be here next shabbes, too." (I guess that's the part about it being shabbes whether or not we happen to be observing it, and how.) "And even though Yossi and Brooke won't be here, we can demonstrate that Rabbi Yossi was right when he said he hoped they'd left something behind to inspire us. And if *you* and *you* and *you* and *you* and *you* and I come, or even only some of us, there's going to be some very special people here." I know it's schmaltzy, but I really felt it when I said it. I want the shul to keep going strong, even when a rabbi isn't leaving.

Several folks, including a couple whom I didn't know by name, came up to me to inquire how Elissa was doing. One was a middle-aged, short, somewhat stocky woman with dyed blonde hair who certainly addressed me as though she assumed I knew who she was. After asking about Elissa, she volunteered that when Rabbi Pollak had come, she told him that she didn't think this should be transformed into a "Modern Orthodox" shul but that the ways of the old congregation should be continued, because if it had not been for them, the shul would not have existed thus far. It was clear to her that Rabbi Pollak had not taken her advice; she was the only person I've spoken to who clearly expressed relief that he is moving on. What I think: Most of the changes, including loss, over the past few years have been inevitable, some desirable, others regrettable. "If things are to stay the same, things are going to have to change."

Dudi wasn't in shul at all this shabbes: he may have been dealing with pressing family matters again, but he might also not have had the stomach for the adulation of the rabbi. Certainly a tenable position.

Benny Sauerhaft wasn't there this shabbes, either, of course, since his son forbade him to walk to Stanton Street on shabbes after a fainting episode about a year ago. Instead, therefore, he made a remarkably long-winded going-away speech for Rabbi Pollak after this morning's min-yan, full of affection tied with rambling reminiscences, a late reprise of the weekly speeches Benny used to give when he was still strong enough to act in the ceremonial role of shul president, which he retains today (and presumably for life). For posterity, I'll record his mention that he is ninety-three now and first came to the shul when he was forty-eight: forty-five years ago was around 1963. I'm not sure why he mentioned at some length his former employer at the Upper West Side kosher butcher, Fischer Brothers and Leslie, whom he recalled with fondness: "He bought a house near the store for $180,000, now it's worth six million dollars. He was a millionaire, now he's a poor man"—that is, dead, possibly a play on the Talmudic saying *ani khashuv kemet*, "a poor man is considered as a dead man." In Paris, decades ago, a Polish Jewish immigrant told me that was because neither is responsible for his own debts. And this: "Thank God, I have a pension from the butcher's union. Today, it's hardly worth anything."

For the record: at a somewhat difficult shul board meeting Thursday night, in which Elissa participated by conference call and much of which I listed in on as well (any synagogue member is permitted to attend board meetings), Pinchas Duber was elected the new vice president—effectively, the congregation's chief executive officer for the coming year.

### Day Six of Parshas Masay, August 1, 2008

I volunteered to give the *dvar torah*, the sermon, tomorrow. Here's the text of what I wrote this afternoon:

> *Eyle masay vney yisroel asher yotso me'erets mitsrayim l'tsivosom beyad moshe ve'aharon.* These are the stages of the children of Israel, by which they went forth out of the land of Egypt by their hosts under the hand of Moses and Aaron.

It's almost too easy. These are the stages of the congregation of the Stanton Street Shul:

They left Brzezany, a small town in Galicia. It wasn't where they'd started from; rather, as our shul's new vice president Pinchas Duber has remarked to me recently, a Jew is never from just one place: It's always Berzhan, and before that, and before that . . . But let's start with this group of people from Berzhan, who left Europe at the turn of the twentieth century. Not all of them traveled together, and some of them went to places other than New York. Indeed, we know that when Jews left a shtetl called Narayev—very close to Berzhan, almost a suburb—some went to New York, and others went to Toronto. The ones who went to Toronto established a shul that still exists there. It's called the First Narayever Congregation. Why? Because the Narayev Jews who got to Toronto got their shul built before their *landslayt*, their fellow townspeople, who had emigrated to New York, were able to construct theirs. "We built our Narayever Shul first—ha!"

Our own Berzhaner Shul isn't only the most important living trace of a once-thriving Jewish community; it's also one of the last living remnants of that common pattern by which groups of immigrants, having completed one of the "stages" of the children of Israel, would find solidarity with each other and with the place they'd left by coming together to worship. Not all of them went to the same place, as I've said, and of course, many of their families and friends always stayed behind.

Some of our shul's oldest members, and let us never forget what a treasure they are to have among us, are likewise marked by their lifelong loyalty to their hometowns and to the people from their hometowns who joined them here in the New World: Gedalye Getsler, from the Bluzhever-Rimenever Society; if you've never noticed them, take a look at the two eternal lights up front here, and the small plaques to the Jewish communities of those two towns that now hang over the menorah. Benny Sauerhaft is from Lancut: If you've never heard him share his loving memories of that hometown, come to shul some morning and ask him: he's ninety-three, *kine hore*,[2] and still stubbornly comes every day.

Most of us younger, or at least relatively younger members have made our own journeys here, big ones for us, even if they seem less historic and less heroic: I'm from New Jersey, and at this point in my life, I'm

2. No evil eye.

no longer ashamed to admit it. Some of us were born and raised on the Lower East Side, and I imagine understand fully well how choosing to stay when so many others leave is a difficult journey of its own kind. Melech Goldfeld is from Staten Island; Jason Frankel is all the way from Chicago; there's *something* that has made each of us journey to this neighborhood and to this shul, and at least for a time, to sojourn here. And some of us will soon be continuing our journeys elsewhere.

Or I could take an entirely different tack. These are the stages of Congregation Anshei Brzezan: There was a time before Rabbi Singer, but there is virtually no living memory of that time in the life of the shul. There were the decades of Rabbi Singer's stewardship, which contained much warmth and love along with poverty and ended with great and unexpected pain. Out of that experience, it might almost be said, a new Congregation Anshei Brzezan was born, though no one here today, and no one on the congregation's current membership rolls, so far as I know, was actually born or even has roots in that town. There was a stage, which was longer than it seems in retrospect, when we were leaderless and we learned that Stanton Street isn't just some rabbi's shul. Then there was what I might call the "intern stage," when we were blessed to have with us—at least every other shabbes—Zach Geller and then, for two more years, Meir Goldfeld, both of whom helped guide and teach us as we helped them grow in turn. We all know that yet another stage ended last shabbes, in a rich, crowded, and emotional send-off for Rabbi Yossi Pollak and his wife Brooke.

Another stage in our journey is about to begin. We don't know exactly where we're headed, and here, at least, is one difference between our journey and that of our ancestors. We haven't got a Moses, and even, God willing, when we do have a new rabbi soon, he won't be Moshe Rabeynu: God's not going to tell him exactly where we should be going, and he won't be able to tell us, either. And our journey is even more complicated than that: We don't all go in the same direction, God knows, and we don't all wind up in the same place. But it seems that there are some powerful things that we do have in common, things that bring us together, things that keep us devoted to a shul that isn't the closest, or the most beautiful, or the biggest one we could walk to every morning, or every week: I would venture to say that for each of us, sharing the journey— figuring out how our own journey can also be a Jewish one, figuring out how a Jewish journey can also be our own—is something that we've found we can do best together, and here at the Stanton Street Shul, Congregation Anshei Brezan. But with no immediate instructions from the Most High, with no prophet to tell us where and how to go—ultimately, while we continue to listen for the still, small voice, we have to rely on ourselves and each other. There's a lot of work to be done if we want to continue this journey; let's get together and do it.

*A gutn shabbes.*

# Works Cited

Aviv, Caryn, and David Shneer. *New Jews: The End of the Jewish Diaspora*. New York: New York University Press, 2005.

Berman, Marshall. *All That Is Solid Melts Into Air: The Experience of Modernity*. New York: Simon and Schuster, 1982.

Boyarin, Daniel. *Carnal Israel: Reading Sex in Talmudic Culture*. Berkeley: University of California Press, 1993.

Boyarin, Jonathan. *Thinking in Jewish*. University of Chicago Press, 1996.

———. *Polish Jews in Paris: The Ethnography of Memory*. Bloomington: Indiana University Press, 1991.

Boyarin, Jonathan, ed.. *The Ethnography of Reading*. Berkeley: University of California Press, 1993.

Calvino, Italo. *Invisible Cities*. Trans. William Weaver. San Diego: Harcourt Brace Jovanovich. 1974.

Kugelmass, Jack. *The Miracle of Intervale Avenue: The Story of a Jewish Congregation in the South Bronx*. New York: Schocken, 1986.

Kugelmass, Jack, and Jonathan Boyarin, trans. *From a Ruined Garden: The Memorial Books of Polish Jewry*. New York: Schocken, 1983.

Myerhoff, Barbara. *Number Our Days*. New York: Simon and Schuster, 1980.

Redlich, Shimon. *Together and Apart in Brzezany: Poles, Jews, and Ukrainians, 1919–1945*. Bloomington: Indiana University Press, 2002.

Yuter, Alan. "The State of the Jewish Polity: A Modern Orthodox Perspective." *Conversations: Orthodoxy and Kelal Yisrael* 1 (Spring 2008).

# Glossary

*aleynu.* Concluding prayer to most traditional services, declaring our duty to praise God and acknowledge His grandeur as Creator.

*aliyah.* Summons to approach the bima and recite prayers before and after a portion of the Torah reading.

*amida.* The central prayer of daily, Sabbath, and holiday services, given this name because recited standing; also known as shemona esrei.

*amud.* Prayer lectern.

*anthropologist.* Someone who studies and writes about distinctive groups and their identities, especially (but not necessarily) one who is paid to do so.

*aron kodesh.* "Ark" or armoire in which Torah scrolls, sometimes along with other sacred items, are kept.

*ArtScroll.* The most successful contemporary publisher of books oriented toward Orthodox Judaism, especially in the Anglophone world.

*Ashkenazi.* Relating to the Jewish cultures of Central and Eastern Europe, historically those whose vernacular language was Yiddish.

*asur.* Forbidden.

*av beis din.* Chief (literally "father") of a rabbinical court.

*baal kore.* One who performs the public reading of the Torah during specified synagogue services.

*baal tefila (baalei tefila).* Prayer leader.

*batlan, batlonim.* Idler or, in other contexts, one who is free to devote himself to Torah study.

*bayit, bayis.* House (in modern Israeli and traditional Ashkenazi pronunciation).

*beis din.* Rabbinical court.

*beis medresh.* Study hall.

*bench.* Recite grace after meals.

*ben toyre.* Someone steeped from childhood in the study of Torah and Rabbinic literature.

*bikkur cholim.* Society for visiting the sick.

*bima.* Platform or table on which the Torah scroll is placed when read.

*bris.* Circumcision ceremony.

*brokhe.* Blessing.

*cherem.* Ban.

*Chofetz Chaim.* Rabbi Yisroel Meir Kagan, 1838–1933, known by this name, which was the title of his first book, reviewing the Jewish laws concerning gossip and slander.

*chok.* Law of the Torah that is not necessarily subject to rational understanding.

*cholent.* A slow-cooked stew that can be eaten hot on the Sabbath day without violating laws against cooking on the Sabbath.

*Chovevei Torah.* An "open Orthodox" yeshiva recently established on Manhattan's Upper West Side.

*Conservative.* A modern branch of Judaism devoted to tradition but regarding halakha as subject to historical evolution.

*daven.* Pray.

*din torah.* Case brought before a rabbinical court.

*drosha.* A sermon or homily, often on the weekly Torah reading, given by a rabbi or other learned person.

*dvar torah.* Sermon, often based on the weekly Torah portion.

*el mole rakhamim.* "God full of mercy," a memorial prayer often recited on the anniversary of a loved one's death.

*eruv.* Boundary line that permits observant Jews to carry out of doors on the Sabbath.

*gabbai.* Here, the member responsible for making sure the service runs smoothly and for distributing roles among the participants.

*gadol.* A "great one," specifically, someone considered a leading Torah scholar of his generation.

*gelila.* The task of rebinding and covering the Torah scroll after the reading is completed.

*gemara.* The Talmud; Rabbinic elaborations of the Mishna, which is the foundational ancient code of Jewish law.

*haftora.* Reading from the Prophets or Writings, immediately after the Torah reading on the Sabbath and holidays.

*halakha.* Jewish law.

*haredi.* Traditionalistic and strictly following halakha; considered to the "right" of Modern Orthodoxy in religious terms.

*hashkofe.* Viewpoint, outlook, philosophy.

*Hasid.* Follower of the Hasidic movement and/or member of a community of Hasidim.

*Hasidism.* A movement among East European Jews started in the later eighteenth century, stressing proper intention in the performance of commandments, close community among (especially male) Jews, and devotion to a communal leader.

*heymish, heymishkeyt.* Familiar, homey, down-to-earth.

*kabbalat shabbat (kabboles shabbes).* Prayer service "welcoming the Sabbath," preceding maariv on Friday evening.

*kaddish.* Memorial prayer for the dead.

*kavone.* Here, the proper intention when reciting a prayer or performing another commandment of Judaism.

*kashrut.* Jewish dietary laws.

*kedusha.* Central portion of the "reader's repetition" of the amida (or shemona esrei), declaring God's Oneness, Kingship, etc.

*khumesh.* Five Books of Moses.

*kiddush.* "Sanctification" of the Sabbath or holidays, performed through special blessings over wine or grape juice (and occasionally whiskey or other liquor).

*kine hore.* No evil eye! An old-fashioned expression.

*kippa.* Modern Israeli term for a round, often smallish, head covering worn by a male Jew.

*kippa sruga.* Knitted kippa, often indicating Modern Orthodox identity.

*kloyz.* Modest-scaled space for Hasidic worship.

*kohen, kohanim.* Male Jew descended from the priestly clan.

*kugel.* "Pudding" made of various ingredients, especially noodles or potatoes, plus eggs, spices, and so on.

*landslayt.* Emigrés from the same hometown or region.

*landsmanshaft.* Society of émigrés from the same hometown or region.

*layen.* Shortened form of Yiddish verb *leyenen*, to recite aloud from a Torah scroll or other part of the Jewish Scriptures in manuscript scroll form.

*levi, levi'im.* Male Jew descended from the tribe of Levi.

*Litvak.* As an adjective, belonging to the culture or population of Jews from the historical region of Lithuania in the early modern period; as a noun, a member of this group.

*Lubavitch.* Hasidic group currently centered in Crown Heights, Brooklyn, distinctive for its outreach to nonobservant Jews and for its Messianism.

*maariv.* "Evening"; here, the evening service.

*mara d'asra.* Local rabbinic authority.

*mashgiach.* Someone who supervises the preparation and service of food to assure its kosher status.

*mazoles.* Literally "constellations;" here, the astrological symbols sometimes used to decorate East European and immigrant synagogues.

*mechitza.* Barrier separating men's from women's sections of an Orthodox synagogue.

*megillah.* Scroll, often in particular the Scroll ("Book") of Esther.

*Menachos.* Here, the tractate of the Babylonian Talmud dealing with laws concerning offerings of flour in the Temple in Jerusalem.

*mentsh.* Here, a proper, decent person.

*meshulach, meshulachim.* Here, someone who makes the rounds of Jewish homes and communities raising money for a Jewish charity.

*midrash, midrashim.* Genre of Rabbinic narrative and interpretation, often addressing gaps in the Torah text, composed from late antiquity through the early medieval period.

*mikva.* Ritual bath.

*mincha.* Afternoon prayer.

*minhag.* Custom.

*minyan.* Quorum of ten male Jews needed to perform a full prayer service.

*Mishna Berura.* Compendium of Jewish law relating to daily practice, compiled by the Chofetz Chaim.

*mishpat.* Law of the Torah comprehensible according to human logic.

*mitzvah, mitsvos.* Comandment of Jewish law.

*Modern Orthodox.* The relatively more "progressive" wing of Orthodox Judaism, associated in the United States with Yeshiva University and professing the synthesis of Torah and worldly knowledge.

*mohel.* Ritual circumciser.

*musaf.* Additional prayer on Sabbath and certain holidays.

*Noahide.* Non-Jewish adherent of the idea that, in conformity with the Torah, there are seven divine commandments incumbent upon non-Jews.

*nusach.* Version or variety, here pertaining to styles of Jewish prayer.

*Orthodox.* General designation for a range of more traditionalist varieties of religious Judaism that consider Rabbinic authority continually binding.

*parasha.* Weekly Torah portion read in the synagogue.

*parnassa.* Livelihood.

*paroches.* Covering, generally of cloth, for the ark of the Torah.

*parve.* With respect to categories of Jewish dietary law, neither meat nor dairy.

*pidyon haben.* Redemption of the firstborn son.

*Purimshpil.* Folk theater on the occasion of the joyous holiday of Purim.

*Rabad.* Twelfth-century Provençale Talmudist.

*Rabbi Nachman of Braslov.* A great-grandson of the Baal Shem Tov, founder of the modern Hasidic movement.

*Rosh Chodesh.* The new moon, beginning of the lunar month.

*Sefardim.* Jews descended from the medieval Iberian communities.

*sefer, sforim.* Volume of scripture or other Jewish religious book.

*sefer torah.* Torah scroll.

*shabbes.* The Jewish Sabbath, in the traditional pronunciation of Ashkenazi Hebrew or Yiddish.

*shabbes shmues.* "A conversation on the Sabbath."

*shacharis.* The morning prayer service.

*shales-sudes:* The ritual "third meal" on the Sabbath afternoon.

*Shavuos.* The Feast of Weeks in late spring, understood as the festival of the giving of the Torah on Mount Sinai.

*shema.* The declaration "Hear, O Israel, the Lord our God, the Lord is One," with related Bible paragraphs and blessings before and after.

*shemona esrei.* Literally "Eighteen," another name for the amida; sometimes this name is used because the prayer is said to contain eighteen blessings (though it actually contains nineteen).

*shiur, shiurim.* Lesson in Rabbinics or some other aspect of Jewish lore, practice, and text.

*shtibl, shtiblech.* Modest prayer room, usually Hasidic.

*shtreiml, shtreimlekh.* Traditional fur hat worn by male Hasidim on festive days.

*Shulchan Aruch.* The authoritative code of Jewish law, composed by Joseph Karo.

*simcha.* Happy occasion.

*sofer.* Jewish scribe of Torah scrolls and other ritual items.

*sukka.* Temporary "booth" or hut in which traditional Jews eat (and sometimes sleep) on the holiday of Sukkot.

*tachanun.* Penitential prayers.

*tallis, talleisim.* Prayer shawl.

*tefillin.* Phylacteries.

*Torah leshmah.* (The study of) Torah for its own sake.

*Tosafot.* A group of Ashkenazic Talmudists of the twelfth and thirteenth centuries, whose commentary is still widely studied.

*treif.* Nonkosher, usually pertaining to food.

*tsitsis.* Fringes on a ritual garment.

*tume.* Impure.

*vort.* Literally "word," often used in Hasidic culture to refer to an aphorism or brief homily conveyed by a Hasidic leader or learned community member.

*Writings.* Here, the third major component of the Jewish Bible, along with the Five Books of Moses and the Prophets.

*ya'ale ve'yavo.* Prayer inserted into the amida on Rosh Chodesh and festivals asking God to remember us favorably.

*yarmulke.* Traditional (or not so traditional, but distinctive) male Jewish head covering; see kippa.

*yishtabach.* Prayer immediately preceding the first recitation of kaddish in the morning service.

*Yisroel.* Here, male Jew who is neither a kohen nor a levi.

*yizkor.* Memorial service, recited on four occasions during the Jewish year.

*yontev.* Jewish holiday.

*yortsayt.* Anniversary of the death of a close family member.

*Zevachim.* Here, the tractate of the Babylonian Talmud dealing with the laws of animal and bird offerings in the Temple in Jerusalem.